MW01041277

# The Antiquity of Proverbs

## Fifty Familiar Proverbs and Folk Sayings with Annotations and Lists of Connected Forms, Found in All Parts of the World

Dwight Edwards Marvin

**Alpha Editions**

This edition published in 2020

ISBN : 9789354172779 (Hardback)

ISBN : 9789354173943 (Paperback)

Design and Setting By
**Alpha Editions**
www.alphaedis.com
email - alphaedis@gmail.com

We count him wise who knows the mind and the insides of men, which is done by knowing what is habitual to them.

*Bishop Lancelot Andrews, A.D. 1555-1626*

# CONTENTS

Contents

## AUTHORITIES CONSULTED

ABBOTT, G. F. *Macedonian Folk-Lore.* Cambridge, 1903.

*Apocrypha, Old Testament.*

BAILY, NATHAN. *Diverse Proverbs.* London, 1721, Reprint 1917.

BAYAN, G. *Armenian Proverbs.* Venice, 1897.

BENAS, B. L. *On the Proverbs of European Nations.* Literary and Philosophical Society of Liverpool, 1878.

BENHAM, W. GURNEY. *A Book of Quotations, Proverbs, Phrases and Names.* London, 1907.

BERNARD, HENRY; SLAVEIKOFF; PENCHO; AND DILLON, E. J. *The Shades of the Balkans.* London, 1904.

BIGELOW, JOHN. *The Wit and Wisdom of the Haytians.* New York, 1877.

BLAND, ROBERT. *Proverbs Chiefly Taken from the Adagia of Erasmus.* London, 1814.

BOHN, HENRY G. *A Polyglot of Foreign Proverbs.* London, 1884.

BURCKHARDT, JOHN LEWIS. *Arabic Proverbs.* London, 1875.

BURKE, ULICK RALPH. *Sancho Panza Proverbs.* London, 1872.

BURKE, ULICK RALPH. *Spanish Salt.* London, 1877.

BURTON, RICHARD F. *Wit and Wisdom from West Africa.* London, 1865.

CARR, M. W. *A Collection of Telugu and Sanskrit Proverbs.* Madras and London, 1868.

CHAMBERS, R. *Book of Days.* 2 volumes, London, 1869.

CHEVIOT, ANDREW. *Proverbs, Proverbial Expressions and Popular Rhymes of Scotland.* London, 1896.

CHRISTIAN, JOHN. *Behar Proverbs.* London, 1891.

CHRISTY, ROBERT. *Proverbs and Maxims and Phrases of all Ages.* 2 volumes, New York and London, 1907.

COHEN, A. *Ancient Jewish Proverbs.* New York, 1911.

COHEN, HENRY. *Talmudic Sayings.* New York, 1910.

COLLINS, JOHN. *A Dictionary of Spanish Proverbs.* London, 1823.

COWAN, FRANK. *A Dictionary of Proverbs and Proverbial Phrases Relating to the Sea.* Queensburgh, 1894.

DAVIS, E. J. *Osmanli Proverbs and Quaint Sayings.* Originally collected by Ahmed Midhat Effendi. London, 1897.

DAVIS, JOHN FRANCIS. *Chinese Moral Maxims.* Macao and London, 1823.

DAVIS, W. A. *Japanese Songs and Proverbs.* Kyoto, 1913.

DISRAELI, ISAAC. *Curiosities in Literature.* 4 volumes. Art. The Philosophy of Proverbs. London and New York, 1838.

DYKES, OSWALD. *Moral Reflections upon Select English Proverbs.* London, 1708.

ELLIS, GEORGE W. *Negro Culture in West Africa.* New York, 1914.

FALLON, S. W. *Dictionary of Hindustani Proverbs.* Benares and London, 1886.

FIELDING, THOMAS. *Select Proverbs of All Nations.* London.

FULLER, THOMAS. *Gnomologia, Adages and Proverbs.* London, 1732.

GORFINKLE, JOSEPH I. *The Sayings of the Jewish Fathers.* New York, 1913.

GROSE, FRANCIS. *A Proverbial Glossary.* London, 1787.

GURDON, EVELINE CAMILLA. *Country Folk-Lore: Suffolk.* London, 1893.

GURDON, P. R. T. *Some Assamese Proverbs.* Shillong, 1903.

HALLIWELL, JAMES ORCHARD. *The Merry Tales of the Wise Men of Gotham.* London, 1840.

*Haw Kiow Choaan.* London, 1761.

HAZLITT, W. CAREW. *English Proverbs and Proverbial Phrases.* London, 1906.

HEARN, LAFCADIO. *Gombo Zhebes.* New York, 1885.

HENDERSON, ALFRED. *Latin Proverbs.* London, 1869.

HENDERSON, ANDREW. *Scottish Proverbs.* London, 1876.

HEYWOOD, JOHN. *A Dialogue of the Effectual Proverbs in the English Tongue Concerning Marriage.* London, 1562. Reprint.

HEYWOOD, JOHN. *Proverbs, Epigrams and Miscellanies.* London, 1562. Reprint.

HISLOP, ALEXANDER. *The Proverbs of Scotland.* Edinburgh, n. d.

HULME, F. EDWARD. *Proverb Lore.* London, 1906.

INWARDS, RICHARD. *Weather Lore.* London, 1898.

KELLY, JAMES. *A Complete Collection of Scottish Proverbs.* London, 1707.

KELLY, WALTER K. *Proverbs of All Nations.* London, 1870.

KNOWLES, J. HINTON. *A Dictionary of Kashmiri Proverbs and Sayings.* Bombay, 1885.

LEAN, VINCENT STUCKEY. *Collectanea.* 5 volumes. London, 1904.

LONG, JAMES. *Eastern Proverbs and Emblems.* London and New York, 1881.

LONG, JAMES. *On Russian Proverbs.* Transactions of the Royal Society of Literature. Reprint, 1876.

MACCULLOCH, EDGAR. *Guernsey Folk-Lore.* London, 1903.

MACKINTOSH, DONALD. *Collection of Gaelic Proverbs and Familiar Phrases.* Edinburgh, 1819.

MACLEAN, ARTHUR JOHN. *Grammar of the Dialect of Vernacular Syriac, Proverbs, etc.* Cambridge, 1895.

MANWARING, ALFRED. *Marathi Proverbs.* Oxford, 1899.

MASAYOSHI, OTO. *Japanese Proverbs.* 1893.

MAXWELL, WILLIAM STERLING. *Miscellaneous Essays and Addresses.* London, 1891.

MENDIS, MUDALIYAR NICHOLAS. *Sinhalese and European Proverbs.* Colombo, 1890.

MOORE, A. W. *The Folk-Lore of the Isle of Man.* London, 1891.

MORTON, W. A. *A Collection of Bengali and Sanskrit Proverbs.* Calcutta, 1832.

MUGGE, MAXIMILIAN, A. *Serbian Folk Songs, etc.* London, 1916.

MUIRGHEASA, ENRINA. *Sean-focla Uladh.*

NEGRIS, ALEXANDER. *A Dictionary of Modern Greek Proverbs.* Edinburgh, 1831.

NICOLSON, ALEXANDER. *A Collection of Gaelic Proverbs and Familiar Phrases.* Edinburgh and London, 1881.

PALMER, SAMUEL. *Moral Essays on Some of the Most Curious and Significant English, Scotch and Foreign Proverbs.* London, 1710.

PERCIVAL, P. *Tamil Proverbs.* Madras, 1874.

RAMSAY, ALLAN. *A Collection of Scots Proverbs.* Edinburgh and Glasgow, 1797.

RAPAPORT, SAMUEL. *Tales and Maxims from the Midrash.* London and New York, 1907.

RATTRAY, R. SUTHERLAND. *Ashanti Proverbs.* Oxford, 1916.

RAY, JOHN. *A Complete Collection of English Proverbs.* Various Editions.

RIIS, H. N. *Collection of Proverbs of the Natives of the Oji Tribe of Africa.* Basel, 1854.

ROBERTS, J. R. *The Proverbs of Wales.* Penmaenmawr, 1885.

ROEBUCK, THOMAS. *A Collection of Proverbs and Proverbial Phrases in the Persian and Hindustani Languages.* Calcutta, 1824.

SEGAL, LOUIS. *Russian Proverbs.* London, n. d.

SINGER, MRS. A. P. *Arabic Proverbs.* Cairo, 1913.

SKEAT, WALTER W. *Early English Proverbs.* Oxford, 1910.

SPIERS, JAMES. *The Proverbs of British Guiana.* Demerara, 1902.

STAPLETON, ALFRED. *All About the Merry Tales of Gotham*, Nottingham, 1900.

THOMAS, NORTHCOTE W. *Proverbs, Narratives, Vocabularies and Grammar of the Ibo-speaking People of Nigeria.* London, 1913.

THORBURN, S. S. *Bannu.* London, 1876.

TOY, CRAWFORD H. *Critical and Exegetical Commentary on the Book of Proverbs.* New York, 1908.

TRENCH, RICHARD CHENERIX. *Proverbs and their Lessons.* London and New York, 1905.

*Turkish Proverbs.* Published by the Armenian Monaster of St. Lazarus. Venice, 1844.

UPRETI, PANDIT GANGA DATT. *Proverbs and Folk-Lore of Kumaun and Garhwal.* London, 1894.

WILKINSON, R. J. *Malay Proverbs on Malay Character.* Kwala Lumpor, 1907.

## MAGAZINES

*Blackwood's Magazine.* 1864.
*Gentlemen's Magazine.* Various Dates.
*Household Words.* 1852.
*Journal of the American Oriental Society.* 1902.
*London Quarterly Review.* 1868.
*North British Review.* 1858.
*Notes and Queries.* Various Dates.
*Southern Workman.* 1905.
*Westminster Gazette.* 1918.

I said that I loved the wise proverb,
   Brief, simple and deep;
For it I'd exchange the great poem
   That sends us to sleep.

I'd part with the talk of a neighbor
   That wearies the brain,
Like the rondo that reaches the end, and
   Beginneth again.

*Bryan Waller Procter, A.D. 1787-1874*

# The Antiquity of Proverbs

# The Antiquity of Proverbs

## INTRODUCTION

THE origin of most proverbs is unknown. "They were anterior to books," says Disraeli, "and formed the wisdom of the vulgar, and in the earliest ages were the unwritten laws of morality." As a nation's proverbs predate its literature it is impossible to trace them to their beginnings. "They spring from an unknown source, increase in volume as they roll on and are adopted by all as unconsciously as they have sprung into existence." It is a mistake to assume that the earliest known record of a saying indicates its origin. Many with which we are familiar were, so far as we know, first used by the Romans, but the Latin language was the medium of innumerable Greek phrases that predate their Roman use and they may have been the utterances of unknown philosophers, the fragments of lost historic records, the attributed responses to ancient oracles or the accepted lessons of forgotten myths and fables.

Articles sometimes appear in public print that

refer to sententious phrases that are found in modern volumes, as proverbs, in forgetfulness of the fact that sayings, no matter how wise or clever they may be, never become proverbs until they are made so by common repetition. "Many grubs never grow to butterflies," says a *North British Review* contributor, and a maxim is only a proverb in its caterpillar stage—a candidate for a wider sphere and larger flight than most are destined to attain. A sentence must be accepted by the people and used by them in every day speech before it is entitled to a place among the folk sayings of a nation. The process by which a saying is converted into a proverb is slow and may take decades if not centuries.

## THE ANTIQUITY OF PROVERBS

In youth we thought that the proverbs quoted by our elders were mere "ways of speaking," borrowed from others of their own generation. As we grew older and sought to discover from whence they came we were surprised to learn that many, if not all of them, had been used for centuries not only by our forbears but all over the world. Some we learned were used eighteen centuries ago by Plutarch the biographer and moralist, others by Menander the poet, who died over three hundred years before Plutarch was born; others by Theognis the elegiac poet of

Megara five hundred years before Christ. Theognis' poems contained so many proverbs that a large number of them were selected and used as precepts for the conduct of the young. Others were repeated by Theophrastus, Aristotle, Plato and Pythagoras, the Greek philosophers.

Our surprise was great when we were told that Pindar, the Lyric poet, and friend of Theron and Hieron had, a half millennium before the Christian era, penned the words that Paul heard from the illumined heavens when on his way to Damascus—"It is hard for thee to kick against the goad."

Then we read the fables of Æsop, who belonged to an age a little earlier than that of Pindar, and found that all his wonderful stories were in a sense amplified proverbs and from which we may have derived our "One swallow does not make a summer," "Heaven helps those who help themselves," "You cannot wash a blackamoor white," and "Look before you leap."

Searching still further we found evidences that some of our proverbs may have been familiar to Solon, the lawgiver and poet, and to the Seven Sages of Greece. Did not Periander declare that "Nothing is impossible to industry" and Thales say that "He that hateth suretyship is sure, or secure?" A phrase that Solomon, King of Israel, listed among his wise sayings three hundred years before the time of Thales. We found also that among the goodly number of men who strengthened their utterances with well-chosen proverbs was the Greek poet Hesiod, and before him Homer, the author of the Iliad and Odyssey.

But our surprise was greatest when we discovered that the phrases, "He who is wrong fights against himself" and "Thou hast the advantage of the angry when thou keepest silence," were found in "The Precepts of Ptah-hotep," dating back to a period three thousand and more years before the advent of our Lord.

Who knows but that all the men to whom reference has been made, and a multitude of others who lived in by-gone ages borrowed their wise sayings from the talk of the firesides and the conversations of the market places; so that the origin of many proverbs now flippantly quoted in the converse of men is lost in the mists of forgotten centuries.

## THE ANCESTRY AND INFLUENCE OF PROVERBS

Though many of our common sayings seem crude and even coarse to modern ears, they have an honored ancestry and have been used not only by rough and uncouth people but by the wisest and noblest of teachers, so that Lord Chesterfield's slurring statement was out of place that they were the flowers of the rhetoric of vulgar men and characteristic of bad company.

By them parents encouraged their children, teachers instructed their pupils, authors impressed their readers, orators moved their auditors and preachers warned and guided their congregations in ways of uprightness and truth. Leaders of men in all departments of life have used them with confidence and power, and quoted them freely in their conferences and counsels. They have enriched the tales of travelers, strengthened the convictions of moralists, been received as warnings by the wayward, furnished rules of conduct for tradesmen, consoled the downtrodden and depressed and stimulated the young to earnest endeavor. "Sermons of the Reformation are full of them," says a contributor to the *North British Review*. "Latimer often clinched his argument with a text from this oral Bible of the multitude; and Jewel mingled them with aphorisms almost as good of his own invention with the ready wit of these 'wise saws,' John Knox had his quiver richly furnished. . . . There is nothing of which Jeremy Taylor does not contain something, consequently his works are spiced over with a good sprinkling of proverbs."

In olden times the influence of proverbs over the hearts and lives of men was second only to the Bible. Few there were who dared to question their usefulness or authority. Sir William Sterling-Maxwell reminds us that "the qualities which have shaped the destinies of Scotland are those which are mainly inculcated in her proverbs" and adds "The story of Bruce's Spider, often baffled, never disheartened, and at last successful, points the moral which pervades nearly the whole of our proverbial philosophy," and Mr. Benas is no less explicit regarding their influence in America when he says that Motley, the historian and diplomatist, declared "that the earnestness, manliness and resolute character of the American people, that enabled them not only to win their independence, but to suffer with patience the many trials and disappointments inseparable from the task of building up a new commonwealth, was as much due to Benjamin Franklin as to George Washington; and that *Poor Richard's Almanac*, with its maxims, proverbs and teachings, had almost a biblical tendency in moulding the character of the young colonists. When troubles hovered over many an American household, Poor Richard's advice was resorted to as their dearest solace." Franklin himself tells us that the sayings of *Poor Richard's Almanac* "contain the wisdom of many ages and nations." He was not their author so much as their paraphraser and distributor.

## OLD TESTAMENT PROVERBS

The proverbs attributed to Solomon closely resemble those in use by the roving Arabs. It is not surprising that it should be so as the Jews in olden times intimately associated with them.

Yet if one were to compile a large number of Bedouin sayings and place them side by side with those of the Israelitish King he wou'd observe a wide difference in the two collections. Though like them in form, they would be found as a rule to be sensual. Sometimes they might show reverence for the unseen God and teach the most exalted morals, yet to a large extent they would be of the earth earthy.

In studying Solomon's proverbs the first thing that we observe is that they appear to be arranged without regard to consecutive thought. They are unrelated as though thrown together in a hasty manner; but the arrangement is not so haphazard as appears, for, on closer examination we find that the compiler had a distinct plan in mind according to which he classified his material. There are in all six different titles containing five groups of proverbs, each having sayings of the same general type, but slightly differing in form. One dominant purpose is manifest throughout the entire book; never for an instant does the compiler depart from it. His aim from beginning to end is to develop by means of sententious parallelisms a true conception of wisdom. All the proverbs have a certain dignity and impressiveness not found in other collections and bear the marks of inspiration. "All the heathen moralists and proverbialists joined together," says Professor Stuart, "cannot furnish us with one such book as that of the Proverbs in the Sacred Scriptures." John Ruskin tells us that his mother made him learn by heart in his childhood, the third, fourth, eighth and twelfth chapters of the book and that he regarded this commitment to memory as "the most precious and on the whole essential part of all my education."

One peculiarity of Solomon's collection is that there are scarcely any historical allusions in it; the proverbs are all world wide in their application. This is striking when it is remembered that the Jews were always religiously exclusive, narrowly patriotic and passionately enthusiastic for their race and worship. It would have been natural for the collector of such a series of proverbs as is found in his book, to have chosen or formed his material under the influence of national prejudices, but not one of the entire number of recorded sayings is exclusively applicable to Israel. God is frequently referred to but it is not the God of the chosen people but the God of the whole world. "If for the name 'Yahweh' we substitute 'God' says Professor Toy, "There is not a paragraph or a sentence in Proverbs which would not be as suitable for any other people as for Israel." The Messianic hope, so dear to the hearts of the Sons of Jacob, was, with apparent intention, set aside by the compiler that nothing might interfere with the widest application. There are no allusions to the history of Israel, to the nation's oppressions and victories. Such words as "Israel," "Priest" and "Temple" are not mentioned. Even Jerusalem, the sacred city, is not referred to. Solomon wrote as a king, not as the King of Israel, but as an appointed instructor of all nations and generations. While all the wise sayings found in the book are familiar many have remained in common use among men. How often one hears, for example, such phrases as these taken from this wonderful collection: "Out of the heart are the issues of life," "Ponder the path of thy feet," "Go to the ant thou sluggard," "As an ox to the slaughter," "The fear of the Lord is the beginning of wisdom," "Stolen waters are sweet," "The hand of the diligent maketh rich," "A false balance is abomination to the Lord," "In the multitude of counsellers there is safety," "There is that scattereth and yet increaseth," "The liberal soul shall be made fat," "Hope deferred maketh the heart sick," "Righteousness exalteth a nation," "A soft answer turneth away wrath," "Pride goeth before destruction and a haughty spirit before a fall," "The hoary head is a crown of glory," "A fool when he holds his peace is counted wise," "A man that hath friends must show himself friendly," "A faithful man who can find," "A good name is rather to be chosen than great riches," "Train up a child in the way he should go," "Buy the truth and sell it not" and "Where there is no vision the people perish."

### OTHER OLD TESTAMENT PROVERBS

In Old Testament times men used proverbs freely and it is not surprising that many ancient maxims crept into the sacred text. It is not improbable that Malachi had one in mind when he charged Israel with disloyalty to Jehovah, saying, "When ye offer the blind for sacrifice, it is no evil, and when ye offer the lame and sick it is no evil" (Mal. 1: 8). The Spaniards today have substantially the same thought in mind when they say "Let that which is lost be for God." In the book of Job (34: 29) we find a reference to the eagle's or vulture's practice of feeding on carrion, which was alluded to by our Lord (Matt. 24: 28, Luke 17: 37). The vulture's liking for putrefying flesh was well known to the ancients which furnished them with a saying closely resembling the Latin phrase: "Where the corpse is there will the vulture be." In the same book (Job 14: 19) we find the expression—"The waters wear the stones"—which corresponds to our modern saying, "Constant dropping wears the stone." The question of Jeremiah (13: 23) "can the Ethiopian change his skin or the leopard his spots?"—has become a proverb, if it was not one in the prophet's time. Many nations have phrases akin to it. For example, the Turks say: "Washing a negro we lose our soap," the Persians declare that "A black cat will not wash white by soap"; the

Behar people ask each other the question: "Can the crow become white by eating camphor?" A phrase that George Herbert (1639) rendered "The bath of a blackamoor hath sworn not to whiten." The phrase "Skin for skin" (Job 2:4) was probably a well-known expression, which Satan emphasized by the addition of the statement "All that a man hath will he give for his life." The old Hebrew proverb "Is Saul also among the prophets" (I Sam. 19:24) had its origin in a well-known incident recorded in I Sam. 10:12. The phrase "As the mother, so the daughter" (See Psa. 106:35–40; Ezek. 16:44) has its parallel in a multitude of modern maxims. The words of the wise woman recorded in II Sam. 20:18: "They shall surely ask counsel of Abel"—*i.e.* Abel-beth-maacah, a place in upper Galilee celebrated for the wisdom of its inhabitants, was a familiar saying long before she repeated it. Zebah and Zalmunna probably quoted a proverb when they said "As the man is so is his strength" (Judges 8:21). The axiom—"A living dog is better than a dead lion—found in Ecclesiastes 9:4 is still in common use not only in England and America but in other lands. It must have been very expressive to the men of Solomon's day, who thought only of the undomesticated, prowling dog of the streets and the lion, king of all beasts. David quoted a well-known proverb, if not the oldest one in existence, when he vindicated himself with the words "Out of the wicked cometh forth wickedness" (I Sam. 24: 13) which was equivalent to saying character determines conduct, or as Isaiah put it—"The fool will speak folly" (Isaiah 20: 11) and as Christ declared—"The corrupt tree will bringeth forth evil fruit" (Matt. 7: 17). The phrase, "Dead flies cause the oil of the perfumer to send forth an evil odour" found in Ecclesiastes 10: 1 is equivalent to the French, Spanish and Italian saying "A little gall spoils a great deal of honey," the Dutch, "One rotten apple in the basket infects the whole quantity," the German, "One rotten egg spoils the whole pudding," the Danish and Italian, "One mangy sheep spoils the whole flock" and the Russian "A spoonful of tar in a barrel of honey and all is spoiled."

> "Now if some flies perchance, however small,
> Into the alabaster urn should fall,
> The odours of the sweets enclosed would die;
> And stench corrupt, sad change their place supply."
>
> *Matthew Prior.*

It was common in Old Testament times for men to refer to those of their number who were celebrated for proverbs as "Like Nimrod," who we are told was a mighty hunter before the Lord. "Like Nimrod" was a proverbial simile that was suggestive of a multitude of legends, stories of impossible achievements, and folk tales repeated among the people—some of which are preserved in the Talmud.

Scattered throughout the Sacred Oracles are sayings borrowed from every-day life. Some are now unrecognized as popular dicta, others are spoken of as parables, while a few are distinctly designated as proverbs.

### NEW TESTAMENT PROVERBS

Many of the proverbs found in the New Testament are of pure Hebrew origin, but not all. The Jews, in their intercourse with men from other lands, borrowed a large number of maxims. The precepts of the common people are always great travelers, and pass easily from one district to another. Those that were quoted in Palestine in the days of Christ included some that came from Assyria, Babylonia, Persia and Greece.

A few centuries ago the people of England laughed at the men of Gotham and counted them as fools. Today their children make merry over their fathers' prejudice and repeat the nursery rhyme:

> "Three wise men of Gotham went to sea in a bowl,
> If the bowl had been stronger, my tale would have been longer."

So in New Testament times the Jews taunted

the men of Nazareth and quoted the proverb, "Can any good thing come out of Nazareth?" (John 1:46) to prove the untrustworthiness of our Lord's claim. Nazareth had an evil reputation and its inhabitants were compelled to live under reproach.

Jesus, who understood the hearts of his countrymen, said to them, "Doubtless you will say unto me this parable or proverb: 'Physician heal thyself' (Luke 4:23) and then added another familiar saying "A prophet is not without honor save in his own country and in his own house" (Matt. 13:57) which has its parallel in all parts of the world under various forms. The same thought is quaintly expressed in Hindustan by their phrase "A Jogee is called a Jogra in his own village, but one from another village is called Sidh." No less striking is the Telugu dictum—"The tree in the back yard won't do for medicine."

Sitting by Jacob's well the Master referred to a familiar observation, when he asked His disciples, "Say ye not there are yet four months and then cometh harvest?" (John 4:35) and then proceeded to speak of the need of laborers in the field of service.

The excuse maker, who refused to follow Christ, plead that he must first go and bury his father, not because his father was dead or even was nearing death, but because the p overbial expression furnished him a convenient pretext for delay. The saying then current is still used in the East.

To another excuse maker Jesus said, "No man having put his hand to the plow and looking back is fit for the kingdom" (Luke 9: 62), thus suggesting to his hearer the picture of a laborer seeking to drive his plow while at the same time he continually turned to look back at some object that interested him instead of keeping his eyes on the furrow. Such a familiar picture would naturally lead to some proverb indicative of divided attention, which would be similar to the phrase used by Jesus.

Our Lord, in his Sermon on the Mount, declared that "One jot or tittle of the law" (Matt. 5: 18) would not pass until all was fulfilled. In so speaking he repeated a common aphorism. The people were wont to use the phrase "one jot or tittle" whenever they desired to emphasize the impossibility of detraction.

In that same hillside sermon Jesus joined two proverbs when He declared that "With what measure ye mete it shall be measured unto you" (Matt. 7: 2) and asked "Why beholdest thou the mote that is in thy brother's eye, but considerest not the beam that is in thine own eye?" (Matt. 7: 3). The first of these is found in the Talmud and corresponds to the Persian phrase "As he does to others so he will be done by" and the other is paralled by a large number of modern sayings.

"In other men we faults can spy
And blame the mote that dims their eye
Each little speck and error find
To our own stronger error blind."

*John Gay.*

In the fable of *The Fisherman Piping* Æsop furnished not only his countrymen, but the world beside, with an expression that was well known in Christ's day and which He probably quoted when He compared His own generation to children in the market place calling to their playmates, "We have piped unto you and ye did not dance" (Matt. 11: 17).

It is probable that Jesus had in mind a gnome or set of gnomes when he encouraged His disciples to pray saying: "Of which of you that is a father shall his son ask a loaf and he give him a stone, or a fish and he for a fish give him a serpent, or if he ask for an egg will he give him a scorpion" (Matt. 7: 9, 10). Long before His day the Greeks used the phrase "A scorpion for a perch."

At one time Christ admonished His disciples regarding the Pharisees. "Let them alone," He said, "They are blind guides" (Matt. 15: 14). It was not uncommon to use the term "blind guides" when speaking of false teachers and He frequently applied it to the Pharisees. On this occasion He added a proverb, saying, "If the blind guide the blind both shall fall into a pit." The Bengalese in the same way speak in derision of "blind torch bearers." Then quoting another common saying He charged the Pharisees with "straining out a gnat and swallowing a camel" (Matt. 23: 24).

Camels were frequently referred to in the street expressions and by words of the people and we find Him in the current language of the day declaring that it was "easier for a camel to go through a needle's eye than for a rich man to enter the kingdom of heaven" (Matt. 19: 24)—a phrase which is still used in the Orient under various forms.

On another occasion He denounced the lawyers and charged them with loading burdens on others that they themselves would not "touch with one of their fingers" (Matt. 23: 4) reminding us of Cicero's expression "to touch, so to speak with the finger." Presumedly the phrase was in common use in Christ's day as it was in that of the Roman orator.

Seeing the husbandman scattering his seed, He thought of another proverb that had been current eight hundred years, as we find Hesiod using it in his "Theogony," and said, "One soweth and another reapeth" (John 4: 37).

With marvelous power of character delineation Jesus pictured in parable a certain servant to whom a trust had been committed and who, being unfaithful, excused himself on the ground that he knew his master to be a hard man and then added a proverb in certification of his statement, "Reaping," said he, "Where thou didst not sow and gathering where thou didst not scatter" (Matt. 25:24).

In our Lord's charge to His disciples of all time, that they should refrain from anxiety because of the Heavenly Father's knowledge of their desires and needs He closed His plea with a well-known proverbial expression—"Sufficient unto the day is the evil thereof" (Matt. 6:34) which Tyndale (A.D. 1534) quaintly rendered "The daye present hath ever ynough of his awne trouble."

At a feast at which Jesus was present, we read that a certain man was so impressed with His wisdom that he lifted up his voice and praised Him in the presence of the assembled guests repeating a common saying of the day "Blessed is he that shall eat bread in the kingdom of God" (Luke 14:15).

In turning the pages of the gospels one may meet phrases that were on the lips of the people. Some were real proverbs, others proverb germs. Men spoke, for example, of "the gates of Hades" as a symbol of power, of "hanging a millstone about the neck and casting into the sea" as a dire punishment for a transgressor, of a "grain of mustard seed" as representing something exceedingly small, of a "tree being known by its fruit" as appropriately illustrating the relation of reputation to character and of "fearing not God nor regarding man" as indicating the mental state of one who disregarded spiritual and material powers.

We also find in the epistles frequent quotations of familiar maxims. The apostles like their master were men among men and the common people heard them gladly. When Paul said that "A little leaven leaveneth the whole lump" (Gal. 5: 9) he was quoting a popular saying not unlike the Old Testament proverb "Dead flies cause the oil of the perfumer to send forth an evil odor" (Eccles. 10: 1), already referred to, and when he declared that "Evil communications corrupt good manners" (I Cor. 15: 33) he was doing the same thing.

In writing to the Romans (12: 19) he said: "It is written vengeance belongeth unto me I will recompense saith the Lord"—which H. A. W. Meyer tells us had become in Paul's day a familiar proverbial warning formula. The phrase "Whatsoever a man soweth that shall he also reap" (Gal. 6: 7) was also an axiom which has continued in use until the present time and which the inhabitants of the Malabar district of India quaintly render "When anyone has learned to steal, he must also learn hanging."

The Apostle Peter probably quoted current sayings in his epistles. He wrote "Love covereth a multitude of sins" (I Peter 4: 8), "A dog turns to his own vomit again" (II Peter 2: 22) and "A sow that is washed to wallowing in the mire" (II Peter 2: 22).

Were we more familiar with the popular dicta of the Holy Land in the first century we would recognize many sayings no longer used even by the Jews. No more accurate portrait of life among the common people is to be found anywhere than is given in the pages of the Old and New Testaments. It is natural therefore to expect to find there quoted expressions that were habitually used.

### OTHER ANCIENT PROVERBS

The apocryphal books of the Bible like the Bible itself contain many by-words and phrases that were in use at the time of their composition. Ecclesiasticus has perhaps more than the others. There one will find the quotation "A slip on the pavement is better than a slip with the tongue" corresponding to the English saying "a slip of the foot may be soon recovered but that of the tongue never." "A faithful friend is a strong defence" corresponding to our familiar precept. "A friend in need is a friend indeed" and "Birds of a feather resort unto their like" corresponding to the often repeated "Birds of a feather flock together."

In the early centuries of the Christian era, the Jews collected a large number of aphorisms that are now found in the Talmud, intermingling them with the sayings of the Rabbis, many of which in turn have become a part of the world's store of proverbial wisdom. In the Talmud we find for example the phrase "The camel went to seek horns and its ears were cut off" corresponding to our "To go for wool and return shorn." "Every pumpkin is known by its stem" corresponding to "Like father like son," "When the barley is consumed from the pitcher strife knocks and enters the house" corresponding to our "When poverty comes in at the door, love flies out through the window," "The talk of the child in the street is that of his father or his mother," corresponding to our "What the child hears at the fireside it repeats in the market place." "Should the castle totter, its name is still castle; should the dunghill be raised, its name is still dunghill," "Should the peasant become king the soup does not leave his neck," and "Hang the heart of a palm tree around a sow and it will act as usual"—all corresponding to our "Set a beggar on horseback and he will gallop" and "Apes are apes although clothed in scarlet." "In the field where there are mounds talk no secrets" corresponding to our "Fields have eyes and woods have ears." The three Talmudic sayings "Approach the perfumer and thou wilt be perfumed," "The governor took us by the hand and the scent came into the hand" and "The servant of a king is like a king"—all corresponding to our "Walk with a cripple and you will learn to limp."

We are told in the Exodus Rabba that when Moses performed miracles to convince Pharaoh of his divine commission the king only ridiculed wonder works saying sarcastically "Art thou bringing straw to Eprayne" and again "Who carries muria (which was a kind of salt) to Spain, or fish to Acco?" These sayings put in the mouth of Pharaoh correspond to our "Carrying coals to Newcastle," and "Owls to Athens."

The Apostle Paul in his letter to the Thessalonians said "If any will not work neither let him eat" and in the Genesis Rabba we find it written "God designed man to work—work for his own sustenance; he who does not work shall not eat."

The following well-known proverbs are all found in the Talmud: "He whom a serpent hath bitten is terrified at a rope," "When the ox falls they sharpen their knives," "Cast no mud into the well from which thou hast drunk," "The rose grown among thorns," "Rather be the tail among lions than the head among foxes," "Few are they who see their own faults," "When wine enters the head the secret flies out," "Say little and do much," "The soldiers fight and the kings are heroes" and "The dog follows thee for the crumbs in thy pocket."

## PROVERB CHANGES

As proverbs pass from one country to another and continue in use through successive generations local conditions and carelessness of repetition frequently cause slight changes in their forms without altering their character or purport. The Englishman, for example, will say of the exaggerator that he makes "a mountain out of a molehill" while the North Indian will declare that he makes it out of a mustard seed. We say that "they who live in glass houses should not throw stones" while Chaucer wrote, "Who that has a head of glass from casting stones let him beware." Long before Chaucer was born the Spaniards were repeating the same proverb in the phrase, "He that has a roof of glass should not throw stones at his neighbor"—which so far as is known is the oldest form. The mountaineer will naturally change a lowland proverb so that it will be adapted to his own habits of life and the ranchman will alter a seafarer's maxim so that it will be understood by his associates: As ' there is no difference between bread and milk and milk and bread," as the residents of Old Britany say, so there is no real difference between altered proverbs that contain the same thought and have the same application.

Sometimes the form of a proverb will remain unaltered from one generation to another while the meaning will change. Take the saying, for example, "The more haste the less speed" which we understand to mean, one does not gain by hurrying. But our forefathers did not so understand it, for "speed" was used by them in the sense of "prosper," giving the phrase an entirely different purport. The adage "Kissing goes by favor" is another saying that has altered its meaning. To us it signifies that selected people alone are kissed, but in olden times the word "favor" was applied to looks or general appearance, which changed the meaning of the phrase. We find this old meaning of "favor" in our English Bible where it is written "Rachel was beautiful and well favored" (Gen. 29:17). Notwithstanding such changes, proverbs travel from one district to another and are handed down by parents to children in substantially the same form.

It must be remembered, however, that although slight alterations take place with the passing of years proverbs always remain complete. Fragments are without significance and popular sayings always have a definite meaning to those who use them. Agricola called them condensed rules of life, James Howells styled them weighty material in small packages and quaint Thomas Fuller spoke of them as decoctions. It is true that Aristotle declared them to be remnants which because of their shortness and correctness had been saved from the wreck and ruin of ancient philosophy, but he never intended to imply that they were incomplete.

### WHAT PROVERBS TEACH

J. G. Holland tells us that "the proverbs of a nation furnish the index to its spirit and the results of its civilization." While this may to some extent be true, it must not be inferred that all the proverbs of a country are indicative of its character or that any collection of a nation's sayings is a safe guide to its inner life, for many phrases that are thus properly listed are of common heritage and belong as truly to one nation as another. Sometimes phrases that are used in one district have been borrowed not from the people of another adjacent district but from an entirely alien race. "Mushrooms never grow after they are seen" is an old saying attributed to the Irish and understood as indicating a certain Celtic superstition, but its real significance is that mushrooms are so desirable that they are gathered as soon as they make their appearance. It is the same with proverbs. A short, crisp sentence that is exact and pointed is sure to be adopted so soon as it is heard. This is particularly true of witty sayings. The nations of the world are at all times taking proverbs from each other and adding them to their store. It therefore follows that only such as have been in constant use among the people of any district for a long period of time and are particularly adapted to their daily life are of any value to the ethnologist in determining the thoughts, feelings and purposes of such people. The fact that proverbs are modified and toned by the prevailing characteristics of the nation that uses them is true but it is no less true that they in turn influence the nation's habits of thought and the influence is so subtle and shows itself so gradually that while those in constant use throw light on the character of the people only students are able to discern their bearing. This, however, may be known to anyone who reads even superficially the folk sayings of the world. All nations and tribes belong to one human family and have the same characteristics and ambitions, no matter how much one may claim superiority over another. Conditions of life cause variant habits of speech but that does not indicate that there is any intrinsic difference in nature. The heart of the sturdy fisherman who braves the storms on the coast of Labrador and the indolent dependent on the natural products of the tropics, the intensive trader competing with his fellows on the noisy exchange and the lonely woodsman dwelling in the depths of the forest are all brothers, with common selfish and religious instincts and all reveal their brotherhood by repeating the same saws and maxims.

### WHY PROVERBS ARE NOT USED

It has been thought strange that proverbs are not as commonly used as they were in olden times. They were frequently quoted in the pulpit by preachers of the Reformation, cited in argument by authors of the seventeenth and eighteenth centuries and constantly repeated in conversation at the firesides and market places in the middle ages. Today they are seldom heard. This is not because the present generation does not appreciate wise and witty phrases or is loath to quote bright and instructive expressions. Epigrammatic sayings are regarded with favor everywhere, yet proverbs, no matter how wise and pertinent they may be, are rarely used. The extension of commercial relations and the enlargement of experience has had much to do with this change in habits of speech. "When Scotland began to have cities and seaports," it has been said, "she almost ceased to produce proverbs"—so has it been everywhere. In olden times the repetition of popular observations regarding the weather, health and ways of living, though more common in rural districts than in the more thickly populated sections, was general. Men everywhere stored their minds with precepts and counsels both for self-direction and instruction and admonition, but commerce and association with the outside world enlarged the vision and made the use of gnomes less necessary.

There is another and greater reason why proverbs are not so popular as in olden times. The printing press has wrought a change in the thoughts and habits of men. While the printing press has, according to a well-known authority, sought to continue the use of proverbs by the production of no less than two thousand books that directly relate to them, many of which have been compilations, its influence has been greater in stimulating the thoughts and enlightening the minds of people and has therefore been far more potent in causing their disuse than their use. Yet the work of proverb compilers has not been in vain for by the preservation of phrases once used in the affairs of life we learn the manner of men who lived and wrought in the world. "They being dead yet speak" and we enter into a large inheritance by reason of their wisdom.

Books, pamphlets and periodicals have given the people a more practical knowledge of the world than it would have been possible for them to obtain in any other way, broadened their visions so that they have been able to understand the bearing of natural laws on their daily lives and taught them to think for themselves and express their opinions more clearly and forcefully than they could by the repetition of set phrases. In past ages, when few could read, it was necessary to memorize wise and terse forms of speech and repeat wise adages but that need has passed. Superstition, that haunted the lives of our fathers and expressed itself in a myriad folk sayings, has been superseded to a large extent by reason. Men no longer accept a saying as true because it is old or is constantly repeated; they ask for the reason of things and will not be satisfied until they know.

Furthermore, people have learned that a proverb cannot be always true. "I am of opinion that there are no proverbial sayings which are not true," said Cervantes, "because they are all sentences drawn from experience itself, which is the mother of all sciences." But proverbs at best are only half truths. For that reason we find some that contradict the teaching of others. "A rolling stone gathers no moss" but it is equally true that "A setting hen never gets fat." "Friends and mules fail us in hard places" but that does not prevent our declaring with emphasis that "A friend is best found in adversity." "Honesty may be the best policy" yet "Honesty is praised and starves." How often have parents warned their children with the words "Marry in haste and repent at leisure" and fail to remind them that "Happy is the wooing that is not long in doing." Proverbs can be depended upon as statements of truth when viewed from a certain angle, and are properly used and forcefully quoted only when thus considered. This use of proverbs is clearly marked in Solomon's wise admonition to "Answer not a fool according to his folly lest thou also be like unto him" (Prov. 26:4) and his no less wise advice to "Answer a fool according to his folly, lest he be wise in his own conceit" (Prov. 26:5).

THE VALUE OF PROVERBS

Though proverbs are no longer treasured in the mind and used on all occasions they still have their value and Allan Ramsay's advice may be repeated: "As naething helps our happiness mair than to have the mind made up wi' right principles, I desire you for the thriving and pleasure of you and yours, to use your een and lend your lugs to these guid auld saws, that shine wi' wail'd sense, and will as lang as the world wags." The good old saws with their admonitions and warnings are of value still for thriving and pleasure and worth storing in the mind for thought and guidance. Gifted poets of bygone ages, profound philosophers, eloquent preachers, faithful students and men of letters have collected and used them with appropriateness and power, and we may well follow their example. "In whatever language it may be written," said Max Muller, "every line, every word is welcome that bears the impress of the early days of mankind."

Through them as through the old legends, songs, ballads, traditions, rhymes, superstitions and customs, we trace the moral and ethical development of the races, and learn the workings of the mind amid conditions other than our own. They are the "wisdom of the ages," but their wisdom is not found in their depth of thought or breadth of vision but rather in what Coleridge called their "commonsense in an uncommon degree." Their wisdom is not the wisdom of the schools but of the street, the farm and the cottage.

Education and enlightenment have not in the

least degree depreciated their value; they have only changed the character of their service. They may no longer be appealed to as authority but they still contain truths that are as old as man and suggest to both writers and public speakers lines of thought that bear on the problems of the present age. "They are the safest index to the inner life of a people," says Mr. A. Cohen, "with their aid we can construct a mental image of the conditions of existence, the manners, characteristics, morals and *Weltanschauung* of the community which used them. They present us with the surest data upon which to base our knowledge of *Volkspsychologie*." But more than an index they are of value to all who seek to serve their fellowmen in revealing to them the forces that move their consciences and wills. "A really good proverb," says Sir William Sterling-Maxwell, "is a coin as fine as any that ever was struck in the mint of Sicily."

As few people realize the antiquity of the common proverbs, I have selected a few of the most familiar sayings and sought to indicate in some degree their great age and the high esteem in which they have been held not alone by the common people but by literary workers of the past and present. I have added a few groups of folk sayings that indicate how widely they or their equivalents have been used by people in all parts of the world. It need hardly be said that the proverbs selected are only representative. There are a multitude of other common phrases that are just as old and that have been just as popular in the past, but enough examples have been given to enable the reader to realize the large place that proverbs have held in the esteem of men, for the development of character and wise direction in the affairs of daily life.

The original renderings of foreign phrases have not been given as such renderings would add to the size of the book without increasing its usefulness to the general reader, but care has been taken to use only such renderings as have been approved by competent translators.

The languages and dialects indicated in parenthesis after the proverbs quoted are not intended to signify that such proverbs are found only in the languages and dialects given but rather to show their most pronounced affiliation.

The small figures following the proverb headings refer to pages in *Curiosities in Proverbs* where the same saying is quoted and in many cases annotated.

It is hoped that the book will be found interesting and instructive and will lead to a greater appreciation of the value of the sayings of our fathers who helped to give us the heritage of wisdom and truth.

# Proverbs Annotated

## A BIRD IN THE HAND IS WORTH TWO IN THE BUSH

Certainty is better than uncertainty, possession is better than prospect.

Though caution and prudence are commendable, the truthfulness of the proverb under all circumstances may be questioned. The refusal to take business risks would stop the wheels of industry and prevent social, political and commercial advancement. While possession may sometimes be better than prospect, "prospect is often better than possession" (English).

The Teluges compare men who give up a certainty for an uncertainty to a jumping leech that never lets go its head in its forward movement, till it grasps its feet, and say that he is "like the leaping leech," while the Osmanli peasants decline to use a simile and substitute the proverb, "Forty birds that are in the mountain are worth one farthing"; but the Italians give the thought a religious turn and affirm that "God helps him who is in possession."

Mr. F. Edward Hulme draws attention to

the difference in our English rendering of the proverb and that of the Scotch. He says that the leading idea in both the Scottish version: "A bird in the hand is worth twa fleeing bye" and the English declaration that "A bird in the hand is worth two in the bush" "is the greater value of a small certainty than a larger possibility; but while the twittering of the free birds in the bush may be provoking there is at least the possibility of their capture, while the Scottish version gives a still greater value to our possession, seeing that even as we grasp it, the possibility of increasing our store is rapidly passing away.

As to the origin of the saying, it belongs to that class of proverbs that spring spontaneously into popularity among widely separated people. Nathan Bailey, early in the eighteenth century, was of the opinion that it was borrowed from the Hebrews or Greeks but gave no reason for his opinion. The thought was undoubtedly expressed in proverbial form by both the Greeks, and the Romans long before the Christian era. Some have thought that it originated in the well known Cuckoo story of the Gothamites which Mr. J. O. Halliwell gives in the following words:

"On a time the men of Gotham, fain would have pinn'd in the cuckoo, whereby she should sing all the year; and in the midst of the town they had a hedge made round in compass, and they had got a cuckoo, and put her into it, and said, 'Sing here, and you shall lack neither meat nor drink all the year.' The cuckoo when she perceived herself encompassed within the hedge, she flew away. 'A vengeance on her,' said the wise men, 'We made not our hedge high enough.'"

Alfred Stapleton, who made a study of Nottingham lore, said that he sometimes wondered whether the cuckoo story, or some similar tradition, may not have had something to do with the origin of the saying "A bird in the hand is worth two in the bush." If the proverb sprang from some such tale we must not forget that all the Gothamite stories predate their application to the fools of that town.

Lord Surrey, we are told, at one time gave a kingfisher to Sumers, the jester to King Henry VIII. Learning afterwards that Lord Northampton desired the bird he asked Sumers to return it to him and promised that if he would do so he would compensate him later with the gift of two kingfishers; but the jester thinking that possession was better than prospect refused to comply with Lord Surrey's request saying, "A bird in the hand is worth two in the bush."

Æsop (B.C. 561) has several fables bearing on the lesson of the proverb, as for example, *The Fisherman and the Sprat* and *The Partridge and the Fowler*, but the most striking one is the story of *The Nightingale and the Hawk,* which runs as follows:

A nightingale was sitting, according to custom, on the bough of an oak singing. A hungry hawk that was watching for prey heard the nightingale's song and swooped down on her, seized her in his talons. "Spare me," cried the poor little songster, "I never did you wrong, I am only a little bird, so very little that I could not satisfy your hunger. There are other birds in the woods that are larger and better than I am." "Spare you," returned the hawk, "Not I, for I have been on the watch for you all day and I am not foolish enough to give up a certainty for an uncertainty."

> "Better one bird in hand, than ten in the wood
> Better for birders, but for birds not so good"
>
> JOHN HEYWOOD, A.D. 1497–1580.

"Come, master, I have hair enough in my beard to make a counsellor, and my advice is as fit for you as your shoe is for your foot; a bird in the hand is worth two in the bush."—MIGUEL DE CERVANTES SAAVEDRA, A.D. 1547–1616, *Don Quixote.*

"As they were at supper, 'Well, Sir,' quoth the squire, 'What a rare fool I have been, had I chosen for my good news the spoils of your first adventure, instead of the breed of the three mares! Troth, commend me to the saying 'A bird in hand is worth two in the bush.'"—CERVANTES, *Don Quixote.*

"*Interpreter*, so he said, these two lads are figures; Passion, of the men of this world, and Patience, of the men of that which is to come: for as here thou seest, Passion will have all now, this year, that is to say, in this world; so are the men of this world; they must have all their good things now; they cannot stay till the next year, that is, until the next world, for their portion of good. That proverb, 'A bird in the hand is worth two in the bush' is of more authority with them than are all the divine testimonies of the good of the world to come."—JOHN BUNYAN, A.D. 1628–1688, *Pilgrim's Progress*.

" 'Tis not always true, that the bird I have in my hand, is justly my own, but if nobody else has a better claim to't, I would not part with it for forty birds that are in the bush only, and far enough out of my reach. A person may be pretty sure then of the thing he possesses; 'tis safe in his keeping but if he once lets it slip through his fingers, by grasping at more airy prospects, he may bid adieu to the ever having of it any more in his clutches. There will be no catching of the bird again, after it is once flown out of his power. . . . All men, I suppose, whether Greeks, Latins, Italians, French or English, who ever read or wrote of proverbs will readily grant me that it is better to have an egg today than a hen tomorrow; that the present pleasure is more eligible than a future enjoyment; that it is safer to stick to certainty than to chance; that what's in the fist is worth two in the fen; or that one horse in the stable is more useful for present service than three in the pasture. . . . Who but a knight errant would not accept of a real competent estate in possession, and hug himself in the enjoyment of it, rather than live fictitiously expecting the imaginary monarchy of the world of the moon in reversion."—OSWALD DYKES, A.D. 1707, *Moral Reflections*.

"This proverb intimates that possession is a mighty matter and precautions us not to run the hazard of a certain loss for an uncertain gain; and teaches us that futurities are liable to disappointments; no depending on shall or will hereafter, and no commanding things out of our hand five tenses distant from fruition."—NATHAN BAILEY, died A.D. 1724, *Diverse Proverbs*.

"The Italians say: 'Better be bird of the wood than bird of the cage.' This is rightly enough the bird's point of view; but the owner of the cage puts things rather differently, and declares: 'Better one bird in the hand than ten in the wood.' The Italians say that, 'It is better to have an egg today than a hen tomorrow,' but this surely is rather overdoing the thing. Even though present gain may outweigh future grander possibilities, the policy may be too narrowly pinched, and does away with legitimate hope." —F. EDWARD HULME, A.D. 1841–1909, *Proverb Lore*.

"This proverb turns up in several forms but it always means that we are to prefer that which we have to that which we only expect. It is a proverb of this world only and is not true on the broad field of eternal things. There our bird in the bush is worth all the birds that ever were in mortal hand."—CHARLES H. SPURGEON, A.D. 1834–1892, *The Salt Cellars*.

"There is a race of narrow wits that never get rich for want of courage. Their understanding is of that halting, balancing kind which gives a man just enough light to see difficulties and start doubts, but not enough to surmount the one or to remove the other. They never get ahead an inch, because they are always hugging some coward maxim, which they can only interpret literally. 'Never change a certainty for an uncertainty,' 'A bird in the hand is worth two in the bush,' are their favorite saws; and very good ones they are too, but not to be followed too slavishly. Of what use is it 'to be sawing about a set of maxims to which there is a complete set of antagonist maxims?' Proverbs, it has been well said, should be sold in pairs, a single one being but a half truth."—WILLIAM MATHEWS, *Getting on in the World*.

"'A bird in the hand is worth two
In the bush'—so the proverbs say;
But then, what on earth can you do,
If the bird in your hand flies away?"
*Harper's Bazar*, June 23, 1877.

VARIANT PROVERBS

**A beggar—who comes—to foot quickly is better than a master who comes to hand late.** (Osmanli).

**A bird in the hand is worth a dozen on wing.** (Gaelic).

**A bird in the cage is worth a hundred at large.** (Italian).

**A bird in the hand is better than a hundred—or thousand—flying.** (Spanish).

**A bird in the hand is worth two fleeing by.** (Scotch, Dutch, Portuguese).

**A bird in the hand is worth two in the wood.** (English).

**A bird in the hand is worth two on the wing.** (Guernsey).

**A captured bird is worth a thousand on the green.** (Latin).

**A crown in the pocket doth you more good than an angel spent.** (English).

**A feather in the hand is better than a bird in the air.** (English).

**An egg of today is better than the fowl of tomorrow.** (Osmanli).

**A pullet in the pen is worth a hundred in the fen.** (English).

**A small benefit obtained is better than a great one in expectation.** (Latin).

**A sparrow in the hand is better than a bustard on the wing.** (Spanish).

**A sparrow in the hand is better than a crane in the air.** (Persian).

**A sparrow in the hand is better than a hawk in the air.** (Persian).

**A sparrow in the hand is better than a peacock in expectation.** (Persian).

**A sparrow in the hand is better than a pigeon on the roof.** (German).

**A sparrow in the hand is better than a pigeon on the wing.** (French).

**A sparrow in the hand is worth a pheasant that flieth by.** (Latin, English).

**A sparrow in the hand is worth more than a goose flying in the air.** (French).

**A trout in the pot is better than a salmon in the pool.** (Irish-Ulster).

**A thousand cranes in the air are not worth one sparrow in the fist.** (Egyptian, Arabian).

**A titmouse in hand is better than a duck in the air** (Welsh).

**A titmouse in the hand is better than a crane in the air.** (Persian).

**A worm in my hand is better than a crane in the air.** (Persian).

**A wren in the hand is better than a crane to be caught.** (Irish).

**A young pumpkin now is better than a full grown one later on.** (Ancient Hebrew).

**Better a bird in the hand than four—or ten—in the air.** (Latin, Ashanti, Dutch).

**Better a finch in the hand than a parrot in the Indies.** (Portuguese).

**Better a fowl in the hand than two flying.** (English, Scotch).

**Better a lean lintie in the hand than the fat finch on the wand.** (Scotch).

**Better a leveret in the kitchen than a wild boar in the forest.** (Levonian).

**Better an egg today than a hen tomorrow.** (Italian, Modern Greek).

**Better an egg today than a pullet tomorrow.** (Italian).

**Better a sparrow in hand than a falcon in the forest.** (Serbian).

**Better a sparrow in hand than a vulture on the wing.** (Latin, Spanish).

**Better a wren in the hand than a crane in the air.** (French).

**Better is a wren in your fist—that is your property—than a crane—or heron—on loan.** (Irish-Ulster).

**Better one bird tied up than a hundred flying.** (Hebrew).

**Do not part with your ready money for future profit.** (Hindustani).

**Eggs now are better than chickens tomorrow.** (Latin).

**Even the bush which is near is preferable to a relation who lives at a distance.** (Singalese).

**Even the crow flesh that is to be had near is better than the peacock flesh that is far off.** (Singalese).

**Give me wool today and take sheep tomorrow.** (Arabian).

**Hoping for something still in the womb, while abandoning that which is in the lap.** (Assamese).

**I'd rather have balaow—horn fish—today than tazard—a kind of mackerel—tomorrow.** (Martinique Creole).

**It is better to haif ane brade in hand nor twa in the wood fleande.** (Scotch).

**Lungs at hand are better than a sheep's tail in expectation.** (Persian).

**Near us we have the puthi and khaliana, the ro and barali are far away—It is better to catch small fish that are near than to let the mind dwell on large and fine fish that are distant.** (Assamese).

**Oat bread today is better than cake tomorrow.** (Serbian).

**One bird in the dish is better than a hundred in the air.** (German).

**One bird in the hand is better than four outside it.** (Latin).

**One bird in the hand is worth ten in the sky.** (Belgian).

**One bird in the hand is worth two on the roof.** (Dutch, Portuguese).

**One bird in the net is better than a hundred—or thousand—flying.** (Hebrew).

**One bird in your hand is better than ten birds in the sky.** (Ashanti).

**One "here it is," is better than two "you will get."** (Irish).

**One " take this " is better than two " will give."** (French, Spanish).

**One hour today is worth two tomorrow.** (Latin).

**One quill is better in hand than geese upon the strand.** (Dutch).

Sheeps trotters in the hand are better than a leg of mutton a year hence. (Bannu).

The flow of cash is better than the sweetmeats of credit. (Persian).

The egg of today is better than the goose of tomorrow. (Osmanli).

Today's fowl is better than tomorrow's goose. (Osmanli).

Why let the bird in hand go and snare one in the jungle? (Tamil).

ALLIED PROVERBS

A clear loss rather than a profit of distant expectation. (Arabian).

A friend at hand is better than a relative at a distance. (Japanese).

A palm of the hand never deceives me. (African, Youba).

Better good afar off than evil at hand. (English).

Forty birds that are in the mountain are worth one farthing. (Osmanli).

God send you readier meat than running hares. (English).

He left the half and did not overtake the whole. (Hindustani).

He that leaves certainty and sticks to chance, when fools pipe, he may dance. (Latin, English).

The moon is with thee, thou needest not to care about the stars. (Arabian).

I'm like the piper's cow, gie me a pickle pea-stae and sell your wind for siller—said to a promiser or boaster. (Scotch).

It's a rash bargain to sell the bird on the bough. (Italian).

I will not change a cottage in possession for a kingdom in reversion. (Latin, English).

Like a leaping leech. (Telugu).

Milk the cow you have caught, what's the good of following the runaway. (Latin).

Sour milk which has been tried is better than untried curds. (Syriac).

The fish binny said, "If thou canst find a better than myself do not eat me"—the binny fish is regarded as one of the best tasting fishes that are to be caught in the Nile. (Arabian).

The sheep says they too get the child, but the shaking sickness is what takes it. (Ibo-Nigeria).

They don't sell the duiker walking in the bush. (Ibo-Nigeria).

This is better than the thing we never had. (Irish).

PROVERBS FROM THE BIRD'S POINT OF VIEW

Better be a bird in the wood than one (or ten) in the cage. (Italian).

Better be a free bird than a captive king. (Danish).

It is a old sayin' dat one bird in de han' is wuth two in de bush.

It may be wuth more ter de man, but it ain't wuth half as much ter de bird. (Negro Plantation Proverb).

The figs on the other side of the hedge are sweeter. (Serbian).

## A BURNT CHILD DREADS THE FIRE

This old English proverb, or its equivalent, is found in all lands. Lafacadio Hearn heard it repeated by the Creoles of Louisiana in their *Chatte brille pair di few*, and David Livingston met with it among the Bechuanas who said of those who received injury from some foolish act, "You will not go into those coals a second time."

The saying is lengthened in Denmark by adding "and a bitten child a dog."

A child's book of the eighteenth century entitled *Proverbs Exemplified* illustrated the phrase by a picture of two boys, one standing near a beehive from which he had sought to take honey. He is represented as lifting his foot and sucking his thumb in agony, because of the stings that he had received. The other boy is shown running away from the place of danger.

While the proverb is intended to indicate that "Experience is the best teacher" its English form states that the burnt child *dreads* the fire, which is not always true.

The old Romans expressed the same thought in their saying, "A fisherman once stung will be wiser," which is believed by some to have been the original form of the proverb. If this were true the Romans probably borrowed it from the inhabitants of some seacoast district where it was used in referring to over-anxious fishermen who in seeking to ascertain the contents of their nets were stung by scorpions or by fish with sharp finned backs.

"A dog was lying in the sun before a farmyard gate when a wolf pounced upon him and was just going to eat him up but he begged for his life and said, 'You see how thin I am and what a wretched meal I should make you now; but if you will only wait a few days my master is going to give a feast. All the rich scraps and pickings will fall to me and I shall get nice and fat; then will be the time for you to eat me.' The wolf thought this was a very good plan and went away. Some time afterward he came to the farmyard again and found the dog lying out of reach on the stable roof. 'Come down,' he called, 'and be eaten: You remember our agreement.' But the dog said coolly, 'My friend, if ever you catch me lying down by the gate there again don't you wait for any feast.'"—ÆSOP, died about B.C. 561 *V. S. Vernon Jones translation.*

Another of Æsop's fables tells us that a certain house was infested by mice and that the occupants, being greatly annoyed by their presence, secured a cat that caught some of them every day. The mice, finding their number rapidly decreasing, consulted with each other as to the best method of protecting themselves against their enemy and decided to remain on the upper shelf where they could not be reached. The hungry cat noticing that the mice did not run about on the floor as usual, sought to outwit them by strategy; so she laid hold of a peg with her hind feet and hung against the wall as though she were dead. She had not remained long in that position when a cunning mouse looked over the edge of the upper shelf and said: "So you are there, are you, my good friend? There you may stay. I would not come down on the floor though I saw your skin stuffed with straw."

"The fish which has once felt the hook suspects the crooked metal in every food which offers."—Publius Ovidus Naso, B.C. 43–A.D. 17.

"He that has been shipwrecked shudders at still water."—Publius Ovidus Naso.

"So soon upon supper, said he, no question
Sleep maketh ill and unwholesome digestion:
By that diet a great disease once I gat
And burnt child fire dreadeth; I will beware of that."

John Heywood, A.D. 1497–1580, *A Dialogue*.

"*Gloucester*: Suspicion always haunts the guilty mind;
The thief doth fear each bush an officer.

4

*King Henry:* The bird that hath been limed in a bush,
With trembling wings misdoubteth every bush;
And I, the hapless male to one sweet bird,
Had now the fatal object in my eye,
Where my poor young was limed, was caught and kill'd."

WILLIAM SHAKESPEARE, A.D. 1497–1580, *King Henry VI, Pt. III.*

"What, wouldst thou have a serpent sting thee twice?"

WILLIAM SHAKESPEARE, *The Merchant of Venice.*

"He who has suffered shipwreck fears to sail
Upon the seas, though with a gentle gale."

ROBERT HERRICK, A.D. 1591–1674, *Hesperides: Shipwreck.*

"'Tis certain, Ulysses had no great kindness for the sea, after he had been dangerously toss'd in it by storms and tempests for the space of ten years, or upwards before he could arrive at the haven of his own wishes, and land safe in his own native country; for no doubt he would have dreaded the thought of renewing those terrible hazards and repeating that perilous voyage over again, as much as ever he rejoiced at his own safety upon an unexpected deliverance from the fury of a merciless ocean."—OSWALD DYKES, A.D. 1707, *Moral Reflections.*

"Not seldom will there be an evident superiority of a proverb in one language over one, which, however, resembles it closely, in another. Moving in the same sphere, it will yet be richer, fuller, deeper. Thus our own, *A burnt child fears the fire*, is good; but that of many tongues,

*A scalded dog fears cold water*, is better still. Ours does but express that those who have suffered once will henceforward be timid in respect of that same thing from which they have suffered; but that other the tendency to exaggerate such fears, so that now they shall fear even where no fear is. And the fact that so it will be, clothes itself in an almost infinite variety of forms."—RICHARD CHENEVIX TRENCH, A.D. 1807–1886, *Proverbs and Their Lessons*.

"We are all like burnt children. We have all suffered more or less by our ignorance, our wilfulness or our folly, in tampering and meddling with that which we should have left alone. We are all (begging our several pardons) like scalded urchins; running continually into mischief, smarting from the consequences, and then howling or growling at what we are pleased to term our misfortunes."—JEFFERYS TAYLOR, A.D. 1827, *Old English Sayings*.

"If those are wise who learn caution from their own experience, those are wiser still who learn it from the experience of others. If the burnt child dreads the fire, it is well; but if the unburnt child dreads it, it is better; for he has obtained the benefit of experience without the expense of it."—JEFFERYS TAYLOR, *Old English Sayings*.

VARIANT PROVERBS

**A beaten dog is afraid of the stick's shadow.** (Italian).

**A beaten soldier fears a reed.** (Japanese).

**A bitten child dreads a dog.** (English).

**A burnt cat dreads the fire.** (Louisiana Creole).

**A burnt cat shuns the fireplace.** (Tamil).

**A burnt child dreads the fire and a bitten child dreads a dog.** (Danish).

**A crane, frightened at the roar of thunder, fears even a jackal's howl—cranes are said to fall on the ground when they hear thunder.** (Pashto).

**A dog once struck with a firebrand dreads even the sight of lightning.** (Behar).

**A dog that has been beaten by a stick is afraid of its shadow.** (English).

**A fisherman once stung will be wiser.** (Latin).

**A man once struck with a firebrand runs away on seeing a glow worm.** (Bengalese).

**A man who has once been bitten by a snake is afraid of every piece of rope.** (Assamese, Japanese).

**A scalded cat dreads cold water.** (English, Scotch, French, Spanish, Portuguese, Malay, Behar).

**A scalded dog fears cold water.** (English).

**A snake bite you, an' you see a lizar (lizard), you mus' run.** (British Guiana).

**Burnt bairns dread the fire.** (Scotch).

**Having burnt his mouth with milk he now blows even on buttermilk before drinking it.** (Marathi).

**He that has been bitten by a serpent fears a rope.** (Hebrew, Hindoo, Assamese, English, Persian).

**He that has been scalded with milk blows when he drinks buttermilk.** (Persian, Hindustani, Behar, Kumaun, Garhwal).

**He that is bitten by a snake is terrified by a cord.** (Persian).

**He who has been bitten by a serpent is afraid of an eel.** (English, Danish).

**He who has been bitten by a serpent is afraid of a lizard.** (Italian, Serbian).

He who has been burnt by the hot blows even upon the cold. (Modern Greek).

He who has been kicked by a bear fears the sight of one who sells cucumbers. (Tamil).

He who has been stung by a scorpion is afraid of its shadow. (Spanish).

He who has once burnt his mouth always blows his soup. (English, German).

He who has seen a black serpent is afraid of a black stick. (Armenian).

He whom a serpent has bitten dreads a slow worm—The slow, or blind, worm of West Africa is a harmless reptile. (Oji-West Africa).

Once bitten by a snake fears a rope. (Marathi, Assamese).

Once bitten, twice shy. (English).

Singed by lightning he runs from a burning stick. (Hindustani).

The animal escapes the trap and stands in dread of a bent stick. (Efit, West Africa).

The cow that has been burnt out of its shed sees the evening sky red (with the setting sun) and trembles. (Bengali).

The horse that is struck in the head will be full of fear—he will expect a blow when none was intended and start when his owner moves. (Gaelic).

The man who has been beaten by a firebrand runs away at the sight of a firefly. (Cingalese).

When a cat has been once burned by the fire it is even afraid of cinders. (Mauritius Creole).

Who has burnt himself with hot food blows at cold. (Pashto).

### ALLIED PROVERBS

A blind man loses his staff only once. (Hindustani).

A dog steals a leg (of mutton) from the butcher's shop, but he cuts off his own leg—i.e. He will not be allowed to go to the butcher's shop again. (Syriac).

**A fox is not caught twice in a snare.** (Greek).

**A man deceives a man only once.** (Osmanli).

**A scalded dog thinks cold water hot.** (Italian).

**After mischance everyone is wise.** (French).

**Boys avoid the bees that stung 'em.** (English)

**By falling we learn to go safely.** (Dutch).

**Do not show a man that is hanged, a rope; nor a burnt man fire.** (Syrian).

**Experience keeps a dear school, but fools learn in no other.** (English).

**Experience is the best teacher.** (English).

**Experience is the great baffler of speculation.** (English).

**Experience makes fools wise.** (English).

**Experience purchased by suffering teaches wisdom.** (Latin).

**Experience teaches fools and he is a great one that will not learn by it.** (English).

**Having had experience he fears it.** (Latin).

**He knows the water best who has walked through it.** (Danish).

**He remembers the burning of his finger.** (Gaelic).

**He starts at sight of a log whose relative was devoured by a crocodile.** (Bengali).

**He who has been burned fears.** (Latin, English).

**He who has been hurt fears.** (Latin).

**He who has crossed the ford knows how deep it is.** (Italian).

**He who has led a wicked life is afraid of his own memory.** (English).

**He who is a man does not make a mistake twice.** (Osmanli).

**He who is deceived once is (not) deceived again.** (Osmanli).

**He whose father was killed by a bear is afraid of a black stump.** (Hindi).

**If a snake bite you an' you see lizar you mus' run.** (British Guiana).

If the timid sees a glow worm he shouts: Fire! (Armenian).

Is the weaver so mad that he will again steal wool? (Kashmiri).

It is shameful to stumble twice against the same stone. (Greek).

None know the danger of the fire more than he who falls into it. (English).

The fish which has once felt the hook suspects the crooked metal in every food which offers. (Latin).

The fisherman when stung will learn wisdom. (Latin, Greek).

The leaf cracked and you have fled. (Hindi).

Trembling at a bit of rope thinking it to be a snake. (Tamil).

Will the woman with a shaved head go under the bel tree? —The answer being, No! as the fruit of the bel tree is a wood apple that is believed by the natives to be attracted by bald heads. (Behar).

You will not go into those coals a second time. (Bechuana, South Africa).

A CHIP OF THE OLD BLOCK
LIKE FATHER, LIKE SON
LIKE MOTHER, LIKE DAUGHTER.

The resemblance of children to their parents has been observed for untold ages and has been expressed in many phrases. Among primitive races various rites and ceremonies are performed by the parents before and after the birth of a child to cause it have commendable traits of character. It is believed that by such rites and ceremonies the father and mother are able to communicate their virtues to their offspring.

The three proverbs indicate that the child bears a physical resemblance to one or both of its parents or that his way of thinking, speaking or acting is similar to theirs. They do not indicate that a child may not be inferior or superior in physical strength, intellectual power or business acumen. Brewer reminds us that in English history King John was the son of Henry II, Edward II was the son of Edward I, Richard II was the son of the Black Prince, Henry VI was the son of Henry V and Lord Chesterfield's son was a disappointment to his father; that in French history Louis VIII was the son of

Philippe *Auguste*, Charles *the Idiot* was the son of Charles *le Sage* and that Henry II was the son of François I; and that in German history Heinrich VI was the son of Barbarossa; and that Albrecht I was the son of Rudolf.

If it is true that a father of great talents has a son who has less ability, it may also be said to be true that that son probably had a grandfather inferior to his son.

The phrase, "A chip of the old block" has been in common use for many centuries. Edmund Burke said of William Pitt that he was not merely a chip of the old block, but the old block itself.

Twenty-five hundred years ago Ezekiel, Prophet of Israel, declared that "As is the mother, so is her daughter" (Ezek. 16:44) this was a common proverb. That being the case its corresponding saying, "As is the father, so is his son" must also have been well known in his day.

Bible References: I Sam. 24:13; Isa. 24:2; Ezek. 18:2.

"An old crab said to her son, 'Why do you walk sideways like that, my son? You ought to walk straight.' The young crab replied: 'Show me how, dear mother, and I'll follow your example.' The old crab tried, but tried in vain, and then saw how foolish she had been to find fault with her child."—ÆSOP, B.C. 561, *V. S. Vernon Jones' translation.*

"Falsehood her father is with fickle tongue
That since he came to earth, never said sooth,
And Meed is mannered after him, as nature will
Like father, like son: Every good tree maketh
good fruit."

WILLIAM LANGLAND, A.D. 1300–1400.

"*Gloucester*: No doubt, no doubt: O 'tis a parlous boy;
Bold, quick, ingenious, forward, capable:
He is all the mother's from top to toe."

WILLIAM SHAKESPEARE, A.D. 1564–1616, *King Richard III.*

"*Paulina*: It is yours;
And might we lay the old proverb to your
charge,
So like you, 'tis the worse. Behold, my lords,
Although the print be little, the whole matter
And copy of the father, eye, nose, lip;
The trick of's frown; his forehead; nay, the
valley
The pretty dimples of his chin and cheek; his
smiles;
The very mould and frame of hand, nail,
finger."

WILLIAM SHAKESPEARE, *Winter's Tale.*

"*Constance*: Thou monstrous injurer of heaven and earth!
Call not me slanderer; thou and thine usurp
The dominations, royalties and rights
Of this oppressed boy; this is thy eld'st son's
son,
Unfortunate in nothing but in thee:
Thy sins are visited in this poor child;
The canon of the law is laid on him,
Being but the second generation
Removed from thy sin—conceived womb."

WILLIAM SHAKESPEARE, *King John.*

"Treason is but trusted like the fox,
Who, ne'er so tame, so cherish'd and lock'd up,
Will have a wild trick of his ancestors."
WILLIAM SHAKESPEARE, *King Henry IV., Pt. I.*

"Impossible suppositions produce impossible consequences, 'As is the mother, so is the daughter.' Therefore surely God's Holy Spirit would not suppose such a thing but what was feasible and possible, but what either had, did, or might come to pass."—THOMAS FULLER, A.D. 1608–1661.

FATHER AND SON PROVERBS

**A branch brings forth a fig.** (Ancient Hebrew).

**A chip of the old block, like the seed of the trooper, if he is not up to very much, still he is above the average.** (Behar).

**A lion's whelp resembles its sire, but tell me in what respect do you resemble a prophet?** (Persian).

**A monkey's young ones.** (Kashmiri).

**As the father so the son.** (Sanskrit, Telugu, Kumaun, Garhwal).

**As flour so the gruel.** (Tamil).

**As the nest so the bird, as the father so the child.** (Serbian).

**As the old cock crows so the young bird chirrups.** (English).

**As the old bird sings so the young ones twitter.** (German, Danish).

**As the potter so the pitcher and as the father so the son,** (Marathi).

**Even in animals there exists the spirit of their sires.** (Latin).

**Even the child of a thief is characterized by thievish propensities.** (Tamil).

**Foxes sons of foxes.** (Hebrew).

**He has of his father—i.e. He is like his father.** (Russian.)

**He is a child of his father.** (Modern Greek).

**He is a lion the son of a lion.** (Hebrew).

**He is cut out of his father's eyes—i.e. He is like his father.** (Frisian).

**He is his father's son.** (Telugu, Latin).

**He is the son of his father?** (Latin, English).

**If the father is a fisherman the children look into the water.** (Russian).

**Is he not the son of that father?** (Telugu).

**My father was a thief, I am of the same nature.** (Assamese).

**Such a father such a son.** (English, Portuguese, Telugu).

**Such as his—referring to his likeness to his father.** (Kumaun, Garhwal).

**The big dog's nature will be in the pup.** (Gaelic).

**The brave are born from the brave and good.** (Latin).

**The child for whom the father dances Ufie dances Agidi.** (Ibo).

**The father is known from the child.** (German).

**The fish is rotten from the head—i.e. The child partakes of the nature of its parents.** (Persian).

**The old one sings, the young ones pipe.** (Dutch).

**The rope dancer's son is always turning summersaults.** (Indian).

**The son of a brave is brave.** (Osmanli).

**The son of a tailor will sew as long as he lives.** (Behar).

**The son of a tyrant will be a tyrant as the sword when broken becomes a dagger.** (Persian).

**The son of a wolf will be a wolf even if it grows up with man.** (Osmanli).

**The son of Hyn is a Jinn—i.e. a bad man.** (Osmanli).

**The son resembles his father and the colt his sire, if not exactly so, yet in a certain degree.** (Hindustani).

**The young ravens are beaked like the old.** (Dutch, Arabian).

**Thou art thy father's own son.** (English).
**Vessels of the same kiln.** (Hindustani).
**Weights of the same bag.** (Kumaun, Garhwal).

MOTHER AND DAUGHTER PROVERBS

**As is the mother such is the child; as is the yarn such is the cloth.** (Tamil).
**As mother so daughter; as the mill so the flour.** (Pashto).
**Bad crow, bad egg.** (Greek, Sanskrit).
**Durag's stick (i.e. according to her height) and as mother so daughter.** (Kashmiri).
**Ewe followeth ewe, as the acts of the mother so are the acts of the daughter.** (Hebrew).
**From the sow comes but a little pig.** (Gaelic).
**Gusie sow, gudely calf.** (Scotch).
**Like crow, like egg.** (English).
**Mother a witch, daughter also a witch.** (German).
**Pull a girl by her sleeve she always resembles her mother —i.e. try to pull or influence a girl to be like someone else, she will still be like her mother.** (Arabian).
**See the mother comprehend the daughter.** (Pashto).
**She hath a mark after her mother.** (English, Telugu).
**She's her mother over again.** ((Scotch, English).
**That which is the mother's is the daughter's.**

This proverb is used to refer not only to the daughter's property but also to her disposition and habits. (Tamil).

**The leaf that the big goat eats the kid eats.** (Ibo).
**The skein corresponds with the thread and the daughter resembles her mother.** (Hindustani).
**The young ones of the duck are swimmers.** (Arabian).
**The young pig grunts like the old sow.** (English).
**Turn the jar on its mouth and the daughter will come up like her mother.**

The Syrian water jar is shaped so that whether it stands on its base or on its mouth it looks about the same. (Syrian.)

## ALLIED PROVERBS

A branch bringing forth a fig. (Hebrew).

A calf takes after its mother and a foal its sire, if not in all points still in a few. (Behar).

A child is a child though the son of a prophet. (Persian).

A herb grows according to its root. (Syriac).

Arrows from one quiver. (Hindustani).

As the auld cock crawd the young cock learns. (Scotch, English).

As the seed so the sprout. (Sanskrit).

As the teacher so will the scholar be. (Kashmiri).

As the king such are his subjects. (Tamil).

At last the wolf's cub becomes a wolf. (Pashto).

A wild goose never laid a tame egg. (Irish).

Before taking a woman in marriage ascertain the character of her mother; before buying a cow ascertain the quality of its milk. (Tamil).

Being born a tiger will it become a cat? (Tamil).

Being born a tiger will it be without claws? (Tamil).

Big and small baskets and fans are made of the same bamboo. (Kumaun, Garhwal).

By the child one sees what sort of a man his father is. (German).

Choose cloth by its edge; a wife by her mother. (Persian).

He is not the son of that father. (Telugu).

He that is born of a hen must scrape for a living. (English, French).

He who takes his lineage from the ground himself becomes ox-tender—i.e. He who is low born must engage in some lowly occupation. (Osmanli).

If you put sour milk into a leathern bag, for one hundred years, it will still be sour milk—i.e. as sour milk will remain sour milk, so bad blood will remain bad blood through successive generations. (Persian).

If you wish to know a prince look at his ministers; if you wish to understand the man himself look at his

**parents, but if you wish to know a father observe his son.** (Chinese).

**It is "pan" from the same tree, how will it be different?** (Assamese).

**Let it be torn, let it be broken; it is still a scarf of fine silk; let him be young, let him be old; he is still the son of Bhuiya** (n).

The silk referred to in this proverb is of a fine quality and obtained from the cocoons of mulberry fed worms. The scarf that is made of this silk is often beautifully embroidered with red and sometimes with gold threads. Being a son of Bhuiya (n) is an honor because of their position as landholders and their relation to the government. (Assamese).

**Like priest like people.** (English).

**Look at the mother before affiancing the daughter.** (Serbian, Tamil).

**Look at the mother take the daughter.** (Osmanli).

**Nature will out.** (English).

**Observe the edge and take the linen; observe the mother and take the daughter.** (Turkish).

**Plant a mango and eat a mango; plant a tamarind and eat a tamarind.** (Hindustani).

**That which does not resemble its master is spurious.** (Syriac).

**The branch of a rose wherever it grows is always a rose.** (Persian).

**The calf is like the cow and the colt is like its father—if not entirely yet certainly in some degree.** (Hindustani).

**The child had a rid tongue like its father.** (English).

**The comparison of a gray goose to his mother.** (Gaelic).

**The daughter of a bad cow, the grandchild of a good one.** (Gaelic).

**The daughter of a crab does not give birth to a bird.** (Chinese, Oji).

**The devil is like his dam.** (English).

Dam in this proverb refers to a mother, though the word is sometimes applied in old literature to a wife.

**The devil is the father of lies.** See John 8:44 (English).

**The devil's child the devil's luck.** (English).

**The donkey colt by force of growing becomes a donkey.**

This proverb is generally applied to one who exaggerates in telling a story.

**The faults of a mother are visited on her children.** (Tamil).

**The future crop is known in the grain.** (Tamil).

**The hen scratches and the chickens learn.** (Kashmiri).

**The mother a radish, the father an onion and the son a saffron flower—i.e. The son of a worthless father and mother will be worthless.** (Panjabi).

**The mother was an innkeeper and the son is Fatteh Khan —i.e. The mother is of a common grade and her son puts on the airs of a conqueror though he himself is common.** (Panjabi).

**The muddy fountain spurts forth muddy water.** (English).

**The rose from rose is born, the thorn from thorn.** (Pashto).

**The serpent brings forth nothing but little serpents.** (Arabian).

**The spawn of frogs will become frogs.** (Japanese).

**The thieving dog's pup may not be a thief yet, but he will sniff about—i.e. The thieving dog's pup may not be an actual thief but he will have a thieving propensity.** (Pashto).

**They are all loaves of one batch or cakes of the same griddle, whether small or great—i.e. They are all of the same descent or family.** (Hindustani).

**They are seeds out of the same bowl.** (Telugu).

**The young of a cuckoo will be a cuckoo and cause the crow grief and disappointment—i.e. will put ashes on the face, that being the common sign of mourning and distress of mind in the East.**

The meaning is that a cuckoo will be a cuckoo even though brought up by a crow foster-mother. (Behar).

**The young of a snake is a snake and its young one is a scorpion.** (Tamil).

**What is bred in bone won't out of the flesh.** (English).

**We may not expect a good whelp from a bad dog.** (Hebrew).

**Whence is this twig? From this shrub.—i.e. Bad children spring from bad parents, and good children from good parents.** (Modern Greek).

**Who shall teach young fish to swim?** (Hindustani).

**Will a plant differ from the seed?** (Telugu).

**Will a child—daughter—fail to follow its mother's track?** (Telugu).

### CONTRADICTING PROVERBS

**A beggar's son struts like a peer.** (Hindustani).

**A diligent mother has a lazy daughter.** (German).

**A dog had a young one which grew worse than his father.** (Syrian).

**A light heeled mother makes a heavy heeled daughter.** (English).

**A skitting cow has often had a good calf.** (English).

**A son like the mother, and the daughter like the father.** (Gaelic).

**Diligent mother, idle daughter.** (Portuguese).

**From good parents a black calamity was born.** (Pashto).

**From the thorn bush comes the rose.** (Hebrew).

**He died as a dog and freed us of service, but he left a whelp behind that was worse than his father.** (Hindustani).

**Many a good cow hath but a bad calf.** (English).

**Many a good father has a bad son.** (English).

**Parched maize is the excellent offspring of millet—i.e. A good child of worthless parents.** (Hindustani).

**Parents who have no equals rear children unlike themselves—i.e. Good parents rear children unlike themselves.** (Hebrew).

**The active mother makes the lazy daughter.** (Gaelic).

**The father, a petty merchant, the son a lord.**

This proverb is used contemptuously in speaking of an upstart. (Hindustani).

**The father wore a mallet about his neck, the son a precious necklace.** (Hindustani).

**The wise man is father of the fool.** (West African).

**What does the beetle beget? Insects worse than itself.**

Sometimes this proverb is quoted: "What does the scorpion beget? Insects worse than itself." (Hebrew).

**You are no son like the father.** (Gaelic).

**You'll never fill your father's shoes.** (English).

36, 99, 155, 302

## A FRIEND IN NEED IS A FRIEND IN DEED

Friendship shows itself by love and ministry.

The origin of this proverb is unknown but as its thought has been expressed by a multitude of writers in olden times we may well believe that it has been known and used for more than two thousand years. Plautus, the Roman dramatist, two hundred years before the coming of Christ, declared that "Nothing is more friendly to a man than a friend in need," which is but another form of the proverb.

The saying, "He that's no my friend at a pinch is no my friend at a'" is another form of the phrase, "He that's no my friend at a pinch is not worth snuff," or as we would say "a pinch of snuff," which expresses in a quaint way the thought that the test of friendship is helpfulness in time of need. When the Telugus ask for proof of friendship they say, "Would you comfort me or remove my grief, or if necessary would you plunge?" That is, plunge in the water to save me were I in peril of drowning. This understanding of the proverb is in accord with the universal conception of true friendship.

"Just as the yellow gold is tested in the fire," said the Roman poet Ovid, "So is friendship to be proved in an evil time."

"I praise you when you regard the trouble of your friend as your own."—PLAUTUS, B.C. 254–184.

"A true friend is distinguished in the crisis of hazard and necessity, when the gallantry of his aid may show the worth of his soul and the loyalty of his heart."—ENNIUS, B.C. 239–169.

"The swallows are at hand in summer time, but in cold weather they are driven away—so false friends are at hand in life's clear weather but as soon as they see the winter of misfortune they all fly away."—CICERO, B.C. 106–43.

"Prosperity is no just scale, adversity is the only balance to weigh friends."—PLUTARCH, A.D., 46–120.

"Some man is a friend for his own occasion and will not abide in the day of wrath."—ECCLUS., 6: 8.

"A friend cannot be known in prosperity and an enemy cannot be hid in adversity."—ECCLUS., 12: 8.

"Forget not thy friend in thy mind and be not unmindful of him in thy riches."—ECCLUS., 37: 6.

"Nother love levere, ne lever freonds
Than after werre and wreck."
WILLIAM LANGLAND, A.D. 1330–1400.

"As hatred is the serpent's noisome rod,
So friendship is the living gift of God:
The drunken friend is friendship's very evil;
The frantic friend is friendship for the devil;
The quiet friend, all one in word and deed,
Great comfort is, like ready gold, in need.
Hast thou a friend the heart may wish at will?
Then use him so, to have his friendship still.
Would'st have a friend? Would'st know what friend is best?
Have God thy friend, who passeth all the rest."

THOMAS TUSSER, A.D. 1524–1580.

"He that is thy friend in deed
He will help thee in thy need:
If thou sorrow he will weep;
If thou wake he cannot sleep;
Thus, of every grief in heart
He with thee doth bear a part:
These are certain signs to know,
Faithful friend from flattering foe.'

RICHARD BARNFIELD, A.D. 1574–1627.

"By friendship you mean the greatest love, the greatest usefulness, the most open communication, the noblest sufferings, the severest truth, the heartiest counsel and the greatest union of minds of which brave men and women are capable."—JEREMY TAYLOR, A.D. 1613–1667.

THE CHARACTERISTICS AND HABITS OF FRIENDS

**A courageous is better than a cowardly friend.** (English).
**A rat and a cat friendship.** (Gugerat).
**A rich friend is a treasure.** (English).
**Friends are one soul in two bodies.** (Turkish).
**Friends 'gree best at a distance.** (Scotch).

Friendship consists not in saying: " What's the best news." (English).

Friendship is love with understanding. (German).

Friends may meet, but mountains never greet—i.e. Friends may agree but haughty people seldom do. (English).

Friends tie their purses with cobweb threads. (Italian).

Friendship with a fool is the embrace of a bear. (Persian).

The ass's friendship is kicking. (Afghan).

The friend looks at the head; the enemy at the foot. (Turkish).

There can be no friendship where there is no freedom. (English).

When friendship goes with love it must play second fiddle. (German).

### THE VALUE OF FRIENDS

A friend at court is worth a penny i' the purse. (Scotch).

A friend at hand is better than relations at a distance. (Japanese).

A man without a friend is a left hand without the right. (Hebrew).

A thousand friends are few, one foe many. (Turkish).

A true friend is better than a relation. (Turkish).

It is as bad to have too many friends as no friends at all. (Latin).

It is with the eye of others we see our own defects. (Chinese).

I would rather have a dog my friend than enemy. (German).

One God no more, but friends a good store. (English).

One enemy can harm you more than a hundred friends can do you good. (German).

One enemy is too much for a man in a great post, and a hundred friends are too few. (English).

One enemy can do more hurt than ten friends can do good. (English).

Rather have a little one for your friend than a great one for your enemy. (Italian).

There is no living without friends. (Portuguese).

They are rich who have friends. (Latin, English, Spanish, Portuguese).

True friends are of service to one in prison or (in distress), since at one's table even enemies appear friends. (Persian).

We can live without a brother, but not without a friend. (German).

We can live without our friends but not without our neighbors. (English).

When friends meet hearts warm. (Scotch).

Where friends, there riches. (German, Portuguese).

Who has no friends only half lives. (German).

Without a clear mirror a woman cannot know the state of her face; without a true friend a man cannot discern the nature of his actions. (Chinese).

## CHOOSING OF FRIENDS AND MAKING FRIENDSHIPS

A broken friendship may be soldered but will never be sound. (English).

A friend is to be taken with his faults. (Portuguese).

A new pair of breeches will cast down an old coat—i.e. A new friend may take the place of an old one. (Scotch).

A hedge between keeps friendship green. (German).

Can't I be your friend but I must be your fool too. (English).

Friendships are cheap when they can be bought by dropping the hat. (Italian).

Friendship is not to be bought at a fair. (English).

Give out that you have many friends and believe that you have but few. (French).

Happy men should have many friends. (English).

Have but few friends though much acquaintance. (English).

He that would have many friends should try a few of them. (Italian).

He who seeks to have many friends never has any. (Italian).

In poverty one learns to know his friends. (German).

Let not one enemy be little in thy eyes nor a thousand friends be many in thy sight. (Hebrew).

My friend's enemy is often my best friend. (German)

Sudden friendship sure repentance. (English).

Who makes friends of all keeps none. (German).

### THE TESTING OF FRIENDSHIP

A bad friend is like a smith, who, if he does not burn you with fire will injure you with smoke. (Arabian).

A fool or unlearned is an enemy to himself, how is he a friend to others? (Arabian).

A friend is best known in adversity. (English, Portuguese, Arabian, Turkish).

A friend is never known till a man has need. (English, Scotch, French, Italian, Dutch).

An untried friend is like an uncracked nut. (Russian).

A sure friend is known in a doubtful matter. (Latin).

At marriages and funerals friends and kinsfolk are known. (English).

Before you make a friend eat a peck of salt with him. (Scotch).

Better lose a jest than a friend. (English).

Fall sick and you will see who is your friend and who is not. (Spanish).

Friends are like fiddle strings; they must not be screwed too tight. (English).

Good neighbors and true friends are two things. (English).

He is not a friend who in the time of distress and helplessness takes his friend by the hand. (Persian).

He is a relation or friend who renders essential service. (Hindustani).

He is my friend who succoreth me, not he that pitieth me. (English).

He is my friend who grinds at my mill—i.e. He is my friend who shows me a real kindness. (English, Spanish, Portuguese).

He who has no enemy has no friend. (German).

In poverty one learns to know his friends. (German).

In times of prosperity friends will be plenty; in times of adversity not one in twenty. (English).

My friend is he who helps me in time of need. (German).

One should fly a laughing enemy and a flattering friend. (German).

Prosperity gets followers but adversity distinguishes them. (English, French).

Prove thy friends ere thou have need. (English).

Three things are not known except in three points: courage except in war, the wise except in anger and a friend except in adversity. (Arabian).

Trust not the praise of a friend nor the contempt of an enemy. (Italian).

Try your friends before you have need of them. (Scotch).

Try your friend ere you trust him. (English).

Try your friend with a falsehood and if he keeps it a secret, tell him the truth. (Italian).

Who would have many friends let him test but few. (Italian).

### THE TREATMENT OF FRIENDS

A dear bargain, a dear friend. (Italian).

A friend's faults may be noticed but not blamed. (Danish).

A friend's faults should be known but not abhorred. (Portuguese).

Aft counting keep friends lang thegither. (Scotch).

By requiting one friend we invite many. (English).

Even reckoning maketh long friends. (English).

Fall out with a friend for a trifle. (English).

Friendship should be unpicked not rent. (Italian).

**He who is wanting but to one friend loseth a great many by it.** (English).

**Is it right to forsake old friends in reliance on new ones?** (Tamil).

**It is more disgraceful to suspect our friends than to be deceived by them.** (French).

**It is no use hiding from a friend what is known to an enemy.** (Danish).

**Keep your mouth and keep your friend.** (Danish).

**Let our friends perish provided our enemies fall with them.** He cannot be a true friend who permits those he calls friends to be sacrificed that he may secure the downfall of his enemies. (Latin, Greek).

**Make not thy friend too cheap to thee, nor thyself to thy friend.** (English).

**Old friends and new reckonings.** (French).

**Old friends and old ways ought not to be disdained.** (Danish).

**Old friends are not to be paid with gold.** (German).

**To preserve a friend three things are necessary: To honor him present, praise him absent, and assist him in his necessities.** (Italian).

**When a friend asks, there is no tomorrow.** (Spanish).

**Friendship is a plant which one must often water.** (German).

**Little presents maintain friendship.** (French).

**One should sacrifice everything to friendship except honor and justice.** (French).

**Patched up friendship seldom becomes whole again.** (German).

**Reconciled friendship is a wound ill salved.** (Italian, Danish).

**To preserve friendship one must build walls.** (Italian).

**Friendship canna stand aye on one side.** (Scotch).

**Suffering for a friend doubles the friendship.** (English).

## FALSE FRIENDS AND FLEETING FRIENDSHIPS

A dissimilarity of pursuits dissolves friendship. (Latin).

A fairweather friend changes with the wind. (Spanish, Portuguese).

A false friend and a shadow attend only when the sun shines. (American).

A false friend has honey in his mouth; gall in his heart. (German).

A false friend is worse than an open enemy. (English, German).

A friend as far as conscience allows. (English).

A friend is not so soon gotten as lost. (English).

A friend is often best known by his loss. (German).

A friend that you buy with presents will be bought from you. (English).

A friend to everybody is a friend to nobody. (Spanish).

A friend to my table and wine is no good neighbor. (French).

A fu' purse never lacks friends. (Scotch).

All are not friends who speak one fair. (English).

A lost friendship is an enemy won. (German).

A plaster house, a horse at grass, a friend in words are all mere glass. (Dutch).

A ready way to lose your friend is to lend him money. (English).

A reconciled friend is a double enemy. (English).

Better an open enemy than a false friend. (Danish).

Better a toom (empty) house than an ill tenant; better no friend than a false friend. (Scotch).

Between friends a bug in the eye—i.e. In matters of trade do not trust a friend's honesty. (Spanish).

Between two friends, a notary and two witnesses. (Spanish).

Beware of a reconciled friend as of a devil. (Spanish).

Everybody's companion is nobody's friend. (German).

Everybody's friend and nobody's friend is all one. (Spanish, Portuguese).

**Everybody's friend is everybody's fool.** (Dutch, German, Danish).

**Eye friend false friend; eye friend back enemy.** (German).

**Friends and mules fail us at hard places.** (Gallican).

**Friends are far from a man who is unfortunate.** (Latin).

**Friends become foes and foes are reconciled.** (Latin).

**Friends frae the teeth outwith—i.e. Insincere friends.** (Scotch).

**Friends living far away are no friends.** (Greek).

**God keep me from my friends, from my enemies I will keep myself.** (Italian).

**God will remain, friends will not.** (Afghan).

**Having wine and having meat one has many friends; in seasons of misfortune not one is to be found.** (Chinese).

**He is a friend at sneezing time, the most that can be got from him is a "God bless you."** See *Curiosities in Proverbs*, p. 354. (English, Italian).

**He is no friend that eats his own by himself and mine with me.** (Portuguese).

**He never was a friend who ceased to be so for a slight cause.** (Portuguese).

**He never was a friend who has ceased to be one.** (French).

**He that trusts a faithless friend has a good witness against him.** (Spanish).

**He who has a good nest finds good friends.** (Portuguese).

**He who is everybody's friend is either very poor or very rich.** (Spanish).

**I am on good terms with the friend who eats his bread with me.** (Spanish).

**Let him who is wretched and beggared try everybody and then his friends.** (Italian).

**Let us be friends, let our purses be variance.** (Modern Greek).

**Many friends and few helpers in need.** (German).

**Many humble servants but not one true friend.** (English).

**Many kinsfolk and few friends.** (English).

**May God not prosper our friends that they forget us.** (Spanish).

**No friendship lives long that owes its rise to the pot.** (English).

**No longer foster, no longer dear man.** (English).

**One seldom finds white ravens and true friends.** (German).

**Poverty parteth friends.** (English).

**Pylades and Orestes died long ago and left no successors.** (English).

**Save me from my friends.** (English).

**She devoted herself with every demonstration of affection, but when the time of need arrived made her retreat.** (Hindustani).

**So long as fortune sits at the table friends sit there.** (German).

**Table friendship soon changes.** (English).

**Tell nothing to thy friend which thy enemy may not know.** (Danish).

**Tell your friend your secret and he'll set his foot on your neck.** (Italian, Spanish and Portuguese).

**The best friends often become the worst enemies.** (German).

**The false friend is like the shadow of a sundial.** (French).

**The friendship between fire and water.** (Telugu).

**The friendship of the base is a wall of sand.** (Urdu).

**The friendship of the great is fraternity with lions.** (Italian).

**The friendship of a great man is like the shadow of a bush, soon gone.** (French).

**The interested friend is a swallow on the roof—prepared to fly when winter weather comes.** (French).

**There is no more hold of a new friend than of a new fashion.** (English).

**They cease to be friends who dwell afar off.** (Latin).

**When good cheer is lacking our friends will be packing.** (English).

When my vine was laden with grapes my friends were many, when the grapes were finished my friends disappeared. (Arabian).

When there are two friends to one purse, the one sings, the other weeps. (Spanish).

Where shall a man have a worse friend than he brings from home. (English).

While the pot boils friendship lasts. (Latin).

### TRUE FRIENDS AND ABIDING FRIENDSHIP

A father is a treasurer, a brother is a comfort, but a friend is both. (English).

A friend at one's back is a safe bridge. (Dutch).

A friend—even to the altar. (Latin).

A friend in the market is better than money in the chest. (English).

A friend is better than money in the purse. (Dutch).

A friend's dinner is soon dressed. (Dutch).

A friend's frown is better than a foe's smile. (English).

A good friend is better than silver and gold. (German, Dutch).

A good friend is my nearest relation. (English).

A good friend never offends. (English).

A man may see his friend need but winna see him bleed. (English).

An old friend is a mount for a black day. (Osmanli).

An old friend is better than two new ones. (German, Russian).

A true friend is above all things sure capital. (German).

A true friend is better than a relation. (Turkish).

A true friend is known in the day of adversity. (Turkish).

A true friend is the nectar of life. (Tamil).

A true man is he who remembers his friend when he is absent, when he is in distress and when he dies. (Arabian).

Avoid a friend who covers you with his wings and destroys you with his beak. (Spanish).

Better have a friend in the market place than money in your coffer. (Portuguese).

Better have a friend on the road than gold or silver in your purse. (French).

Familiar paths and old friends are the best. (German).

Friendship, the older it grows the stronger it is. (English).

Here's to our friends and hang up the rest of our kindred. (English).

He who has a thousand friends has not a friend to spare; he who has one enemy shall meet him somewhere. (Persian).

If ye wanted me and your meat, ye would want one gude friend. (Scotch).

If you have one true friend you have one more than your share. (English).

In distress will the faithful friend be seen. (Welsh).

It is a good friend that is always giving, though it be ever so little. (English).

Little intermittin' make gude friends. (Scotch).

Many a man is a good friend but a bad neighbor. (Danish).

Old friends are not to be paid with gold. (German).

Quhen (when) welth abounds mony freends we number. Quhen guidis (wealth) decay, then freends fly away. (Scotch).

The best looking glass is an old friend. (German).

The enemy of my friend is often my best friend. (German).

The hireling is gained by money, a true friend by an obliging behaviour. (Chinese).

To a friend's house the road is never long. (Danish).

True love kyths (appears) in time of need. (Scotch).

Who has true friends is rich. (German).

## ALL IS NOT GOLD THAT GLITTERS

Things may not be what they seem. It is easy to be misled by appearances. Pyrites may be taken for gold and reputation for character. The Gibionites came to Joshua as travel-worn ambassadors from a distant land, deceitful workers of iniquity sought St. Paul's approval of their deeds and Satan assumes the guise of an angel of light.

The proverb has been attributed to Shakespeare but it is much older than Shakespeare. It has also been said to have been first spoken by Alain de Lillie, a monk and celebrated scholar of the twelfth century. Whether Lillie was the first man to use it or not similar expressions were frequently quoted by the ancient Romans.

See Æsop's Fables, *The Crow and the Snake*, and *The Vain Jackdaw*.

"And when we be together every one,
Every man seemeth a Salamon,
But all things which that shineth as the gold,
Is nought gold, as that I have herde told;
Nor every appel that is fair at eye,
Is always good, what so men clappe or crye
Right so, lo, fareth it amonges us."

GEOFFERY CHAUCER, A.D. 1340?–1400, *Canterbury Tales*.

"All that glisters is not gold;
Often have you heard that told:
Many a man his life hath sold
But my outside to behold,
Gilded tombs to worms infold."

WILLIAM SHAKESPEARE, A.D., 1564–1616,
*The Merchant of Venice.*

"Something shall shew like gold; at least shall glister"

BEAUMONT AND FLETCHER, A.D. 1584–1616,
*The Pilgrim.*

"A man may wear the Saviour's livery and yet be busied in Satan's drudgery. The skin of an apple may be fair when it is rotten at the core. Though all gold may glitter, yet all is not gold that glitters. The arrantest hypocrite may have the color of gold but not the value of gold. What comparison is there between the gilt tun filled with air and the homely vessel filled with generous wine."—WILLIAM SECKER, A.D. 1660, *The Nonsuch Professor.*

"I was born in the year 1755, in the manor house of a sweet little country village, almost every cottage of which might be seen reflected in a small lake that spread itself over the valley beneath. I seem at this moment to see my Aunt Winifred as she used to stand, as sad as one of the willows which wept over the water, and, pointing to the shadowy mansion beneath, to say, 'Aye, child, all is not gold that glitters.'"—JOHN W. CUNNINGHAM, A.D. 1780–1861, *Sancho.*

"Oh, that teacher! How she looms up in the far off sunny land of my childhood, like the great

6

mournful visaged impenetrable sphynx of the desert: and as it gazes toward the pyramids, so did she look on the world about her—to her it was the mighty tomb of a dead glory. Now I think of her with sadness; yet, can I scarcely forgive her for throwing that unnecessary damper over me when I exhibited to her the gold ring that had been sent me in a letter from a loving grandfather, hundreds of miles away. 'All is not gold that glitters' was the expression from her thin lips; so my pleasure was woefully diluted. I looked with suspicion on the dear little circlet, and was not sorry when my finger outgrew it."—LOUISE V. BOYD, *Arthur's Magazine*, April, 1873.

VARIANT PROVERBS

**All that glitters is not gold.** (Tamil).

**All that's yellow is not gold and all white things are not eggs.** (Gaelic).

**All white stones are not gems.** (Singalese).

**A's no gowd that glitters, nor maidens that wear their hair.**
It was at one time the fashion in Scotland for maidens to go bareheaded. (Scotch).

**Think not all things gold which you see glittering.** (Latin).

ALLIED PROVERBS

**A devotee's face and a cat's claw.** (Spanish).

**A fair face may hide a foul heart.** (English).

**A good name covers theft.** (German).

**A honeyed tongue and a heart of gall.** (French).

**All are not crooks who wear long knives.** (German, Dutch, Danish).

**All are not free who mock their chains.** (German).

**All are not friends that speak us fair.** (English).
**All are not friends who smile on you.** (Dutch).
**All are not hunters who blow the horn.** (English, French, German, Danish).
**All are not merry that dance lightly.** (English).
**All are not saints that go to church.** (English, Italian).
**All are not soldiers that go to war.** (English, Spanish, Portuguese).
**All saint without, all devil within.** (English).
**A man is not always known by his looks, nor is the sea measured with a bushel.** (Chinese).
**A mouth that prays, a hand that kills.** (Arabian).
**An honest look covers many faults.** (English).
**Appearances are deceitful.** (German, English).
**Beauty is but dross if honesty be lost.** (Dutch).
**Beauty is but skin deep.** (English).
**Beauty may have fair leaves, yet bitter fruit.** (English)
**Be what you seem to be.** (English).
**Big words seldom go with good deeds.** (Danish).
**By candlelight a goat looks like a lady.** (French).
**By lamplight every country wench seems handsome.** (Italian).
**Everybody who wears spurs isn't a jockey.** (Martinique Creole).
**Every glowworm is not fire.** (German, Italian).
**Every grain is not a pearl.** (Armenian).
**Every light is not the sun.** (English).
**Every crooked neck is not a camel.** (Arabian).
**Externally a sheep, internally a wolf.** (Modern Greek).
**Externally he is a saint but internally he is a devil.** (Persian).
**Fair hair may hae foul roots.** (Scotch).
**False gold is very bright.** (Telugu).
**Glow worms are not lanterns.** (Italian).
**God in his tongue, a devil in his heart.** (English).
**He has a Bible on his lips but not in his heart.** (Dutch).
**He is a wolf in sheep's clothing.** (English).

**He shows honey—he mixed poison.** (Modern Greek).

**He thinks his penny good silver.** (English).

**If he is in the wilderness he is a robber; if he comes to the village he wishes to be a guru—i.e.** A guru is a religious teacher. (Badaga).

**It is not by saying " honey, honey " that sweetness comes into the mouth.** (Turkish).

**Judge not of men or things at first sight.** (English).

**Like Hindu gods, externally sleek and shining dry glass within.** (Bengalese).

**Never judge by appearances.** (English).

**Never trust to fine promises.** (English).

**Not all those who have long knives are crooks.** (Russian).

**Pleasant on the outside, dark and gloomy on the inside.** (Irish-Ulster).

**Rosary in hand, the devil at heart.** (Portuguese).

**Scented oil on the head; the body so filthy as to drive away sleep.** (Bengalese).

**The cross on his breast and the devil in his heart.** (English).

**The hypocrite has the look of an archbishop and the heart of a miller.** (Modern Greek).

**The mouth of a Buddha, the heart of a snake.** (Chinese).

**The mien of a bishop and the heart of a miller.** (Modern Greek).

**There is no trusting to appearances.** (Latin).

**Things are not what they seem.** (Latin).

**To clothe a wolf in priest's clothes.** (Japanese).

**Truth's cloak is often lined with lies.** (Danish).

**To the jaundiced all things seem yellow.** (French).

**Water under the grass.** (Chinese).

**When gold comes near to you it glitters—i.e. When you see gold you want it.** (Oji-African).

**When you think there are flitches of bacon, there are not even hooks to hang them on.** (Spanish).

**You cannot judge of the wine by the barrel.** (English).

**You can't judge of the horse by the harness.** (English).

### CONTRADICTING PROVERBS

A grave and majestic outside is as it were the palace of the soul. (Chinese).
By the husk you may guess at the nut. (English).
Common fame seldom lies. (Dutch).
Fair feathers make fair fowls. (English).
From one you may judge the whole. (Latin).
No honest man has the leer of a rogue. (English).
You may know a foolish woman by her finery. (French).
You may know by a handful the whole sack. (English).
You may know the horse by his harness. (English).

### OTHER PROVERBS ABOUT GOLD

A gold ring does not cure a felon. (English).
A golden bit makes none the better horse. (German, Italian).
A golden dart kills where it pleases. (English).
A golden gallows is still but a gallows. (German).
A golden hammer breaks an iron gate. (German).
A golden key opens every door. (Italian).
A golden key opens every door save that of heaven. (Danish).
A golden shield is of great defence. (English).
A great load of gold is more burdensome than a light load of gravel. (English).
A hare may draw a lion with a golden cord. (English).
A hearth of your own is worth gold. (Danish).
A lawyer without cunning, a peasant without manure, a merchant without gold remains poor. (German).
A man may buy even gold too dear. (English).
An ass covered with gold is more respected than a good horse with a pack saddle. (English).
An ass is but an ass though laden with gold. (English).
An ass loaded with gold climbs to the top of the castle. (English).
A spoken word is silver; an unspoken word gold. (German).

**As the touchstone trieth gold, so gold trieth men.** (English).

**Beat a woman with a hammer and you'll make gold.**

This ignoble proverb is intended to teach that as a woman is a spendthrift, her subjection is necessary in order to save money. (Russian).

**Before gold even kings take off their hats.** (German)

**Better a good friend than silver and gold.** (German).

**Better gain in mind than lose in gold.** (Italian, Portuguese).

**Better God than gold.** (English).

**Better have a friend on the road than gold or silver in your purse.** (French).

**Better whole than patched with gold.** (Danish).

**Brandy is lead in the morning, silver at noon, gold at night.** (German).

**Chains of gold are stronger than chains of iron.** (English).

**Eloquence avails nothing against the voice of gold.** (Latin).

**Even gold may be bought too dear.** (German).

**Even with gold one cannot buy everything.** (German).

**Everything he touches turns to gold.**

An allusion to Midas the Phrygian.

**Fetters even of gold are heavy.** (English).

**Fetters of gold are still fetters and silken cords pinch.** (English).

**Freedom is above silver and gold.** (German).

**Gold and goods may be lost; a good name endures forever.** (German).

**Gold and silver do not make men better.** (German).

**Gold and silver were mingled with dirt till avarice parted them.** (English).

**Gold does not buy everything.** (Italian).

**Gold goes through all doors except heaven's door.** (German).

**Gold goes in at any gate.** (German).

**Gold goes to the Moor—i.e. Gold goes to the man without a conscience.** (Portuguese).

**Gold is good though it be in a rogue's purse.** (Danish).
**Gold is no balm to a wounded spirit.** (English).
**Gold is proved with fire; friendship in need.** (Danish).
**Gold is the best mediator.** (German).
**Gold is the right nail one must strike.** (German).
**Gold is the snare of the soul.** (German).
**Gold lies deep in the mountain; dirt on the highway.** (German).
**Gold must be beaten and a child scourged.** (English).
**Gold remains gold though it lay in the mud.** (German).
**Gold when present causeth fear; when absent grief.** (English).
**Golden bishop, wooden crosier; wooden bishop, golden crosier.** (French).
**Golden dreams make men awake hungry.** (English).
**Good counsel is not to be paid with gold.** (German).
**Hay is more acceptable to an ass than gold.** (Latin).
**He has killed the goose that laid the golden egg.**

An allusion to Æsop's fable of *The Goose that laid the Golden Egg*. (English).

**He that labors and thrives spins gold.** (English).
**He who would make a golden door must add a nail to it daily.**

Sometimes the word "gate" is used instead of "door" in quoting. (German, Dutch).

**If it were not for the belly the back might wear gold.** (English).
**If it were adamant gold would take the town.** (English).
**I hate fetters though they be of gold.** (Portuguese).
**I will not have any gold but I love to reign over those who have.** (Latin).
**Man must govern, not serve gold.** (German).
**Nature furnishes genuine gold, but art makes false.** (German).
**No fence against gold.** (English).
**Old women's gold is not ugly.** (English).
**Parnassus has no gold mines in it.** (English).
**Rich in gold, rich in care.** (German).

So it goes in the world—one has the purse and the other the gold. (German).

Speaking is silver, silence is gold. (Dutch).

That is all well and good, but gold is better. (Danish).

That is gold which is worth gold. (Italian, Spanish, Portuguese, French).

The ass loaded with gold still eats thistles. (German).

The balance distinguishes not between gold and lead. (English).

The balance in doing its office knows neither gold or lead. (German).

The devil catches most souls with a golden net. (German).

The golden age was never the present age. (English).

The golden ass passes everywhere. (Spanish).

The golden covering does not make the ass a horse. (German).

The golden key opens every door. (Italian).

The morning hour has gold in its mouth. (Dutch, Danish, German).

The purest gold is the most ductile. (English).

The true art of making gold is to have a good estate and spend little of it. (English).

There is no better friend in misfortune than gold. (German).

There is no lock if the pick is of gold. (Spanish).

There is no lock one cannot open with a golden key. (German).

'Tis folly to love fetters though they be of gold. (Latin).

To fish with a golden hook. (Latin).

To withhold truth is to bury gold. (Danish).

Truth is better than gold. (Arabian).

Try your skill in gilt first and then in gold. (English).

Two things govern the world—women and gold. (German).

When gold speaks every tongue is silent. (German, Italian).

When gold speaks you may hold your tongue. (English).

When we have gold we are in fear; when we have none we are in danger. (English).

Where gold chinks arguments are of no avail. (German).

Where there is gold, there the devil dwells. (German).

Who fishes with a golden hook catches what he will. (German).

Who has gold can choose his son-in-law. (German).

Who has gold has ease. (German).

Who has gold is a welcome guest. (German).

Who will prosecute a lawsuit must have much gold, good lawyers, much patience and much luck. (German).

Who will win in a lawsuit must have three sacks—one with briefs, one with gold and one with luck. (German).

Wisdom is better than gold or silver. (German).

With houses and gold men are seldom brave. (German).

Women, fortune and gold favor fools. (German).

You may speak with your gold and make other tongues dumb. (English).

## A MAN IS KNOWN BY THE COMPANY HE KEEPS

(See "Who keeps company with a wolf learns to howl" and "Birds of a feather flock together.")

This proverb was well known to the old Greeks and Romans and was in common use before the Christian era. Æsop, the wise fabulist, told the story of *The Ass and the Purchaser* wherein a man was said to have desired to try an ass that was for sale before buying it, and taking it home placed it in his stable with other asses. The newcomer, Æsop said, began at once to associate with the laziest and greediest ass in the place, whereupon the man returned it to its owner saying that it was unnecessary to test the animal any further as its character was evident from its chosen companion.

Euripides, the Athenian tragic poet a century later than Æsop, declared that "Every man is like the company he is wont to keep."

"Do you see those two boys walking together," said Arnold of Rugby (1795–1842) to one of his assistants. "I never saw them together before; you should make an especial point of observing the company they keep—nothing so tells the changes in a boy's character."

"A husbandman pitched a net in his fields to take the cranes and geese which came to feed upon the new sown corn. Accordingly he took several, both cranes and geese, and among them a stork, who pleaded hard for his life, and, among other apologies which he made, alleged that he was neither goose nor crane, but a poor harmless stork who performed his duty to his parents to all intents and purposes, feeding them when they were old, and, as occasion required, carrying them from place to place upon his back. 'All this may be true,' replies the husbandman, 'but as I have taken you in bad company, and in the same crime, you must expect to suffer the same punishment.'"—ÆSOP, B.C. 561(?), *Samuel Croxall's translation.*

"'Do they never sleep neither?' said Sancho. 'Never,' said Don Quixote; 'At least they never closed their eyes while I was among them.' 'Nor I neither,' quoth Sancho. 'This makes good the saying, "Tell me thy company, and I will tell thee what thou art."—SAAVEDRA MIGUEL CERVANTES, A.D. 1547–1616, *Don Quixote.*

"If you wish to be held in esteem, you must associate only with those who are esteemed."—JEAN DE LA BRUYÈRE, A.D. 1645–1696.

"Who friendship with a knave hath made
Is judg'd a partner in the trade.
'Tis thus that on the choice of friends
Our good or evil name depends."

JOHN GAY, A.D. 1688–1732, *Fables.*

"All men are judged, so I've heard say,
By company they keep;
But this is either very vague
Or else it's very deep.
The information I would seek
Is—if it can be had—
Does one that's bad become thus good
Or good because thus bad?"—ANONYMOUS.

### VARIANT PROVERBS

**A man's character is judged by the character of his companions.** (Arabian).

**A man is judged by his companions.** (Latin).

**Show me your company and I'll tell thee what thou art.** (Spanish).

**Tell me the company you keep and I'll tell you what you are.** (French, Italian, Spanish, Dutch).

**Tell me whom you love and I'll tell you who you are.** (Louisiana Creole).

**Tell me with whom thou goest and I'll tell thee what thou doest.** (English).

**Tell me with whom you go and I'll tell you your value.** (Modern Greek).

**Tell me with whom you live and I'll tell you what you are.** (Spanish, French, Dutch and Italian).

**You may know him by the company he keeps.** (English).

### ALLIED PROVERBS

**A loose horse is sure to stand near the chaff house—i.e. An idle man can be found in the haunts of his associates.** (Behar).

**Attach thyself to honorable people and men will bow to thee.** (Hebrew).

**A wicked companion invites us all to Hell.** (English).

**He who associates with a suspicious person will himself be suspected.** (Arabian).

**If bad be the raven, his company is no better.** (Gaelic).

If you drink milk under a date tree they will say it is toddy. (Telugu).

Join with good men and you will be one of them. (Spanish).

Keep company with the good and you will be one of the number. (Portuguese).

Smoke is no less an evidence of fire than that a man's character is that of the character of his associates. (Arabian).

Take your son to the market place and see with whom he associates. (Syrian).

With whom you are such one you are. (Syrian).

### A MAN MAY BRING HIS HORSE TO WATER BUT HE CANNOT MAKE HIM DRINK

A man, by reason of commercial or political position and power, may be able to force another to obey his will, but he cannot compel him to change his opinions.

> "He that complies against his will
> Is of his own opinion still."
>
> SAMUEL BUTLER, A.D. 1612–1680, *Hudibras.*

The proverb has been attributed to Queen Elizabeth of England, but it could not have originated with her—the thought is almost as old as man. "He who demands, does not command" is an Italian saying that is expressed in many proverbial forms and applied to the management of both men and animals.

> "But that time ye thought me a daw, so that I
> Did no good in all my words then, save only
> Approved this proverb plain and true matter:
> A man may well bring a horse to the water,
> But he cannot make him drink without his will."
>
> JOHN HEYWOOD, A.D. 1497–1580,
> *A Dialogue of Effectual Proverbs.*

"I said I was afraid my father would force me to be a lawyer.

JOHNSON. 'Sir, you need not be afraid of his forcing you to be a laborious practicing lawyer; that is not in his power. For as the proverb says, 'One man may lead a horse to the water, but twenty cannot make him drink.'"—JAMES BOSWELL, A.D. 1740–1795, *Life of Samuel Johnson.*

"'Ruben, the son of my cottar! Very weel, Jeanie lass, wilfu' woman will hae her way—Ruben Butler! He hasna in his pouch the value o' the auld black coat he wears—But it disna signify.' And as he spoke he shut successively and with vehemence the drawers of his treasury. 'A fair offer, Jeanie, is nae cause of feud—A man may bring a horse to the water, but twenty winna gar him drink—And as for wasting my substance on other folk's joes'"—SIR WALTER SCOTT, A.D. 1771–1832, *The Heart of Mid-Lothian.*

"There is the well-known and excellent warning that 'One may take a horse to the water but you cannot make him drink'—a hint that one cannot always have one's own way, and that the co-operation of the other party in the arrangement is an essential point."—F. EDWARD HULME, A.D. 1841–1909, *Proverb Lore.*

VARIANT PROVERBS

**A man may lead a horse to the water, but four and twenty cannot gar him drink.** (Scotch).

**Hwa is thet mei thet hors evettrien the him-self mule drinken?—Who is he that may water the horse and not drink himself.** (English).

**If an ox won't drink you cannot make him bend his neck.** (Chinese).

**In vain do you lead the ox to the water if he be not thirsty.** (English, French).

**One man may lead a horse to water but twelve won't make him drink.** (Gaelic).

**One may lead a horse to the water but twenty cannot make him drink.** (English).

**You cannot make an ass drink if he is not thirsty.** (French).

**You may force a man to shut his eyes but you cannot make him sleep.** (Danish).

**You may bring a horse to the river but he will drink when and what he pleaseth.** (English).

**You may force an ox to water but you can't make him drink.** (Danish).

ALLIED PROVERBS

**He must be strong to pull a rope against a stronger.** (Danish).

**He who demands does not command.** (Italian).

**Law cannot persuade where it cannot punish.** (English).

**Let a horse drink when he will, not what he will.** (English).

**The full belly does not believe in hunger.** (Italian).

**The well fed man does not believe in hunger.** (Italian).

**The will cannot be compelled.** (Latin).

**They may tie a Lingam round a man's neck however much he resists it, but can they make him worship it?** (Telugu).

**Thirty-three crores of gods joined together can make me hold my nose, but can they make me say "Nârâyana?"** (Telugu).

**Undertake no more than you can perform.** (English).

**Who leads an ox to drink must first wet his own feet.** (Chinese).

**Who has no thirst has no business at the fountain.** (Dutch).

**You cannot coax de mornin' glory to clime de wrong way roun' de corn stalk.** (American—Negro).

## A MISS IS AS GOOD AS A MILE

Though a failure may not be great it is a failure. A narrow escape is an escape. Too late is too late. If the train starts on time one may as well be an hour late as ten minutes.

The origin of this proverb is unknown. Some have thought that it was derived from the less familiar "An inch of a miss is as good as a mile of a miss," but it is not probable. Ray's version, however, indicates that there was a close connection between the two. He renders the saying, "An inch of a miss is as good as an ell." Others believe that the proverb originally referred to two legendary soldiers of Charlemagne who resembled each other in character and appearance and who were named Amis and Amile. As they were regarded as martyrs it is said to have become the custom to invoke either of them when desired, hence the saying, "Amis is as good as Amile." Of course such an origin belongs to the realm of fancy and is not reliable.

Martin, Abbot of Asello in Italy, desired an inscription over the gate of his abbey, so the story runs, and selected this sentence for the purpose: "Gate be open. Never be closed against an honest man," but not being proficient in the art of punctuation, he and his copyist placed a period after the word "never" instead of the word "open." The pope on hearing of this strange inscription became indignant and deposed Abbot Martin and gave it to another ecclesiastic who corrected the punctuation and added to the inscription the words: "For a single point Martin lost his Asello"—Asello being not only the name of the abbey but also meaning an ass. The line was translated: "For a single point Martin lost his ass" which soon passed into a proverb among the French. In Italy it assumed the form of "For a point Martin lost the cope."

### ALLIED PROVERBS

**A little too late is much too late.** (German).
**A nod is as good as a wink to a blind horse.** (English).
**For a point Martin lost the cope.** (Italian).
**For a single point Martin lost his ass.** (French).
**Lost by a drop can't be recovered by a pond-full.** (Hindustani).

297

## A NEW BROOM SWEEPS CLEAN

The business man puts energy into a new enterprise, the laborer shows interest in a new line of work, the clerk is anxious to please a new employer, the maid tries to satisfy her new mistress and the child enters with zest on a new game. New responsibilities call forth one's best endeavors.

There is a tradition that in the seventeenth century, when Admiral Tromp sought to defeat the English, he attached a broom to the mast of his vessel to indicate his intention of sweeping his enemies' ships off the seas; but the English Admiral, not to be intimidated by signs and symbols, answered the Dutch Commander by fastening a horsewhip to the mast of his vessel to show that, instead of being swept from the sea, he purposed to horsewhip Tromp and his men. This use of the horsewhip by the English Commander is said to have given rise to the pennant, but a broom fastened to the mast of a vessel now indicates that it is for sale.

It was the custom in olden times, when the mistress of a house was away on a journey or visiting distant kindred or friends, to indicate her absence by hanging a broom outside the window that all might know her household services had been suspended.

The origin of the proverb is unknown.

"Some laughed, and said: All things is gay that is green
Some thereto said: The green new broom sweepeth clean;
But since all things is the worse for the wearing,
Decay of clean sweeping folk has in fearing."
JOHN HEYWOOD, A.D. 1497–1580.

"New broom sweepeth clean, which is thus understand—
New broom sweepeth clean in the clean sweeper's hand."
JOHN HEYWOOD.

VARIANT PROVERBS

**A new bissome soupe's clean.** (Scotch).
**A new broom is good for three days.** (Italian).
**A new broom's a clean broom.** (Mauritius Creole).
**A new broom sweeps clean but the old brush knows the corners.** (Irish-Farney).
**A new broom sweeps clean but the old one is good for corners.** (Dutch).
**A new broom sweeps the room well.** (Italian).
**A new servant never transgresses the commands of her mistress but if too obsequious, she inspires no confidence.** (Sanskrit).
**A new servant will catch a deer.** (Hindustani).
**A new washwoman applies soap to rags even**—Rags are seldom washed in India. (Behar).
**A new washwoman will wash with great care.** (Tamil).
**A new broom sweeps clean.** (English, Italian).
**New servants are swift.** (Persian).
**New things are fair.** (English).

ALLIED PROVERBS

**All that is new is fine.** (French).
**A new pot keeps the water cold for a few days.** (Persian).

**An old ass is never good.** (English).
**An old dog will learn no tricks.** (English).
**An old parrot does not mind the stick.** (Latin).
**An old physician and a young lawyer—are the best.** (English, Italian).
**Flies do not swarm on a new pot.** (Tamil).
**In a thing that is fresh the pleasure is of a different kind.** (Osmanli).
**New dishes beget new appetites.** (English).
**New laws, new deceit.** (German).
**New laws, new frauds.** (English).
**New lords, new laws.** (English).
**New meat begets a new appetite.** (English).
**New pastures make fat sheep.** (English).
**The water of a fresh jar is cold.** (Osmanli).
**Young flesh and old fish are the best.** (English).

CONTRADICTING PROVERBS

**A new government and a drum on a hen's back.**
A proverb expressing contempt for new laws. (Hindustani).
**An old broom is better than a new one.** (Accra—W. Africa).
**An old ox makes a straight furrow.** (English).
**An old wise man's shadow is better than a young buzzard's sword.** (English).
**Old ovens are soon hot.** (English).
**Old shoes are easiest.** (English).
**The prime of youth and weak in the loins.** (Hindustani).

190

## AN OUNCE OF MOTHER WIT IS WORTH A POUND OF LEARNING

**A little common sense is better than a thorough education.**
**A little cleverness counts for more than great scholarship.**
**A little shrewdness is more valuable than much knowledge.**
**A little understanding of men and things is of more benefit than a large acquaintance with books.**
**A little luck leads to success quicker than much striving.**

It has been the common opinion of men in all lands and in all ages, particularly of those who have not had the advantages of education, to disparage the work and achievements of others who have sought wisdom through the training of the mind. There are few folk sayings that commend scholarship, but many that laud natural brightness of mind, keenness of thought, quickness of perceptions and what is termed "good luck." When comparisons are made the relative value of acquired and natural ability is often expressed by pounds and ounces.

SCRIPTURE REFERENCES: Prov., 3: 13–18; 8: 1–21; 17: 16.

> "For all that Nature by her mother-wit
> Could frame on earth."
>
> EDMUND SPENSER, A.D. 1553–1599,
> *Faerie Queene.*

"*Katharina:* Where did you study all this goodly speech?

"*Petruchio:* It is extempore from my mother-wit.

"*Katharina:* A witty mother! Witless else her son."

SHAKESPEARE, A. D. 1564–1616. *The Taming of the Shrew.*

"'An ounce o' mither-wit is worth a pound o' clergy,' says the Scotch proverb, and the 'mother-wit,' *Muttergeist* and *Mutterwitz*, that instructive common sense, that saving light that makes the genius and even the fool in the midst of his folly, wise, appear in folk lore and folk speech everywhere. What statistics of genius seem to show that great men owe to their mothers, no less than fools, is summed up by the folk mind in the word mother-wit."—ALEXANDER F. CHAMBERLAIN, A.D., 1866–1914—*The Child and Childhood in Folk-Thought.*

VARIANT PROVERBS

**A dram of discretion is worth a pound of wisdom.** (German, Italian).

**A drop of fortune rather than a cask of wisdom.** (Latin).

**A grain of good luck is better than an ass load of skill.** (Persian).

**A handful of good life is better than a bushel of learning.** (English, French).

**A handful of good life is better than seven bushels of learning.** (English, French).

**A handful of luck is better than a sack full of wisdom.** (German).

**An ounce o' a man's ain wit is worth ten o' ither folks.** (Scotch).

An ounce o' mither-wit, is worth a pound o' clergy. (Scotch).

An ounce o' wit is worth a pound o' lear. (Scotch).

An ounce of favor goes further than a pound of justice. (English, French).

An ounce of fortune is worth a pound of forecast. (English).

An ounce of discretion is better than a pound of knowledge. (Italian).

An ounce of luck is worth a pound of wisdom. (English, French).

An ounce of mother-wit is worth a pound of school-wit. (German).

An ounce of patience is worth a pound of brains. (Dutch)

An ounce of practice is worth a pound of preaching. (English).

An ounce of state to a pound of gold. (Spanish).

An ounce of wit that's bought (through experience) is worth a pound that's taught. (English).

A pot full of luck is better than a sack full of wisdom. (Russian).

Better an ounce of luck than a pound of intelligence. (Belgian).

Good luck is better than brains. (Serbian).

Half an ounce of luck is better than a pound of sense. (German).

### ALLIED PROVERBS

A cart load of friendship is not worth a barley corn of kin. (Hindustani).

An honest penny is better than a stolen dollar. (English).

A single penny fairly got is worth a thousand that are not. (German).

Better a little good than much bad. (German).

Better a little peace with right than much with anxiety and strife. (Danish).

Better a little with honor than much with shame. (English).

Better to be born lucky than wise. (English).

Better untaught than ill taught. (English).

In one scale the four Veds, in the other natural wit—Erudition weighs lighter than natural wit. (Hindustani).

Learning is worthless without mother-wit. (Spanish).

One penny is better on land than ten on the sea. (Danish).

Patience surpasses learning. (Dutch).

Penny wise and pound foolish. (English).

Science is madness if good sense does not cure it. (Spanish).

Take care of the pence and the pounds will take care of themselves. (English).

Who has luck needs no understanding. (German).

### CONTRADICTING PROVERBS

An ounce of discretion is worth a pound of wit. (English).

An ounce of wisdom is worth a pound of wit. (English).

## A ROLLING STONE GATHERS NO MOSS

This proverb is applied to people who having restless natures frequently change their place of residence or employment in a vain endeavor of bettering themselves. It is found in almost every language and belongs to the same class of proverbs as "Three removes are as bad as a fire" (English) and "A tree often transplanted neither grows nor thrives" (Spanish).

> "I never saw an oft removed tree,
> Nor yet an oft removed family,
> That throve so well as one that settled be."

Mr. Frank Cowan, while acknowledging, in his *Dictionary of Sea Proverbs*, that the saying originated with the Greeks, traces its English form to William Langland as the earliest author known to him, who seemed to have the phrase in mind and quotes the following from *Piers Plowman:*

> "Seldom mosseth the marble stone
> That men oft tread."

Mr. John Tweezer, writing in the *Keystone*,

March, 1894, says that the Spanish form of the proverb is "older than the Court of Isabella (A. D. 1451–1504), older than the Cid (A.D. 1040–1099), older than the earliest traditions of Spanish chivalry"; that the Italian form predates the time of Dante (A.D. 1265–1321) and that the Portuguese rendering is older than the first crusade (A.D. 1096).

The proverb is of great antiquity and there is little doubt but that it was first used by men living in some sea coast district, for the only stones known to be in continual motion are those that are tossed by the waves, rolling to and fro among the rocks with the incoming and outgoing tides. Such stones are worn smooth and not suffered to accumulate any seaweed. That the stones referred to in the proverb were originally such as are found on the seashore is further shown by the earlier Latin form in which it is rendered, "A rolling stone gathers no seaweed."

"Ye merchant! What attempteth you to attempt us,
To come on us before the messenger thus?
Roaming in and out, I hear tell how ye toss;
But son, the rolling stone never gathereth moss."

JOHN HEYWOOD, A.D. 1497–1580, *A Dialogue.*

"The stone that is rolling, can gather no moss,
Who often removeth is surer of loss;
The rich it compelleth to pay for his pride,
The poor it undoeth on every side."

THOMAS TUSSER, A.D. 1524–1580,
*Five Hundred Points of Good Husbandrie.*

"There are a set of people in the world of so unsettled and restless a temper, and such admirers of novelty, that they can never be long pleased with one way of living, no more than to continue long in one habitation; but before they are well enter'd upon one business, dip into another, and before they are well settled in one habitation, remove to another; so that they are always busily beginning to live, but by reason of fickleness and impatience, never arrive at a way of living. Such persons fall under the doom of this proverb, which is designed to fix the volatility of their tempers, by laying before them the ill consequences of such fickleness and inconstancy."—NATHAN BAILEY, A.D. 1742, *Diverse Proverbs*.

"From the time they first gained a foothold on Plymouth Rock they began to migrate, progressing and progressing from place to place and land to land, making a little here and a little there, and controverting the old proverb that a rolling stone gathers no moss."—WASHINGTON IRVING, A.D. 1783–1859.

"As the rolling stone gathers no moss, so the roving heart gathers no affections."—ANNA BRONNELL JAMESON, A.D. 1794–1860, *Studies*.

"One of the members of his (Mr. Shireff) church was John Henderson or Anderson—a very decent douce shoemaker—and who left the church and joined the Independents, who had a meeting in Sterling. Some time afterwards, when Mr. Shireff met John on the road, he said, 'And so, John, I understand you have become an Independent?' 'Dear Sir,' replied John. 'That's true.' 'Oh, John,' said the minister, 'I'm sure ye ken that a rowin' stane gather nae fog (moss).' 'Ay,' said John, 'that's true too; but can ye tell me what guid the fog does to the stane?' Mr. Shireff himself afterwards became a Baptist."—DEAN EDWARD B. RAMSAY, A.D. 1793–1872, *Reminiscences.*

"'You have always been a very good friend of me, Mr. Varden,' he said, as he stood without, in the porch, and the locksmith was equipping himself for his journey home; 'I take it very kind of you to say all this, but the time's nearly come when the Maypole and I must part company.'

'Roving stones gather no moss, Joe,' said Gabriel.

'Nor mile-stones much,' replied Joe. 'I'm little better than one here, and see as much of the world.'"—CHARLES DICKENS, A.D. 1812–1870, *Barnaby Rudge.*

In August, 1829 the following announcement of the marriage of Cotton K. Simpson of Pembroke, N. H. to Miss Sarah R. Marble, appeared in Haverhill, Mass.

"An old calculation of gain and loss
Proves 'a stone that is rolling will gather no moss.'
A happy expedient has lately been thought on,
By which Marble may gather and cultivate Cotton."

"Probably it originated with the Greeks, who lived on a peninsula and an archipelago, and in whose ancient literature it is found. That the above is the proper figure of the proverb appears clearly in several of its foreign forms where such words as Greek *Phukos*, Latin *Fucus*, the modern term for a genus of sea-mosses,—and Latin *Alga*, from which is derived Algæ, the name of the order comprising the sea-weeds—correspond to the English word *moss*, and the Scottish *fog*, which is simply a variation of *phukos*, or *fucus*. The poetic beauty of this proverb is great—much greater than that of most proverbs, which also favors its origin from the æsthetic Greeks."—FRANK COWAN, A.D. 1844–1906, *Dictionary of Sea Proverbs*.

"When my young brother started out into the great world to try his fortunes, instead of a kindly 'God speed,' he only heard, 'A rolling stone gathers no moss,' and when my bankrupt uncle thought to take his stalwart sons and rosy daughters and in the far West begin life anew, his neighbors gravely shook their heads, remarking, 'A drowning man catches at a straw,' or they reminded him by way of discouragement that, 'Three removes are as bad as a fire.'"—LOUISE V. BOYD, A.D. 1873–, *Of Proverbs and Adages*.

VARIANT PROVERBS

**A plant often removed cannot thrive.** (Latin, English).

**A rolling stone gathers no seaweed.** (Latin).
**A rowin' stane gathers nae fog.** (Scotch).
**A stone often removed gathers no moss.** (Polish).
**A tree often removed will hardly bear fruit.** (French).
**A trolling stone gathers no moss.** (English—Yorkshire form).
**A tumlan stann gidders nae moss.** (English—Cumberland form).
**Moss grows not on oft turned stones.** (Gaelic).
**The rolling stone without moss.** (Irish).

ALLIED PROVERBS

**A heavy stone remains in its place.** (Syriac).
**A rugged stone grows smooth from hand to hand.** (English).
**A wheel that turns gathers no rust.** (Modern Greek).
**Old trees must not be transplanted.** (French).
**People often change and seldom do better.** (English).
**Remove an old tree and it will wither to death.** (English).
**Running about gives no scholars.** (African—Wolof).
**Seize one door, and seize it firmly—i.e. Hold firmly to one patron or business and do not change from one to another.** (Persian).
**Three removes are as bad as a fire.** (Italian).
**Today I am going!—Tomorrow I am going! gives the stranger no encouragement to plant the Ahusa.** The proverb refers to the removal of one's residence, giving the planter no encouragement. The Ahusa bears fruit quickly. (African).
**Who often changes suffers.** (French—Yoruba).

CONTRADICTING PROVERBS

**A millstone does not become mossgrown; unlike the rolling stone it performs its work and serves men by motion.** (German).
**A setting hen loses her breast feathers.** (English).

**A setting hen never gets fat.** (English).
**A tethered sheep soon starves.** (English).
**Change of pasture makes fat calves.** (English).
**Seldon moseth the marbelston that ofte treden.** (English as rendered by William Langland).
**Who stands still in the mud sticks in it.** (Chinese).

85, 86, 312.

## AS WISE AS A MAN OF GOTHAM

Though the traditional Gothamites were wise in their folly the proverbial phrase—"As wise as a man of Gotham"—is usually applied to stupid people.

The little town of Gotham, seven miles from Nottingham, England, contains over a thousand people whose intelligence is fully equal to that of other communities of the same size, yet all who dwell in the district have been regarded for centuries as devoid of understanding. There is an old rhyme that says:

> "The little smith of Nottingham
> Who doth the work that no man can."

The rhyme has often been quoted as a taunt, flung at someone in the little community who pretended to have a certain ability others did not possess. Dr. Thomas Fuller in the seventeenth century said that he suspected that the little smith never lived except in the imagination of the rhymester, which is probably true, the rhyme being a taunt at those who lived in the district.

That the Gothamites were not fools, may be seen from the reply of one of their number, a mere boy who, it is said, was interrupted in his work in a field by a passing stranger, who inquired: "Is this the Gotham where the fools come from?" "No, Sir," replied the lad, "this is the Gotham that the fools come to."

No one knows why Gotham was thought to contain more simpletons than other towns. The story that is said to have given rise to the belief is without historic foundation. It may even have been applied to the Gothamites subsequent to the traditions of its simplicity. It is as follows:

In the early part of the thirteenth century King John determined to secure an estate and build a castle in Gotham and sent a messenger to look over the ground. The townsfolk, hearing of the king's purpose and knowing that if it were carried out they would be subjected to heavy expense and loaded with burdens, sought means to circumvent their sovereign's will. After consultation they agreed to the novel expedient of pretending that they were idiots, so that when the messenger arrived he would think that no one in the district was sane. The plan worked as they expected. The King's representative came to the town, examined the ground and conversed with the people. Finding that they were all engaged in some childish employment and talked foolishly he was at first surprised and then disgusted. Returning he reported to his Sovereign that Gotham was not a fit place for a royal estate and castle, as it was inhabited by fools;

whereupon King John gave up his project and permitted the people to live in peace.

This absurd tale gave rise to others that were intended to prove that the people did not pretend to be idiots but acted as they did because they were actually devoid of reason. The best known of these stories is *The Hedging of the Cuckoo*, given in notes on the proverb, "A bird in the hand is worth two in the bush" that gave rise to the old proverbial expression "To fence in the cuckoo."

All the tales used to indicate the stupidity of the people existed long before the sixteenth century when they were brought together and applied to the Gothamites. Mr. W. H. Davenport Adams (A.D. 1829–1891) says, "It is quite possible that the best of the tales of Gotham were foreign in origin, were afterwards naturalized in England and finally located." It is certain that they are all very old and were fathered on the innocent Gothamites as a taunting joke.

Among the Syrians, Homs (the ancient Amasa) was regarded as the dwelling place of dullards. Asiatics declared that there was no district that contained more idiots than Phrygia. The North Africa wandering tribes spoke of Beni Jennad as the place of shallow brained people. The Greeks had their Bœotia, whose citizens were stupid and to whom was attributed many childish deeds and sayings. The Thracians pointed to Abdera in derision as the dwelling place of noodles. The Persians referred to the Geelan townsfolk as fools. The Hindustani regard the Badauns as simpletons and refer to them as children. The Scotch derided the people of Cupar in Fife because of their reputed dullness. The French laughed at Saint Maixent where dizzards dwelt and expressed their opinion of the stupidity of the Champanese by saying, "Ninety-nine sheep and a Champanese make a round hundred." The Germans had their Swabia, also their fabled city of Schildburg where dotards found a home. The Italians compared witless men to the inhabitants of Zago, declaring that the people of Zago sowed needles to raise a crop of crowbars and fertilized a steeple to make it grow higher. Hollanders credited the dwellers in Kampan with all kinds of brainless acts. The Swiss looked at the townspeople of Belmont near Lausanne as blockheads. The Belgians laughed at the inhabitants of Dinant, and the feeling of the Jews toward the people who lived in the home town of the child Jesus was expressed by Nathaniel who asked, "Can any good thing come out of Nazareth?"

There have been few countries that have not made some town or district the object of jest; it is no wonder therefore that Englishmen should have laughed at Gotham and her people.

Washington Irving showed his keen sense of humor when he nicknamed the City of New York, Gotham, because of the presumption of its citizens, who prided themselves on their wisdom. "It so happened by great mischance," he wrote in *Salmagundi*, "that divers light-heeled youth of Gotham, more especially those who are descended from three wise men, so renowned of yore for having most venturesomely voyaged over sea in a bowl, were from time to time captured and inveigled into the camp of the enemy."

"Then to Gotham, where sure am I,
Though not all fools I saw many;
Here a Shee-gull found I prancing,
And in moonshine nimbly dancing,
There another wanton madling
Who her hog was set a saddling."

RICHARD BRAITHWAITE, A.D. 1588–1673,
*Barnaboe Itinerarium.*

"Tell me no more of Gotham fools,
Or of their eels in little pools
Which they, we're told, were drowning;
Nor of their carts drawn up on high,
When King John's men were standing by,
To keep a wood from browning.

"Nor of their cheese shoved down the hill,
Nor of a cuckoo sitting still,
While it they hedged around;
Such tales of them have long been told
By prating boobies, young and old,
In drunken circles crowned.

"The fools are those who thither go
To see the cuckoo bush I trow

The wood, the barn, the pools;
For such are seen both here and there,
And passed by without a sneer
By all but arrant fools."

UNKNOWN EIGHTEENTH CENTURY POET.

"Seamen three! What men be ye?
Gotham's three wise men we be,
Whither in your bowl so free?
To rake the moon from out the sea:
The bowl goes trim. The moon doth shine,
And our ballast is old wine;
And your ballast is old wine.

"Who art thou, so fast adrift?
I am he they call old Care.
Here on board we will three drift,
No: I may not enter there.
Wherefore so? 'Tis Jove's decree.
In a bowl Care may not be;
In a bowl Care may not be.

"Fear ye not the waves that roll?
No: In charmed bowl we swim.
What the charm that floats the bowl?
Water may not pass the brim.
The bowl goes trim. The moon doth shine
And our ballast is old wine;
And your ballast is old wine."

THOMAS LOVE PEACOCK, A.D., 1785–1866.

"Three wise men of Gotham
Went to sea in a bowl;
And if the bowl had been stronger
My song would have been longer."

OLD NURSERY RHYME.

ALLIED PROVERBS

**As learnt as a scholar o' Buckhaven College.**
Used ironically as there is no such such institution as Buckhaven College. (Scotch).

**As wise as an ape.** (English).
Used ironically.

**As wise as a daw.** (English).
Used ironically.

**As wise as a hare.** (English).
Used ironically.

**As wise as a woodcock.** (English).
Used ironically.

**As wise as a wren.** (English).
Used ironically.

**As wise as the Mayor of Danbury who would prove that Henry III was before Henry II.** (English).

**As wise as Waltam's** (sometimes written: Waltham's, Watton's or Wudsie's) **calf.** (English).
Various writers have extended this proverb thus, "As wise as Waltam's calf that ran nine miles to suck a bull."

**A wise man and a fool together know more than a wise man alone.** (Italian).

**A wise man may look ridiculous in the company of fools.** (English).

**Children of Badaun. A place where fools live.** (Hindustani).

**He that will to Cupar maun to Cupar.** (Scotch).
"Applied to foolish or reckless persons who persist in carrying on projects in the face of certain failure, of which they have been duly advised. Why Cupar, the capital of the Kingdom of Life should have been selected as typical of such 'pig-headness' we are unable to say."—ALEXANDER HISLOP, A.D. 1862.

**He is not a wise man who cannot play the fool on occasions.** (Italian).

**If a man of Naresh has kissed thee, count thy teeth.** Narish in Babylonia. (Hebrew).

**If wise men play the fool they do it with a vengeance.** (Italian).

**It takes a wise man to be a fool.** (English).

**Nobody is so wise but has a little folly to spare.** (German).

**None can play the fool as well as a wise man.** (English).

**The clown of Geelan. The fools of Geelan.** (Persian).

**'Tis wisdom sometimes to seem a fool.** (English).

**To fence in the cuckoo.** (English).

**To put gates to the fields.** (Spanish).

## A TALE NEVER LOSES IN THE TELLING

Reports of events, when often repeated, are seldom strictly in accord with facts, not only because those who repeat what they hear are frequently ignorant of details, but because many people are prone to secure attention and interest by embellishments. It is for this reason that the chatterings of gossips and the graphic tales of babblers are said never to lose in the telling. Gossip has been well described as putting two and two together and making it five.

The tendency of some people to enlarge upon a story or to make personal adventures seem more wonderful than they were by fictitious additions has been noticed in all ages. St. Paul wrote of tattlers and busybodies who went about from house to house speaking things they ought not (I Tim. 5: 13) and St. James declared that the tongue though little boasted great things (James 3: 5). The proverb is therefore an expression belonging to no particular age or country but is a common observation that springs to the lips of all who have any intercourse with their fellow men.

There is an old story told in India that

illustrates the proneness of some people to exaggerate when they narrate experiences.

A hard working woman who had an idler for a husband sought in every way to induce him to labor, but in vain. He only became angry when she spoke to him on the subject and threatened that if she did not cease her faultfinding he would leave her. As she did not believe that he would carry out his threat, she told him to go. So he left the house and started for the Plains. Seeing him depart she donned the clothes of an officer of the law and, taking a gun and sword, followed him. Managing in some way to pass him without being observed she stood in the path and threatened to kill him if he did not return and promise never again to leave the village by the same road, for she knew that there was no other path by which to reach the Plains. The man not recognizing his wife in her disguise was so frightened that he readily pledged his word and retraced his steps. Seeing that her trick had proved successful she went back to the village avoiding him by the way. On reaching his home he was met by his spouse who asked the reason for his change of mind. "How could I go," he answered, "when a hundred constables stood in the way and threatened to kill me?" Knowing the truth she plied him with questions till he confessed that there were only fifty constables, then that there were only twenty-five, then that there were only ten, then that there were only five, then that there were only two and finally that there was only one.

"These carry elsewhere what has been told them; the proportion of the falsehood increases and the latest teller adds something to what he has heard."—OVID, B.C. 43–A.D. 17.

Who so shall telle a tale after a man,
He moste reherse, as neighe as ever he can,
Everich word, if it be in his charge,
All speke he never so rudely and so large;
Or elles he moste tellen his tale untrewe,
Or feinen thinges, or finden wordes newe."

GEOFFREY CHAUCER, A.D. 1340(?)–1400, *Canterbury Tales.*

"Such difference is there in an oft-told tale;
But truth, by its own sinews, will prevail."

JOHN DRYDEN, A.D. 1631–1700, *Religio Laici.*

"Lest men suspect your tale untrue
Keep probability in view."

JOHN GAY, A.D. 1688–1732, *The Painter.*

"Report, than which no evil thing of any kind is more swift,
Increases with travel and gains strength by its progress."

VERGIL, B.C. 70–19, *Æneid.*

ALLIED PROVERBS

**A crow (another) crow (a third) crow, a hundred crows.** (Kashmiri).
**A good tale ill told is a bad one.** (English).
**A good tale is not the worse for being twice told.** (English).
**A large fire often comes from a small spark.** (Danish).

**A louse exaggerated into a buffalo.** (Kumaun, Garhwal).
**A story grows by telling, a bit of straw makes the hole in the ear larger, a girl grows up best at her mother's house, paddy grows best on the pathar.** (Assamese).
**Falsehood never tires of going round about.** (Danish).
**From long journeys long lies.** (Spanish).
**Great talkers are commonly liars.** (English).
**Hear say is half lies.** (German).
**He may lie boldly who comes from afar.** (French, Italian).
**He who prates much lies much.** (German).
**In the fair tale, is foul falsity.** (English).
**In the report of riches and goodness always bate one-half.** (Spanish).
**Lies and gossip have a wretched offspring.** (Danish).
**Lying and gossiping go hand in hand.** (Spanish).
**Much talking, much erring.** (English, Spanish).
**Old men and far travelers may lie by authority.** (English).
**Report can never be brought to state things with precision.** (Latin).
**Report makes the crows blacker than they are.** (English).
**Report makes the wolf bigger than he is.** (German).
**Talking very much and lying are cousins.** (German).
**The dirt of a jackal is made into a mountain.** (Behar).
**The nimblest footman is a false tale.** (English).
**The tale runs as it pleases the teller.** (English).
**" They say so " is half a lie.** (English).

## A WHISTLING WOMAN AND A CROWING HEN ARE NEITHER LIKED BY GOD NOR MEN

This saying is used in disapproval of women of masculine appearance, or who are thought to be manlike in disposition and habit. In olden times witches were believed to be in league with Satan and to whistle for the wind which blew at their command. Women therefore who indulged in the practice of whistling were regarded as in some way associated with witches and under the influence of the powers of darkness. As the crowing of a hen was, according to a common superstitition, believed to be indicative of calamity and death, the offending barnyard fowl was immediately killed to prevent if possible any resultant evil. The old Normans had a similar superstition regarding crowing hens.

One of the strange freaks of proverb migration is found in the Chinese saying, "A bustling woman and a crowing hen are neither fit for gods nor men," which leads the people after the manner of our own ancestors to slay a crowing hen and thus prevent misfortune. The superstitition has taken such a strong hold on the Chinese that the destruction of crowing hens is enjoyed by their priests and has become a common practice.

According to an ancient legend it is said that when the nails were being forged that were to be used in fastening Jesus to the cross, a woman standing near the smith and watching him at his work, began to whistle, and that because of her act the heart of the Virgin Mary bled afresh.

Mr. T. F. Thiselton-Dyre tells us in his *Folk-lore of Women* that a party of women at one time attempted to go on board a vessel at Scarborough and were prevented by the Captain who said, "No, not that young lady, she whistles." Her whistling prevented her going on the trip that she had planned, as the captain believed, according to a prevailing superstition, that if she went some calamity would come to his craft. As it was his vessel was wrecked on the next voyage. "Had the young lady set foot on it," says Mr. Thiselton-Dyre, "the catastrophy would have been attributed to her."

The old English children's game of "Sally Waters" has a dialogue in which a daughter is told to whistle. Whistling being generally forbidden as a kind of implication that marked a woman out as a witch, she demurred at the proposal. The verses are as follows:

"Whistle, daughter, whistle, whistle for a cradle,
I cannot whistle, Mammy, 'deed I am not able.

Whistle, daughter, whistle, whistle for a cow,
I cannot whistle, Mammy, 'deed I know not how.

Whistle, daughter, whistle, whistle for a man,
I cannot whistle, Mammy; whew! Yes, I believe I can."

Another form of the verses is given by Halliwell as a nursery song as follows:

"Whistle, daughter, whistle, whistle, daughter dear;
I cannot whistle, Mammy, I cannot whistle clear.

Whistle, daughter, whistle, whistle for a pound,
I cannot whistle, Mammy, I cannot make a sound."

VARIANT PROVERBS

**A bustling woman and crowing hen are neither fit for God nor men.** (Chinese).

**A hen which crows and a girl who whistles bring the house bad luck.** (French).

**A whistling wife and a crowing hen will call the old gentleman out of his den.** (English).

**A whistling wife and a crowing hen will come to God, but God knows when.** (English).

**A whistling wife and a crowing hen will fight the devil out of his den.** (English).

**A whistling woman and a crowing hen are neither fit for God nor men.** (English).

**A whistling woman and a crowing hen are two of the unluckiest things under the sun.** (English—Cornwall).

**A whistling woman and a crowing hen will fear the old lad out of his den.** (English).

**A woman who talks like a man and a hen which crows like a cock are no good to anyone.** (French).

**Girls whistling and hens crowing—both are considered unnatural and out of place.** (Gaelic).

**Whistling girls and crowing hens always come to some bad ends.** (English).

**Whistling of women and crowing of hens—two forbidden things.** (Gaelic).

ALLIED PROVERBS

If the hen crows instead of the cock there won't be peace in the fowl yard. (Japanese).

If you be a cock, crow; if a hen, lay eggs. (Persian).

Ill fares the hapless family that shows a cock that's silent and a hen that crows. (English).

It goes ill with the house where the hen sings and the cock is silent. (Spanish).

It is a sad house where the hen crows louder than the cock. (English).

It is a sorry house in which the cock is silent and the hen crows. (French, Italian).

It is said that even the hen reared by a talkative woman crows. (Singalese).

It never goes well when the hen crows. (Russian).

That house is unhappy wherein the hen crows. (Bulgarian).

That were the hen crowing before the cock. (Gaelic).

The crowing of a hen is no rule—i.e. Reliance cannot be placed on the opinion of a woman. (Hindustani).

The hen is not a cock nor a woman a man. (Russian).

The hen should not crow like the cock. (Russian).

The house doth every day more wretched grow where the hen louder than the cock doth crow. (French).

There is little peace in that house where the hen crows and the cock is mute. (Italian).

What trust is there in a crowing hen? (Indian).

When girls whistle the devil laughs outright. (English-Guernsey).

Where the hen crows the house falls to ruin. (Japanese).

Where the cock is the hen does not crow. (Portuguese).

274, 300

## BIRDS OF A FEATHER FLOCK TOGETHER

See "A man is known by the company he keeps."

The age of the proverb is unknown. The fact that it is quoted in substantially the same form that we now use, by Jesus the Son of Sirach, indicates that it was probably known earlier than the second century before the coming of Christ.

The old Jewish Rabbis were wont to say that the degenerate palm went among the unfruitful reeds. The same thought is expressed in our familiar saying, "Like to like the world over." People of similar tastes, habits or interests are everywhere drawn to each other. If it were not so this world would be a lonely place for many.

"The good seek the good and the evil the evil." "He that walketh with the virtuous is one of them" (English), and "No worm-eaten bean remains without finding a half blind measure" (Arabian).

Among the strongest influences at work in drawing men together are those that come from kinship and marriage. One sometimes hears it said in the north of Ireland, "Go nine ridges and nine furrows further to (assist) your own people than you would to the stranger," for "blood is thicker than water," and again we are told that if one marries a mountain girl he marries the whole mountain—that is, he must make friends of his wife's companions.

The proverb finds its parallel in all parts of the world. One of the strangest forms is that used by the Oji-speaking people of the Ashanti district of Africa, who, believing that Satan lives in the dense forest, declare that "When the fiend goes to the Sabbat (or customs) he lodges with the sorcerer," that is, he seeks his kind in association with the devil possessed.

"The birds will resort unto their like; so will truth return unto them that practice in her."—JESUS THE SON OF SIRACH, 27: 9.

"The Jews which believed not, havynge indignacion, take unto them evyll men which were vagabondes, and gathered a company, and set all the cite on a roore, and made asaute unto the housse of Jason, and sought to bringe them out to the people."—THE ACTS, 17: 5, *Tyndale Version*, A.D. 1534.

"'Tis this similitude of manners, which ties most men in an inseparable link, as if they be addicted to the same studies or disports, they delight in one another's companies, 'birds of a feather will gather together'; if they be of diverse inclinations, or opposite in manners, they can seldom agree."—ROBERT BURTON, A.D. 1576–1640, *Anatomy of Melancholy.*

"May not too much familiarity with profane wretches be justly charged upon church members? I know man is a sociable creature, but that will not excuse saints as to their carelessness of the choice of their company. The very fowls of the air, and beasts of the field, love not heterogeneous company. 'Birds of a feather flock together.'"—LEWIS STUCKLEY, A.D. -1687, *Gospel Glass.*

"'Tis natural for cattle of the same kind to go together in herds, upon mountains, in valleys, and in plains all the world over. The sheep follow their bell-wether as forcibly, and as close upon the heel, for good pasture, as rebels do their ringleaders for spoil and booty. The tingling of a bell keeps those together, and the hopes of a golden fleece these; pillage, plunder and rapine, interest and irreligion, being the principal motives to all rebellious cabals or associations."—OSWALD DYKES, A.D. 1907, *Moral Reflections.*

"Every fowler knows the truth of this proverb; but it has a further meaning than the association of irrational creatures. It intimates that society is a powerful attraction, but that likeness is the lure that draws people of the same kidney together. A covey of partridges in the country is but an emblem of a company of gossips in a neighborhood, a knot of sharpers at the gaming table, a pack of rakes at the tavern, etc. That one fool loves another, one fop admires another, one blockhead is pleased at the assurance, conceit and affection of another; and therefore herd together."—NATHAN BAILEY, A.D. 1721, *Diverse Proverbs*.

"Birds of a feather flock together, when free to follow their own inclinations, though rather than remain alone, they will seek out with avidity the fellowship of any, feathered or unfeathered, who may be to be found; but generally speaking persons of congenial dispositions, characters and pursuits, as they assimilate best, are found in each other's company, and the reason is obvious. Geese and crows, owls and peacocks, ducks and canary birds, from necessity as well as choice, are led divers ways by their divers wants and habits. . . . Whenever various animals or men of sundry sorts are by peculiar circumstances brought together, as in a menagerie, how is it with them? Why, the cackling and the cawing, the quacking and the hissing, the talking and the prating, the confused din of discordant tongues make it plain that the convention is unnatural and compulsory, and that like the individuals mentioned in the Acts, 'When they are let go, they will return to their own company,' and then only is it seen, when men are really at liberty to choose their company, what company it is they really choose."—JEFFERYS TAYLOR, A.D. 1827, *Old English Sayings*.

"Like to like. Gold is found in veins, pockets and places. Trees and plants grow in clumps and 'openings.' Menhaden swim in schools. Birds of a feather flock together. In pursuance of this universal law we should expect to find men drifting into groups as determined by natural affiliations and propensities. Nor are we disappointed in this. The three sons of Noah, going out from Ararat to populate the world, pursue their several ways and produce three distinct races of men. These races in turn are subdivided into nations, which assume their separate and distinct places in history."—DAVID J. BURRELL, A.D. 1844, . . . *An Experiment in Church Union.*

"Let the great seek out the great
While we, the poor, accept our fate."
MALAY FOLK RHYME.

VARIANT PROVERBS

**A bird of the same feather.** (English).
**A dove with a dove, a goose with a goose; for things of the same species always go together.** (Persian).
**A jackdaw always sits near a jackdaw.** (Greek).
**Birds of a feather flock together and so with men—like to like.** (Hebrew).
**Birds of one feather are often together.** (Irish-Ulster).
**Birds of one feather flying together.** (Irish-Ulster).
**Birds of the same kind fly together—pigeon with pigeon and hawk with hawk.** (Persian).
**Each bird draws to its flock.** (Gaelic).
**Every bird goes with its own flock.** (Irish-Ulster).
**Every sheep with its fellow.** (Spanish).
**It is one of its own family that a bird roosts with.** (Ashanti).
**Pigeon with pigeon, hawk with hawk.** (Persian).
**Where geese are, will goslings be.** (Gaelic).

### ALLIED PROVERBS

A bully fights with his peers, not with the grandees. (Oji).
A fly to a fly. (Telugu).
All gems in one place, all the snails in another. (Telugu).
A man is known by the company he keeps. (English).
Blood is thicker than water. (English).
Chicken hawk nebber buil' he nes' wid ground dove. (British Guiana).
Common oysters are in one spot and pearl oysters in another. (Telugu).
Go nine ridges and nine furrows to (assist) your own people than you would to the stranger. (Irish).
He that walketh with the virtuous is one of them. (English).
Like a black faced villain joining an oily legged sinner. (Telugu).
Like packsaddle like quilt. (Telugu).
Likeness is the mother of love. (Greek).
Like to like. (English).
Like to like the world over. (Hebrew).
No worm-eaten bean remains without finding a half blind measure. (Arabian).
One camel kneels in place of another. (Arabian).
One saint knows another. (Hindustani).
One with a shaved head should go to a village of shaved heads. (Marathi).
Set a thief to catch a thief. (English).
The degenerate palm goes among the unfruitful reeds. (Hebrew).
The good seek the good and the evil the evil. (English).
They are hornbills, we are sparrows, how can we possibly fly in the same flock? (Malayan).
Those who resemble each other assemble with each other. (French).
When the fiend goes to the Sabbat, he lodges with the sorcerer—i.e. When the devil goes to customs, he stays with wizards and witches. (Oji).

## CONTRADICTING PROVERBS

**A Babham, a dog and a bhat are always at variance with their own caste.** (Behar).

**Babhams, dogs and bards are always at variance with their own caste.** (Behar).

**Babhams, dogs and elephants càn never agree with their own kind.** (Behar).

**Two birds of prey do not keep company with each other.** (Spanish).

**Two nightingales do not perch on one bow.** (Osmanli).

**Two of a trade seldom agree.** (English, Spanish).

**Two proud men cannot ride on one ass.** (English).

**Two rope dancers do not play on one rope.** (Osmanli).

## BY HOOK OR BY CROOK

This phrase is used both in the sense of "One way or another" and "By fair means or foul." Its origin like most folk sayings is hidden in obscurity.

There are no less than six different sources from which it is said to have been derived. They are as follows:

*First*—In olden times men were accustomed to see in the shepherd's crook an emblem of Christ's beneficent watchful care over His church, for did not the religious pictures represent the Good Shepherd as holding one in His hand? They also saw in the hook held by Satan, with which he was represented in many of the pictures, as dragging men down to the flames of hell, an emblem of the adversary's pitiless malignity and cruel purpose. It was natural therefore to speak of human destiny as settled "by hook or by crook."

*Second*—After the great fire in London, 1666, which obliterated most landmarks and led to many lawsuits for the purpose of determining the boundaries of land holdings, two wise and experienced surveyors were appointed to assist in fixing the rights of claimants. One, it was said, was named Hook and the other Crook. Thus it came to pass that the matter of boundary was settled "by Hook or by Crook."

*Third*—When Waterford harbor was invaded by the ships of Strongbow in 1172 the commander saw on one side of the town a tower that was known as "The Tower of Hook," Hook being the name given to the section where it stood. On the other side of the town he saw a church that was known as "The Church of Crook"—Crook being the name of the other section; so he declared that the town must be taken either "by Hook or by Crook."

Mr. Eliezer Edwards tells us that "In Marsh's Library, Dublin, is a manuscript entitled *Annals Hiberniæ*, written in the seventeenth century by Dudley Loftus, a descendant of Adam Loftus, Archbishop of Armagh. The following extract gives a feasible account of the origin of this popular saying: '1172 King Henry the 2nd landed in Ireland this year, on St. Luke's eve at a place in the bay of Waterford beyond the fort of Duncannon on Munster syde, at a place called Ye Crook over agt the Tower of Ye Hook; whence arose the proverbe to gayne a thing by Hook or by Crook; it being safe to gayne land in one of those places where the winde drives from the other.'"

*Fourth*—As thieves often used a hook to possess themselves of plunder and bishops held a crook in their hand as a crosier, it became the custom in olden times to speak of accomplishing one's purposes by foul means or by fair or "by hook or by crook"; hence we find French rendering of the phrase—"Either with a thief's hook or a bishop's crook."

*Fifth*—In the reign of Charles I (1625–1649), there were two lawyers known by the name of Judge Hooke and Judge Crooke. Their legal standing, professional prominence and the similarity of their names gave rise to the saying that matters would be settled either "by Hooke or by Crooke."

*Sixth*—The phrase refers to an old English law regarding the rights of the poor in securing fuel from the wooded lands adjacent to their homes. They were permitted to carry dead wood, stumps, leaves and rubbish from private lands for use as fuel without asking for the owner's consent, provided they did not use either an axe or a saw. The law only allowed them to secure all that they could "by hook or by crook," that is, by the use of hooked poles known as "crook-lugs," with which dead branches could be pulled down from the trees, or by sickles, known as crooks, with which low brush could be gathered.

This last derivation of the phrase may be considered the most reliable.

"Dynmure Wood was even open and common To the . . . inhabitants of Bodmin . . . to bear away upon their backs a burden of lop, hook, crook, and bag wood."—BODMIN REGISTER, A.D. 1525.

"Nor wyll (they) suffre this boke
By hoke ne by croke
Prynted for to be."

JOHN SKELTON, CIRCA, A.D. 1460–1529, *Colyn Cloute.*

"Come, go we hence, friend! (quoth I to my mate)—
And now will I make a cross on this gate.
And I (quoth he) cross thee quite out of my book
Since thou art cross failed; avail, unhappy hook!
By hook or crook nought could I win there; men say:
He that cometh every day, shall have a cockney;
He that cometh now and then shall have a fat hen."

JOHN HEYWOOD, A.D. 1497–1580.

"Thereafter all that mucky pelfe he tooke,
The spoils of people evil gotten good,
The which her soil had scrap't by hooke and crooke,
And burning all to ashes pour'd it down the brooke."

EDMUND SPENSER, A.D. 1553–1599, *Faerie Queene.*

"Throughe thicke and thin, both over banck and bush,
In hope her to attaine by hooke or crooke."

EDMUND SPENSER, *Faerie Queene.*

"When he, who had so lately sack'd. The enemy had done
the fact,
Had rifled all his pokes and fobs
Of gimcracks, whims, and jiggumbobs,
Which he by hook, or crook, had gather'd,
And for his own inventions father'd:
And when they should, at jail delivered,
Unriddle one another's thievery."

SAMUEL BUTLER, A.D. 1612–1680, *Hudibras.*

"I have a communication from a correspondent, who remarks:—The story about the minister, and his favorite theme, 'The Broken Covenant,' reminds me of one respecting another minister whose staple topics of discourse were, 'Justification, Adoption, and Sanctification.' Into every sermon he preached, he managed, by hook or by crook, to force these three heads, so that his general method of handling every text was not so much *expositio* as *impositio*."—DEAN EDWARD B. B. RAMSAY, A.D. 1793–1872.

ALLIED PROVERBS

**By good means or bad.** (Latin).

**Either by might or by slight.** (English).

**Either with the thief's hook or the bishop's crook.** (French).

**He has made every effort with horse and with dog—i.e. He has tried every way, by hook or by crook.** (Osmanli).

## CONSISTENCY, THOU ART A JEWEL

This saying is so trite that it can scarcely be called a proverb, yet, like, "Every man has his faults" and "Fortune has wings," it has been repeated for generations as a statement of fact, challenging contradiction. Some regard consistency in speech and conduct as indicative of stubbornness or an evidence of arrested intellectual development, but it is rather a sign of loyalty to oneself, of standing firmly by one's life purpose, and shows itself by an unwavering and continued effort to live up to one's ideals. This may involve at times a course of action that is apparently divergent from that which went before. Lange in writing of divine consistency says that it does not lie in God's "carrying out the abstract decrees of His own will, inflexibly and in an exact direction, but in His remaining like Himself, and therefore in His even assuming a different position in relation to the changed positions of man; yet this is, of course, in harmony with the consistency of the principles established and realized by Him." So human consistency does not lie in holding to a fixed line of procedure in the face of changed conditions and greater knowledge, but rather in holding resolutely to one's ideals.

It is not surprising that consistency should be called a jewel. It has been common for ages to speak of various virtues as jewels and loyalty to oneself is one of the greatest virtues.

While there has been considerable discussion regarding the authorship of the phrase no one has been able to discover from whence it came. It was thought at one time to have been taken from some verses entitled *Jolly Robyn Roughhead or The Plowman's Philosophy.* The Dowager Countess of Drumlawrigg is said to have given it to a man by the name of Murtagh, who in the year 1754 published it in a collection of English and Scotch Ballads. But Murtagh is evidently a myth as no trace of him can be found and as to the "ancient" Ballad of Jolly Robbyn, it did not appear in print till 1867 when it was published in an American journal. The third verse that is said to contain the proverb is as follows:

> "Tush! tush! my lassie, such thoughts resigne,
> Comparisons are cruele:
> Fine pictures suit in frames as fine
> Consistencie a jewell.
> For thee and me coarse cloathes are best
> Rude folks in homelye raiment drest
> Wife Joan and goodman Robyn."

"Thou therefore that teachest another, teachest thou not thyself? Thou that preachest a man should not steal, dost thou steal? Thou that sayest a man should not commit adultery, dost thou commit adultery? Thou that abhorrest idols, dost thou rob temples? Thou who gloriest in the law, through thy transgression of the law, dishonorest thou God?—ROMANS, 2: 21–23.

"A young hound started a hare, snapping at her as he ran in pursuit as though he intended to kill her, then he let her run and jumped around her as though he wished to play. At last the hare wearied with his behavior said, 'I wish that you would show your true self. If you are my friend why do you snap at me? If you are my enemy why do you seek to play with me.'"—ÆSOP, DIED ABOUT B.C. 561.

"But whatsoever I have merited, either in my mind or in my means, need, I am sure, I have received none; unless experience be a jewell that I have purchased at an infinite rate."—WILLIAM SHAKESPEARE, A.D. 1564–1616, *Merry Wives of Windsor*.

"As the sails of a ship, when they are spread and swollen, and the way that the ship makes, shows me the wind, where it is, though the wind itself be an invisible thing, so thy actions tomorrow, and the life thou leadest all the year, will show me with what mind thou comest to the Sacrament today, though only God, and not I, can see thy mind."—JOHN DONNE, A.D. 1573–1631.

"Thou callest thyself Christian; but we question whether thou hast a right to the title; thy conduct is too contrary to that sacred name, which is too holy to be written on a rotten post." —WILLIAM GURNALL, A.D. 1616–1679.

"A foolish consistency is the hobgoblin of little minds, adored by little statesmen and philosophers and divines. With consistency a great soul has simply nothing to do. He may as well concern himself with his shadow on the wall. Speak what you think now in hard words and tomorrow speak what tomorrow thinks in hard words again, though it contradict everything you said today."—RALPH WALDO EMERSON, A.D. 1803–1882, *Self Reliance.*

"One of the broadest and best defined experiences that passed under my observation and was imprinted on my memory in early youth was that of a family whose father stood high above all his neighbors in religious profession and gifts, and yet returned from market drunk as often as he had the means."—WILLIAM ARNOT, A.D. 1806–1875, *Illustrations of the Book of Proverbs.*

"Gineral C is a dreffle smart man;
He's ben on all sides that give places or pelf;
But consistency still waz a part of his plan,—
He's ben true to one party—an' that is himself;—
So John P
Robinson he
Sez he shall vote for Gineral C."

JAMES RUSSELL LOWELL, A.D. 1819–1891,
*Biglow Papers.*

"Alas! We cannot think that these orientals live as wisely as they talk. Their words are sententious, brilliant, few—their lives are lazy, aimless, monotonous. O consistency thou art a jewell."—*The Home*, April, 1859.

### ALLIED PROVERBS

**A clean cheese in a dirty cheese-vat.** (Welsh).

**Consistency of action is the measure of greatness.** (Tamil).

**His words accord not with his acts.** (Osmanli).

**Like a chameleon, he changes from color to color.** (Osmanli).

**The government official while laughing at the same time bites.** (Osmanli).

**The healthy seeking a doctor.** (Welsh).

**The mouth of a blackbird with the request of a wolf.** (Welsh.)

**There are words that do not agree with words.** (Osmanli).

**The voice of a lamb with the heart of a wolf.** (Welsh).

**To keep a dog and bark yourself.** (Welsh).

**What! Is it for an evil doer to teach religious precepts?** (Tamil).

**What is this fast? What is this pickled cabbage? Why do you talk about fasting while eating?** (Osmanli).

## DO NOT COUNT YOUR CHICKENS BEFORE THEY ARE HATCHED

Day-dreams are not prophecies, neither are hopes and fancies harbingers of success.

The origin of this proverb though unknown may have arisen from Æsop's fable of *The Milk-maid and Her Pail* which is as follows:

"A farmer's daughter had been out to milk the cows and was returning to the dairy carrying her pail of milk upon her head. As she walked along, she fell a-musing after this fashion: 'The milk in this pail will provide me with cream which I will make into butter and take to market to sell. With the money I will buy a number of eggs and these when hatched will produce chickens and by and by I shall have quite a large poultry yard. Then I shall sell some of my fowls and with the money which they will bring in I will buy myself a new gown, which I shall wear when I go to the fair, and all the young fellows will admire it and come and make love to me, but I shall toss my head and have nothing to say to them.' Forgetting all about the pail and suiting the action to the word, she tossed her head. Down went the pail, all the milk was spilled and all her fine castles in the air vanished in a moment."—*V. S. Vernon Jones' Translation.*

There are two stories closely resembling Æsop's fable. One is an Indian tale of *The Poor Man and the Oil Jar*, and the other an Arabian Nights' tale of *Barber's Story of his Fifth Brother*, or *El-Feshshar's Day-dream* which is believed to have been derived from an Indian fable of remotest antiquity found in the Haetopades of Veeshnu-Sarma.

The first tale is that of a man who was hired to carry a jar of oil which he placed on his head according to custom and started. As he went on his journey he speculated in his mind as to what he would do with the money that he would receive for his errand. "For carrying this oil," he said to himself, "I will get four *annas* with which I will buy a hen, then I will sell the chickens that come from the eggs that the hen lays and purchase a herd of goats. From the sale of the goats and their kids I will receive enough to buy a cow, which I can sell with their calves and so obtain a sum of money which will enable me to purchase a herd of buffaloes. Then I can marry and have children who will say 'Father dear, come and eat your meal,' but I will say, 'No, no!'" Shaking his head to emphasize his refusal he shook the jar of oil and it fell at his feet spilling its contents.

The other story is of a man who took his inheritance of a hundred pieces of silver and purchased a basket of glassware which he placed on a large tray and displayed it for sale. Then he leaned against a wall and began to speculate in his mind what he would do with the money he received from the purchaser of his goods. Letting his thoughts run on he imagined that he would buy more glassware and sell it; with the proceeds he would buy another supply and so on until he had acquired great wealth. Then he would branch out into other lines of trade and live in a fine house and have memlooks and horses with gilded saddles and finally marry the daughter of the chief Wezeer and becoming angry at her he would thrust out his foot at her, and to show himself how he would thus spurn her he kicked and in kicking overturned his tray of glassware and broke all the pieces.

"Many count their chickens before they are hatched; and where they expect bacon meet with broken bones."—MIGUEL DE CERVANTES SAAVEDRA, A.D. 1547–1616, *Don Quixote*.

"Neither ought we to reckon our eggs before they are lay'd. We may count our poultry when we have them, well and good, to keep the tale of 'em, 'tis prudent housewifery, but we ought not to compute upon them in the shell. 'Tis not common discretion to crack of our chickens, to talk of our young turkeys, and to feed ourselves with the fancy of our goslins or cygnets, before they are hatch'd. And yet this is no more than what thousands of people do every day in other affairs of their lives."—OSWALD DYKES, A.D. 1707, *Moral Reflections.*

"Reckoning your chickens before they are hatched. Not a very agreeable occupation but one that is quite inevitable as long as there are sanguine temperaments, speculators and calculators—in fact, as long as there is hope in the world. The unwise part of the performance is, simply, when no sufficient care has been taken to procure sound eggs, and to give attention to the hen who is patiently laboring at the hatching."—*Household Words,* July 7, 1852.

### ALLIED PROVERBS

**Bargaining for fish that is in the water.** (Osmanli).
**Before the bear be struck (slain) his skin is not sold.** (Osmanli).
**Boil not the pap before the child is born.** (English).
**Calculating at home on the fish in the sea.** (Marathi).
**Catch the bear before you sell his skin.** (English).
**Chickens are slow in coming from unlaid eggs.** (German).
**Count not four except you have them in a wallet.** (English).
**Dinna gut your fish till you get them.** (Scotch).
**Do not bless the fish till it gets to land.** (Irish).
**Do not build the sty before the litter comes.** (Irish).
**Do not sell the hide before you have caught the bear.** (Dutch, Italian).
**Do not sell the hide before you have caught the fox.** (Danish).
**Do not speak ill of the year until it be past.** (Spanish).
**Don't cry " chue " to the chick till it be out of the egg.** (Italian, Gaelic).
**Don't sell the skin before the bear is shot.** (Dutch).

**Don't cry " Herring " until they are in the net.** (Dutch).
**Don't cry " Dried Fish " before they are caught.** (Italian).
**Don't reckon your eggs before they are laid.** (Italian).
**Don't skin the deer till you get it.** (Gaelic).
**Eating sweet-meats of fancy.** (Kumaun, Garhwal).
**Estimating the value of the skin before you catch the badger.** (Japanese).
**First catch your hare.** (English).
**Grass at a distance looks thick.** (Bengalese).
**He gave a name to an unborn child.** (Telugu).
**He gives away the deer before it is caught.** (Persian).
**He that lives on hope will die fasting.** (English).
**He that waits for dead men's shoes may go long barefoot.** (English).
**Hol' de cow befo' you bargain fo' sell de beef.** (British Guiana).
**It is ill waiting for dead men's shoes.** (English).
**Like the man who went stooping down from the place where he intended to hang the lamp before he built the house.** (Bengalese).
**Make not your sauce until you have caught your fish.** (English).
**Na 'pread table clot' befo' pat done bile.** (British Guiana).
**Never count the fish till they come out of the sea.** (Irish, Gaelic).
**Never praise a ford till you are over.** (English).
**Of uncut grass there are nine hundred bundles.** (Assamese).
**One must catch the bear before he draws a ring through its nose.** (German).
**One must not make the crib before the calf is born.** (Guernsey).
**Rubbing the lips with oil while the jack fruit is still on the tree.**

When jack fruit, which is a glutinous fruit, is eaten without putting oil on the lips it sticks and produces sores. (Assamese.)

**Sell not the bear skin before you have caught him.** (English, German, French, Italian, Dutch).

**Sune enough to cry " Chick " when it's out of the shell.** (Scotch).

**The child is not born and yet it is called " Moozuffur "—i.e. victorious.** (Persian, Hindustani).

**The cow had not been slaughtered, yet he had put the soup tureen on his head for it.** (Pashto).

**The father is not yet born, but the son has taken his stand behind.**

This is a riddle: The father represents fire; the son, smoke. As smoke generally precedes fire, the son in the proverb is said to come before the father. (Behar).

**The son is not yet born, but a beat of the drum proclaims the event beforehand.**

Similar to above. See also "While the father was still in the womb the son went to a wedding party." (Behar).

**The trees in the orchard have not yet been planted, but the woodworms have settled down there beforehand.** (Behar).

**They don't sell the duiker walking in the bush.** (Ibo).

**To build castles in the air.** (English).

**To celebrate the triumph before the victory.** (Latin).

**To grind peppers for a bird on the wing.** (Malayan).

**To sell the bird in the bush.** (Italian).

**To take off one's boots before seeing the water.** (Persian).

**Trusting to the cloud to cut open the tank.** (Telugu).

**Twist a chain for the boy who is yet in the womb.** (Kumaun, Garhwal).

**Tying beads around an unborn child.** (Telugu).

**Unlaid eggs are uncertain chickens.** (German, Dutch).

**Wait till the hare's in the pot before you talk.** (Mauritius Creole).

**We have no son and yet are giving him a name.** (Spanish).

**While the child is still in the womb, the son is named Somalingam.** (Telugu).

**While the cotton crop was still in the field he said, " Three cubits for Poli and six for me "—i.e. Three cubits of cloth for my cousin and six for me.**

Poli is a girl's name and here stands for cousin. (Telugu).

**While the father is still in the womb, the son went to a wedding party.**

Like the proverb—"The father is not yet born but the son has taken his stand behind." This is a kind of riddle. The father represents the seed of the Safflower still in the pod while the son represents the Safflower dye. (Behar).

**Ye're cawking the claith ere the wab be in the loom.** (Scotch).

**Ye're like the miller's dog; ye lick your lips ere the pock is opened.** (Scotch).

**Ye must not sell the bear skin before the bear is killed.** (English, German, French, Italian, Dutch).

**You cannot contract for the fish in the sea.** (Turkish).

338

## EVERY MAN THINKS HIS OWN GEESE SWANS

Parents are conceited over their children; men love their own country, district and town.

It is natural that in forming this proverb, reference should have been made to geese and swans. The two birds have many things in common, yet they are not held in the same respect. Geese are poor men's possessions while swans are seldom seen save in lakes belonging to parks and gardens.

In olden times the swan was called a royal bird for the sovereigns of England appropriated those that had strayed from their proper estates, so that it became the custom for those in possession to establish a prior claim by marking the beaks of their birds.

Geese belonged to the barnyards and adjacent pools or ponds, were good for food and for prognosticating the approach of foul weather, while swans were held to be sacred. Men looked at their graceful forms and movements as they floated on the water and reverently regarded them as birds of prophecy, to be sheltered and watched over with the greatest care so as to be ready for use in case of need in the taking of oaths and for conjuring. Their feathers were thought to be potent as talismans and their song never heard save when they were about to die. No bird, with the possible exception of the eagle, has been more frequently used in heraldry, and legends and fairy stories are abundant in which people have been temporarily changed to swans. "It may be," says Charles de Kay (A.D. 1848–) "that the great river Elbe that springs from the 'sea coast' of Bohemia splits the realms of Saxony and Prussia in two, and reaches ocean in the ancient free commonwealth of Hamburg, was first named from the magic bird whose name was the same as elf."

A child's book entitled *Peter Prim's Pride*, published in 1810, contained a picture of a mother fondly patting the chin of a stubbed nose daughter, while another ill kept child stood near awaiting parental approval. Beneath the picture was inscribed the old proverbial saying: "Every crow thinks her own young whitest."

Two thousand and more years ago the wise fabulist told a story of an argument between a sow and a dog in which the sow claimed that its children were superior to those of the dog because they could see at birth, whereas the children of his opponent were born blind.

There is a phrase in common use that seems to affirm an opposite truth, for it is said, "All his swans are geese"; but the contradiction is only apparent for the phrase is rarely, if ever, used in referring to children. Its application is generally confined to boasters whose claims cannot be substantiated. The boaster would have others believe that his tales are as true and wonderful as birds in the king's garden, whereas they are more like common geese than royal swans.

"Jupiter issued a proclamation to all the beasts, and offered a prize to one who, in his judgment, produced the most beautiful offspring. Among the rest came the monkey carrying a baby monkey in her arms, a hairless, flat nosed little fright. When they saw it, the gods all burst into peal on peal of laughter, but the monkey hugged her little one to her and said, 'Jupiter may give the prize to whomsoever he likes but I shall always think my baby the most beautiful of them all.'"—ÆSOP, BEFORE B.C. 561, *V. S. Vernon Jones' Translation.*

"At this same ancient feast of Capulet's
Sups the fair Rosaline whom thou so lovest,
With all the admired beauties of Verona:
Go thither, and with unattainted eye
Compare her face with some that I shall show,
And I will make thee think thy swan a crow."

WILLIAM SHAKESPEARE, A.D. 1564–1616,
*Romeo and Juliet.*

"By'r lady, friends! (quoth I), this maketh a show,
To show you more unnatural than the crow;

The crow thinketh her own birds fairest in the wood,
But by your words (except I wrong understood),
Each other's birds or jewels, ye do weigh
Above your own."

JOHN HEYWOOD, A.D. 1497–1580, *A Dialogue.*

"This proverb intimates that an inbred philanty runs through the whole race of flesh and blood, and that self-love is the mother of vanity, pride and mistake. It turns a man's geese into swans, his dunghill poultry into pheasants and his lambs into venison. It blinds the understanding, perverts the judgment, depraves the reason of the otherwise most modest distinguishers of truth and falsity. It makes a man so fondly conceited of himself, that he prefers his own art for its excellency, his own skill for its perfection, his own compositions for their wit and his own productions for their beauty. It makes even his vices seem to him virtues, and his deformities beauties; for so every crow thinks her own bird fairest, though never so black and ugly."—NATHAN BAILEY, A.D. 1721, *Diverse Proverbs.*

ALLIED PROVERBS

**A son, although full of faults, is perfect in his father's eyes.** (Persian).

**A son, although he is a lump of earth (worthless) still is the light of the eyes to his parents.** (Persian).

**Black as the raven, he thinks his children fair.** (Gaelic).

**Black is the berry but sweet, black is my lassie but bonnie.** (Gaelic).

**Ebery John Crow t'inks he own picknie white.** (British Guiana).

Ebery crow cry fo' he own calf. (British Guiana).
Every cow licks her own calf. (Serbian).
Every crow thinks her own birds whitest. (Scotch).
Every crow thinks her own nestlings the fairest. (English).
Every man thinks his own chickens are the best. (English).
Every monkey thinks its young ones pretty. (Tamil, Louisiana Creole).
Every mother's child is handsome. (German).
Every mother thinks it is on her own child the sun rises. (Irish).
Every owl thinks all her children the fairest. (Danish).
Every owl thinks her young ones beautiful. (English).
Fowl tread 'pon he chicken, but he no tread haad. (British Guiana).
If they (my children) were a thousand, they would be dearer than my eyes. (Arabian).
If our child squints, our neighbor's child has a cast in both eyes. (Livonian).
Ilka man thinks his ain craw blackest. (Scotch).
I love my dear one were he a black slave. (Syrian).
Monkey never says its young are ugly. (Trinidad Creole).
My heart is for my child and my child's heart is for a stone. (Syrian).
My own heart (I will sacrifice) rather than my children. (West African).
My own son is a son, a stranger's good for nothing. (Hindustani).
No ape but swears he has the handsomest children. (English, German).
Our own child is tender, another's is (as tough as) leather. Marathi).
Sweepings, but from our own field; halt and lame, but our own child—hence valuable. (Marathi).
The beetle is a beauty in the eyes of its mother. (Arabian, Egyptian).
The beetle is a bride in the arms of its mother. (Arabian).

**The crow likes her greedy blue chick.** (Gaelic).

**The crow's chick is dear to the crow.** (Telugu).

**The crow thinketh her own birds fairest in the wood.** (English).

**The crow thinks her own ghastly chick a beauty.** (Gaelic).

**The love of the ghoul is for his own son.** (Syrian).

**The monkey is a gazelle in the eyes of his mother.** (Arabic, Syrian).

**The porcupine says, " Oh, my soft little son, softer than butter," and the crow says, " My son, whiter than muslin."** (Pashto).

**The raven always thinks that her young ones are whitest.** (Danish).

**The raven thinks her own bird the prettiest bird in the wood.** (Irish-Farney).

**The scald crow thinks her daughter is the prettiest bird in the wood.** (Irish-Farney).

**They asked the raven, " Who is the beautiful?" " My little ones," he said.** (Osmanli).

**Though but a young crow, it is golden to its mother.** (Tamil).

**Though earthen, one's own child is precious.** (Tamil).

**To everyone his own son appears the most beautiful.** (Persian).

**To the eye of a crow, its young one has milk white feathers.** (Japanese).

**Whether it is black, or dun, or brown; it is to her own kid the goat gives all her affection.** (Gaelic).

ALLIED PROVERBS
(Personal Preference)

**Every bird admires (loves) its own nest.** (Osmanli).

**Every bird thinks her own family the nicest in the world.** (Irish-Ulster).

**Every bird thinks its own nest beautiful.** (Italian).

**Everybody thinks his own cuckoo sings better than another's nightingale.** (German).

**Every man thinks his own copper gold.** (German, Danish).

**Every man thinks his own owl a falcon.** (German, Dutch).

**Every one's own property is precious to himself.** (Osmanli).

**Every peddler praises his own needles.** (Spanish, Portuguese).

**Every peddler praises his pot and more if it is cracked.** (Spanish, Italian).

**Every potter vaunts his own pot.** (French).

**My own crow (is better) than the nightingale of other folk.** (Osmanli).

**No man calls his own dowie sour.**

Dowie is a drink made from curdled milk, water and herbs. (Syrian).

**The hen he has caught has four legs.** (Telugu).

**The beloved is the object that thou lovest—were it even a monkey.** (Arabian).

**To everyone, what belongs to himself, is beautiful.** (Modern Greek).

## GREAT CRY BUT LITTLE WOOL

He who talks the most does the least.

The proverb is said to have been derived from an old miracle play or ancient "mystery," in which Nabal, the churlish Carmelite (I Sam. 25 : 2, 5) was represented as shearing sheep while the devil, standing near, was imitating him by shearing a hog that loudly protests over the work. A proverb predating the one now in use informs us that the present rendering is a repetition of the devil's statement at the time he was engaged in his useless task. It is given thus: "Great cry and little wool, as the devil said when he sheared the hog." The thought of the proverb was in the mind of Æsop who lived several centuries after Nabal, when he told the story of the mountain in labor that brought forth a mouse. John Fortescue who wrote at the time the miracle plays were in vogue in England quoted the saying thus: "Moche Crye and no Wull"—but Cervantes who published his *Don Quixote* when the "mysteries" were on the wane and Samuel Butler in his *Hudibras* a little later gave the modern rendering.

Still another origin has suggested itself to some students, by the Scotch form, "Mair whistle than wo' quo' the soutar when he sheared the sow." *Soughtar* being the Scotch word for shoemaker, the phrase is said to have come from the shoemaker's use of bristles for flexible needles in sewing.

While the proverb may have been in use long before the miracle plays of the middle ages, there is more probability of its having been derived from them than from the Scotch form as suggested.

"'Let me tell you, friend,' quoth the squire of the wood, 'that you are out in your politics; for these island-governments bring more cost than worship; there is a great cry but little wool; the best will bring more trouble and care than they are worth and those that take them on their shoulders are ready to sink under them.'"—MIGUEL DE CERVANTES SAAVEDRA, A.D. 1547-1616, *Don Quixote.*

"A bit of homely advice, quaintly put, is found in this—'Do not drive black hogs at night.' 'Much cry and no wool' is the result of shearing swine, a hopeless task. The adage is often met with in Fortescue's treatise on *Absolute and Limited Monarchy,* written over four hundred years ago. We find a reference to 'the man that shery'd his hogge, moch crye and no wull.' In a book published in 1597 it runs: 'Of the shearing hoggest there is great crie for so little woole' and we find the saying again in *Hudibras* and many other books, and in old plays."—F. EDWARD HULME, A.D. 1842–1909.

### VARIANT PROVERBS

**As the devil said when he clipped the sow.** (Scotch).
**Great cry and little wool, as the man said when he sheared the sow.** (Italian).
**Great cry and little wool, quoth the devil, when he sheared his hogs.** (English).
**Great cry but little wool, as the fellow said when he shore his hogs.** (English).
**Great noise for a little wool.** (Irish-Ulster).
**Mair whistle than wo', quo' the soutar, when he sheared the sow.** (Scotch).
**Much cry and little wool, said the fool as he sheared the pig.** (German, Dutch).
**Muckle din and little 'oo.** (Scotch).

### ALLIED PROVERBS

**A farthing's worth of peas and the sound of grinding all night.** (Hindustani).
**A lofty shop, but the sweetmeats sold there are tasteless.** (Hindustani).
**Great boaster little doer.** (French).
**Great boast small roast.** (English, Dutch).
**Great cries but not a grain in the heap.** (Telugu).
**Great noise and little hurt.** (Gaelic).
**Great smoke little roast.** (Italian).
**Great talkers are little doers.** (French, Dutch).
**Great vaunters, little doers.** (French).
**Great words but small measure.** (Telugu).
**His words leap over forts, his foot does not cross the threshold.** (Telugu).
**I hear the noise of the mill but see no flour.** (Persian).

**Look for a raven and shear its wool.** (Arabian).
**Loud cackle, little egg.** (Gaelic).
**Mickle ado and little help.** (Scotch).
**More bustle than work.** (Guernsey).
**Much ado about nothing.** (English).
**Much bruit, little fruit.** (English).
**Much talk, little work.** (Dutch).
**Muckle whistlin' for little red lan'.** (Scotch).
**Selling and buying and nothing upon the board.** (Arabian).
**Small mouth, big words.** (Pashto).
**The cow is greater than the milking.** (Gaelic).
**The mountain is in labor and will bring forth a mouse.** (Latin).
**The noise is greater than the nuts.** (English).
**There is more noise than nuts to crack.** (Spanish).
**There is more talk than trouble.** (English).
**Would you shear a donkey for wool?** (Latin).
**Your windmill dwindles into a nut-crack.** (Latin).

## HALF A LOAF IS BETTER THAN NO BREAD

If you cannot have what you want take what you can get. A small benefit is better than no benefit at all.

Nothing is known of the circumstances under which this saying was first used. It may have been an expression repeated in time of famine when food was scarce and when small portions were distributed among the people.

It is often true that when one cannot obtain all that he desires it is wise to accept a portion. It is also true that half is better than the whole when a great sacrifice is required to secure all that is needed.

### VARIANT PROVERBS

**A bad bush is better than the open field.** (English).

**A blind mother-in-law is better than none at all.** (Telugu).

**A blind uncle is better than no uncle.** (Assamese).

**A little is bettah dan not'in'.** (British Guiana).

**A man were better to be half blind than have both eyes out.** (English).

**Bannocks (oat cakes) are better than nae bread.** (Scotch).

**Better a bare foot than none.** (English).

**Better a blind horse than an empty halter.** (Dutch).

**Better a lame horse than an empty saddle.** (German).
**Better a lean jade than an empty halter.** (English, Scotch).
**Better a mouse in the pot than no flesh at all.** (Scotch).
**Better a poor horse than an empty stall.** (Danish).
**Better are small fish than an empty dish.** (English, Scotch, Gaelic).
**Better a wee bush than nae beild-shelter.** (Scotch).
**Better coarse cloth than the naked thighs.** (Danish).
**Better half a loaf than none at all. Better a little furniture than an empty house.** (Danish).
**Better half an egg than an empty shell.** (German, English, Dutch).
**Better half an egg than toom doup—i.e. empty bottom of a shell.** (Scotch).
**Better my hog dirty home than no hog at all.** (English).
**Better one eye than stone blind.** (German, Spanish).
**Better rags than nakedness.** (Haytian).
**Better something than nothing.** (German).
**Better straw than nothing.** (Portuguese).
**Kuhl better than blindness—i.e. A sore eye is better than no eye at all.**

The word kuhl indicates a remedy for a diseased eye. It is better to use the remedy even though you have a sore eye than lose your sight. (Arabian).

**Little better than none.** (Arabian).
**Sma' fish are better than naine.** (Scotch).
**The something is better than its want.** (Arabian).

ALLIED PROVERBS

**Better lose the anchor than the whole ship.** (Dutch).
**Better lose the saddle than the horse.** (German, Italian).
**Better lose the wool than the sheep.** (French, Portuguese).
**Better ride a lame horse than go afoot.** (German).
**Better some of a pudding than none of a pie.** (English).
**Chicken-hawk say, he can't get mamma, he tek picknie.** (British Guiana).

**From the debtor accept even bran in payment.** (Ancient Hebrew).

**If I have lost the ring, I still have the fingers.** (Spanish, Italian).

**If you can't get tu'key, you mus' satisfy wid John Crow.** (British Guiana).

**If you find even fourteen annas of lost money, it is well.** (Assamese).

**It is better to lose than to lose more.** (Spanish, Portuguese).

**Many see more with one eye than others with two.** (German).

**One day is better than sometimes a whole year.** (English).

**One foot is better than two crutches.** (English).

**Them that canna get a peck must put up wi' a stimpart—i.e. A quarter of a peck.** (Scotch).

**To whom a little is not sufficient to him nothing will be sufficient.** (Modern Greek).

## HONESTY IS THE BEST POLICY

Archbishop Whately (A.D. 1787–1863), when quoting this proverb added the words, "but he who acts only on that principle is not an honest man."

Some men are honest from principle, others are honest from motives of expediency. The proverb applies to the latter class. To them honesty is not a matter of character but of policy. They say with Mirabeau (A.D. 1749–1791), "We ought to want it (honesty) as the best means of getting rich."

The wise fabulist taught the advantages of honesty in the story of a woodman who, while felling trees by a river, accidentally let his axe slip from his hand and fall into the water. Mercury appearing at the instant drew a golden axe from the stream and presented it to the woodcutter in place of the axe that he had lost. "No, no!" exclaimed the man, "I cannot take that axe for it is not mine. The one I lost was made of iron and this is made of gold." Mercury being pleased with the man's honesty, went into the river and recovered the axe that was lost and restored it to its owner in addition to which he gave him the golden one that he had first offered, as a reward for integrity of character. An acquaintance hearing of his friend's good fortune determined to try the same method of securing a golden axe and went to the river bank to chop trees. After chopping a short time he intentionally let his axe slip from his grasp and fall into the water. Mercury at once appeared and offered to help him find his lost property. Drawing a golden axe from the river he showed it to the man who was so pleased at the apparent success of his scheme that he grasped for the treasure, exclaiming, "Yes, that's mine! that's mine!" "Oh, no," returned Mercury, "That is not yours," and went away leaving the dishonest man's axe at the bottom of the river.

"Providence," wrote Quintilian (A.D. 35?–100?) "has given to men this gift, that things which are honest are also the most advantageous," but centuries before the Roman critic gave expression to the teaching of the proverb King Solomon saw a stronger reason for honesty and declared that "A false balance is an abomination of Jehovah, but a just weight is his delight." —PROV. 11:1 (See PROV. 20:23).

As to the origin of the proverb: The claim has been advanced that it was first used in China and is found in the translation of the novel *Iu-Kiao-Li*. However that may be the saying is of great antiquity and is found in many languages.

On the fifth of April, 1797, a quaint and curious

announcement appeared in the Worcester (Mass.) *Spy*. The advertiser, under the caption of "Honesty is the best policy," stated that a certain thief had stolen some fresh beef from his slaughter house, and that he wished the said thief would come forward in a *gentlemanly like manner* and settle for the same under penalty of being exposed and *complimented* by a warrant.

"Do not consider anything for your interest which makes you break your word, quit your modesty, or incline you to any practice which will not bear the light, or look the world in the face." —ANTONINUS, A.D. 121?–180.

"I am an old cur at a crust, and can sleep dog-sleep when I list. I can look sharp as well as another, and let me alone to keep the cobwebs out of my eyes. I know where the shoe wrings me. I will know who and who is together. Honesty is the best policy, I will stick to that. The good shall have my hand and heart, but the bad neither foot nor fellowship."—MIGUEL DE CERVANTES, A.D. 1547–1616, *Don Quixote*.

"It would be an unspeakable advantage, both to the public and private, if men would consider that great truth—that no man is wise or safe, but he that is honest."—WALTER RALEIGH, A.D. 1552–1618.

"Man is his own star, and the soul that can
Render an honest and perfect man,

Commands all light, all influence, all fate.
Nothing to him falls early or too late,
Our acts our angels are, or good or ill,
Our fatal shadows that walk by us still."

JOHN FLETCHER(?) A.D. 1576–1625, *Honest Man's Fortune.*

"I would recommend our proverb to the reflection of the great; for 'tis pity that integrity and sincerity should be more in esteem among plebeians than among men of birth, honor and employment. However it mustn't be confined to any set of men, for every man in all parts of his life will find occasion for this instruction, and may observe that the saying is exactly true to whomsoever it be applied. 'Tis impossible that trick, artifice and fraud should have any lasting reputation in the world, while there is any virtue in it, and 'tis seldom that a knave carries his design so well off, but his own ill actions come home to him."—SAMUEL PALMER, A.D. 1710, *Moral Essays.*

"Men think there is no sin in that which there is money to be got by and, while it passes undiscovered, they cannot blame themselves for it; a blot is no blot till it is hit (Hos., 12:7, 8) but they are not the less an abomination to God who will be the avenger of those who defraud their brethren."

"Nothing is more pleasing to God than fair and honest dealing, nor more necessary to make us and our devotions acceptable to Him. A just weight is His delight. He Himself goes by a just weight, and holds the scale of judgment with an even hand and therefore is pleased with those that are herein followers of Him. A balance cheats, under pretence of doing right most exactly and therefore is the greater abomination to God."—MATTHEW HENRY, A.D. 1662–1714, *Comment on Prov. 11:1.*

"Honesty is not only the deepest policy, but the highest wisdom, since however difficult it may be for integrity to get on, it is a thousand times more difficult for knavery to get off; and no error is more fatal than that of those who think that virtue has no other reward because they have heard that she is her own."—CHARLES C. COLTON, A.D. 1780–1832, *Lacon.*

With no intention of advocating dishonesty as a state or public policy, but rather to emphasize the necessity of material strength to enforce its laws and protect its citizens, Washington Irving wrote thus:

"Whatever may be advanced by philosophers to the contrary, I am of opinion that, as to nations, the old maxim, that 'honesty is the best policy' is a sheer and ruinous mistake. It might have answered well enough in the honest times when it was made, but in these degenerate days, if a nation pretends to rely merely upon the justice of its dealings, it will fare something like an honest man among thieves, who, unless he have something more than his honesty to depend upon, stands but a poor chance of profiting by his company."—WASHINGTON IRVING, A.D. 1783–1859, *Knickerbocker History of New York.*

"Though an honest man should get no thanks from the world he ought to count it an abundant reward for all his self sacrifice that the world's Judge sees every righteous deed and delights in it."—WILLIAM ARNOT, A.D. 1808–1875, *Honesty is the Best Policy.*

That honesty is the best policy, "is true in the higher sense; but doubtful in the sense usually intended. It is true as to the general good, but not usually for the individual, except in the long run (we pass over the obvious truth, that it is better policy to earn a guinea than to steal one because the proverb has a far wider range of meaning than that). To be a 'politic,' clever fellow, a vast deal more humouring of prejudices, errors and follies, is requisite, than at all assorts with true honesty of character. If, however, we regard this proverb only on its higher moral ground, then, of course, we cannot at once admit its truth."—*Household Words*, February 7, 1852.

"'Ah!' rejoins Mr. Brass, brim full of moral precepts and love of virtue. 'A charming subject of reflection for you, very charming. A subject of proper pride and congratulation, Christopher. Honesty is the best policy—I always find it so myself. I lost forty-seven pound ten by being honest this morning. But it's all gain, it's gain.'"—CHARLES DICKENS, A.D. 1812–1870, *Old Curiosity Shop.*

### ALLIED PROVERBS

A clean mouth and an honest hand will take a man through any land. (German).

A few things gained by fraud destroy a fortune otherwise honestly won. (Latin).

An ill wan penny will cast down a pound. (English).

A thief seldom grows rich by thieving. (German).

Honesty is better than ill gotten wealth. (English).

Honesty makes rich, but she works slowly. (German).

I never saw a tortuous person satisfied, nor a straight forward person in want of food. (Osmanli).

Knavery may serve a turn but honesty is best at long run. (English).

Look not at thieves eating flesh, but look at them suffering punishment. (Chinese).

No honest man ever repented of his honesty. (English).

None can be wise and safe but he that is honest. (English).

Of all crafts, to be an honest man is the best craft. (English).

The best investment for income is honesty. (German).

The thief proceeds from a needle to gold and from gold to the gallows. (Portuguese).

The thief steals until he comes to the gallows. (German).

Virtue triumphs, vice decays. (Bengali.)

### CONTRADICTING PROVERBS

A good honest man now-a-days is but a civil word for a fool. (English).

Can you take ghi (out of a bottle) with a straight finger? (Behar).

Curved (crooked) ship; straight voyage. (Osmanli).

Honest men are easily humbugged. (English).

Honesty is ill to thrive by. (English).

Honesty is praised and starves. (Latin).

## OTHER PROVERBS ABOUT HONESTY

**All the honesty is in the partings.** (English).

**A man never surfeits of too much honesty.** (English).

**An honest countenance is the best passport.** (English).

**An honest look covers many faults.** (English).

**An honest man does not make himself a dog for the sake of a bone.** (Danish).

**An honest man has half as much more brains as he needs; a knave hath not half as much.** (English).

**An honest man is hurt by praise unjustly bestowed.** (French).

**An honest man is not the worse because a dog barks at him.** (Danish).

**An honest man's word is as good as his bond.** (English).

**An honest man's word is as good as the king's.** (Portuguese).

**An honest man's word is his bond.** (Dutch).

**A nod of an honest man is enough.** (English).

**As honest a man as any in the cards when the kings are out.** (English).

**As honest a man as ever broke bread.** (English).

**As honest a man as ever stepped.** (English).

**As honest a man as ever trod on shoe leather.** (English).

**As true as steel.** (English).

**As true as the dial to the sun.** (English).

**Clean hands want no wash ball.** (English).

**He is wise that is honest.** (Italian).

**He leaves his office with the beggar's staff in his hand.** (German).

**He that builds his house with other men's money is like one that gathers himself stones for the tomb of his burial.** (Hebrew).

**Honest men and knaves may possibly wear the same clothes.** (English).

**Honest men are bound, but you can never bind a knave.** (English).

Honest men fear neither the light nor the dark. (English).
Honest men marry soon, wise men not at all. (English).
Honest men never have the love of a rogue. (English).
Honest nobody is to blame for all. (English).
Honesty and plain dealing put knavery out of bias. (English).
Honesty is like an icicle—if once it melts that is the end of it. (American).
Honesty is na a price. (Scotch).
Honesty is the poor man's pork and the rich man's pudding. (English).
Honesty lasts longest. (English, German).
Honesty may be dear bought but can ne'er be an ill pennyworth. (Scotch).
Many an honest man stands in need of help that he has not the face to beg for. (English).
No honest man has the leer of a rogue. (English).
Too much honesty never did man harm. (English).
Truth and honesty have no need of loud protestations. (English).
Truth and honesty keep the crown o' the causey. (Scotch).
We are bound to be honest, but not to be rich. (English).
You may trust him with untold gold. (English).

## PROVERBS ABOUT DISHONESTY

As honest as the cat when the meat is out of reach. (English).
First a turnip, then a sheep, next a cow, and then the gallows. (English).
He that resolves to deal with none but honest men must leave off dealing. (English).
He that steals an egg will steal an ox. (English, German).
He that steals once is never trusted. (Spanish).
He that will steal a pin will steal a better thing. (English).
He that will steal a pin will steal an ox. (English).
Honesty has stolen the cow. (German).

**Hypocritical honesty goes upon stilts.** (English).

**If he is very straight, he is still like a sickle.** (Behar).

**If I am seen I am joking: if I am not seen I steal.** (German).

**It is a shame to steal, but a worse to carry home.** (English).

**It is a sin to steal a pin.** (English).

**It is not enough to know how to steal, one must know how to conceal.** (Italian).

**I would not trust him—no, not with a bag of scorpions.** (English).

**Never trust a black Brahmin or a white Pariah.** (Hindoo).

**Steal a horse and carry home the bridle.** (German).

**Straight as a sickle.** (English).

**They are all honest men but my cloak is not to be found.** (Spanish).

**To hold the bag is as bad as to fill it.** (English).

**Trust him no further than you can see him.** (English).

**When it thunders the thief becomes honest.** (Italian).

**Who steals a calf will steal a cow.** (German).

**You are a fool to steal if you cannot conceal.** (English).

**You measure every man's honesty by your own.** (English).

## IT IS AN ILL WIND THAT BLOWS NOBODY ANY GOOD

The date and place from which this old proverb came is unknown. It was probably first used by seamen who knew that the wind that drove one ship into the wrecker's power helped another to pursue its course to the desired haven. Nathan Bailey (A.D. 1721) remarks that the "proverb intimates that the dispensations of providence are never entirely and universally ill in themselves, though they may be very afflicting to some particular persons," and quaintly illustrates the fact by the physician who profits by an epidemic, the builder who secures work because of the destruction of property by fire, and the pirate who is benefited by having the sinking merchant ship fall into his hands.

It is true that the sun shines on the evil and on the good, bringing discomfort to many but at the same time blessing the earth with light and warmth. The war devastates many districts, bringing pain and sorrow to the people but at the same time it stirs the hearts of multitudes with a new patriotism and purpose.

"There is not an evil which fails to bring benefit to someone," says the Midrash.

"Except wind stands as never it stood
It is an ill wind turns none to good."

THOMAS TUSSER, A.D. 1524–1580.

"How now, Pistol!

*Pistol:* Sir John, God save you!

*Falstaff:* What wind blew you hither, Pistol?

*Pistol:* Not the ill wind which blows no man to good. Sweet Knight, thou art now one of the greatest men in this realm."—WILLIAM SHAKESPEARE, A.D. 1564–1616, *King Henry IV.*

"Ill blows the wind that profits nobody.
This man, whom hand to hand I slew in fight,
May be possessed with some store of crowns;
And I, that haply take them from him now,
May yet ere night yield both my life and them,
To some man else, as this dead man doth me."

WILLIAM SHAKESPEARE, *King Henry VII.*

"Nane were keener against it than the Glasgowfolk, wi' their rabblings and their risings, and their mobs, as they ca' them now-a-days. But it's an ill wind blaws naebody gude—Let ilka ane roose the ford as they find it."—SIR WALTER SCOTT, A.D. 1771–1852, *Rob Roy.*

"Everything in the world is of some use but it would puzzle a doctor of divinity, or a philosopher, or the wisest owl in our steeple, to tell the good of idleness; that seems to me to be an ill wind, which blows nobody any good."—CHARLES H. SPURGEON, A.D. 1834–1892, *To the Idle.*

### VARIANT PROVERBS

**It is an ill wind that blows naebody gude.** (Scotch).
**It is an ill wind that blows no good to Cornwall.** (English).
**It is a bad wind that does not blow good for somebody.** (Irish-Ulster).
**It's an ill wind that blows no man good.** (English).
**It's an ill wind that turns none to good.** (English).

### ALLIED PROVERBS

**A bad son and a bad coin will save you sometime or other.** (Hindustani).
**I broke my leg perhaps for my good.** (Spanish).
**Ill comes not to one without good to another.** (Welsh).
**Ill luck is good for somebody.** (French).
**Misfortune is good for something.** (French).
**No weather is ill if the weather is still.** (English).
**No wind ever blew that did not fill some sail.** (Gaelic).
**Often out of a great evil a great good is born.** (Italian).
**One dog's death, another dog's grace.** (Manx).
**One man's death is grace to another.** (Gaelic).
**One person's house burns that another may warm himself.** (Hindustani).
**Talk and laugh about—talk and cry about—i.e. That which causes laughter to one causes tears to another.** (Ashanti).
**The lady who found the ear ornament was as glad as the lady who lost it was sorry.** (Telugu).
**The misfortunes of some people are advantageous to others.** (Arabian).
**There is no misfortune that comes on the country that someone is not the better for it.** (Irish).
**There is nothing so bad in which there is not something of good.** (Hebrew).

**Were it not for the fractures there would be no pottery.** (Arabian).

**What is bad luck for one man is good luck for another.** (Ashanti).

**What makes one abbot glad makes another abbot sad.** (Gaelic).

**When the father cried for his child the sexton cried for his money.** (Telugu).

**When the owner cried for the cow the shoemaker cried for the hide—i.e. The death of the cow caused the owner to weep but the shoemaker to rejoice.** (Telugu).

258

## IT IS TOO LATE TO SHUT THE STABLE DOOR WHEN THE HORSE IS STOLEN

It is too late to prevent injury or loss after injury or loss has been sustained. The proverb was in common use both in England and France during the fourteenth century. How much earlier it was freely quoted is not known.

The Chinese use a saying that is more dramatic. Picturing to themselves a horse driven close to the edge of some rocks overhanging a gorge and a boat in which men have set sail and that has a hole in its keel, they say, "Horse having reached descent of precipice receives the rein too late, vessel having reached river's heart, mending the leak too late."

The Telugus desiring to express the same thought have adopted a proverb from an old folk tale. According to a tradition among the people, a certain man saw his son perishing with thirst and let him die rather than give him a cocoanut, but immediately thereafter he offered the corpse all the cocoanuts that he had. When therefore the Telugus see a man exerting himself to prevent an injury sustained through his own carelessness they remark as though addressing a third party, "Alas! my son, drink the water of all the cocoanuts." Sometimes instead of alluding to the tradition they will ask the man directly: "Will you worship the sun after losing your eyes?" in reference to the common practice of worshipping the sun when eyesight begins to fail. At other times they will adopt a more serious tone and advise the offender to "(apply) Collyrium to your eyes while you have them" or "Put all things in order while the lamp is yet burning."

Two Greek sayings closely allied to the proverb are said to have originated as follows: A certain avaricious muleteer sought to save money by underfeeding his mule. As a result the animal became so weak that it was unable to bear a heavy burden. One day the muleteer placed an unusually large load on its back. The mule being unable to carry it fell to the ground whereupon the muleteer removed the burden and sought to raise the beast, but failing in his efforts, sought to induce the animal to rise by an offer of food, holding a handful of corn near its mouth, but it was of no use, the mule was too weak to rise. A passerby, seeing the muleteer's dilemma and knowing his avariciousness, tauntingly called out to him—"Fool, keep the corn farther off"—which became a proverb. Some say that he called out—"Clown, you should have given the corn sooner," which also became a proverb.

"A singing bird was confined in a cage which hung outside a window and had a way of singing at night when all other birds were asleep. One night a bat came and clung to the bars of the cage and asked the bird why she was silent by day and sang only at night. 'I have a very good reason for doing so,' said the bird: 'It was once when I was singing in the daytime that a fowler was attracted by my voice and set his nets for me and caught me. Since then I have never sung except by night.' But the bat replied, 'It is no use your doing that now when you are a prisoner; if only you had done so before you were caught you might still have been free.'"—ÆSOP, B.C. 561(?), *V. S. Vernon Jones' Translation.*

"When you have got into danger it is too late to seek advice."—PUBLIUS SYRUS, B.C. 45(?)

"Too late I grasp my shield after my wound." OVID, B.C. 43–A.D. 18.

"Thrift is too late at the bottom of the purse." —SENECA, B.C. 4–A.D. 65.

"It is too late in refusing to bear the yoke to which he has already submitted."—SENECA.

"It is too late to be cautious when in the very midst of dangers"—SENECA.

Let this proverbe a lore unto you be
"To late y-war," quod Beautee, "whan it paste."

GEOFFREY CHAUCER, A.D. 1328–1400, *Troilus.*

"I know, and knowledge I have wrought mine own pain;
But things past my hands, I cannot call again.
True (quoth Alice), things done cannot be undone,
Be they done in due time, too late, or too soon;
But better late than never to repent this.
Too late (quoth mine aunt), this repentance showed is:
When the steed is stolen shut the stable durre."

JOHN HEYWOOD, A.D. 1497–1580, *Dialogue of Effectual Proverbs.*

"When the steed is stoll'n the groom never reflects upon his own negligence, but falls foul upon the bold adventure of the thief, as if the impudence and knavery of the one upon so inviting a temptation, could excuse the sottishness and folly of the other."—OSWALD DYKES, A.D. 1707, *Moral Reflections.*

ALLIED PROVERBS

**After death, the doctor.** (English, French).

**After meat, mustard.** (English).

**After the act, wishing is in vain.** (French).

**After the carriage is broken many offer themselves to show the road.** (Turkish).

**After the vintage, baskets.** (Spanish).

**Alas! my son, drink the water of all the cocoanuts.** (Telugu).

**An old woman entered a dance by paying a penny; afterwards she would have given two to get out, but she could not.** (Modern Greek).

**Bad servants ask for advice after the deed is done.** (Hebrew).

**Clown, you should have given the corn sooner.** (Modern Greek).

**Collyrium to your eyes while you have them.** (Telugu).

**Digging a well at the time of fire.** (Kashmiri).

**Fool, keep the corn farther off.** (Modern Greek).

**Give losers leave to talk—They can always tell what should have been done.** (English).

**Have not a cloak to make when it begins to rain.** (English).

**He fills the pit when the calf has perished in it.** (Belgian).

**He has done like the Perugian, who, when his head was broken, ran home for his helmet.** (Italian).

**He is wise that is ware in time.** (English).

**He's wise that's timely wary.** (Scotch).

**Horse having reached descent of precipice receives the rein too late; vessel having reached river's heart, mending the leak too late.** (Chinese).

**It is full time to shut the stable when the horses have gone.** (French).

**It is no use cutting a stick when the fight is over.** (Japanese).

**It is too late for the bird to scream when it is caught.** (French).

**It is too late to come with the water when the house is burned down.** (English, Italian).

**It is too late to cover the well when the child is drowned.** (German, Danish).

**It is too late to cry " Hold hard!" when the arrow has left the bow.** (Dutch).

**It is too late to lock the stable door when the steed is stolen.** (French, Dutch, Osmanli).

**It is too late to spare when the bottom is bare.** (English).

**It is too late to throw water on the cinders when the house is burned down.** (Danish).

**It's nae time to stoop when the head's off.** (Scotch).

**It's ower late to lout when the head's got a clout.** (Scotch).

**It's ower late to spare when the back's bare.** (Scotch).

**It's past joking when the head's aff.** (Scotch).

**It's too late to grieve when the chance has past.** (English).

**Let the uncle die, I will find the devil afterwards—i.e. Dispense with the usual exorcism of the evil spirit until after the uncle's death.** (Assamese).

**Lost time and opportunity can never be recovered.** (English).

**Like the wife that ne'er cries for the ladle till the pat rens o'er.** (Scotch).

**One gets clothes after his nakedness has been covered, and food after his hunger is satisfied.** (Kumaun, Garhwal).

**Plenty of words when the cause is lost.** (Italian).

**Praying to have the fire stopped after it is well ablaze.** (Japanese).

**Put all things in order while the lamp is yet burning.** (Telugu).

**Repairing the tank after the water has escaped.** (Sanskrit).

**Repentance does not bring the lost back.** (German).

**Thatch your roof before rainy weather, dig your well before you become parched with thirst.** (Chinese).

**The dam must be made before the flood comes.** (Hindoo).

**The gladiator having entered the list is seeking advice.** (Latin).

**They fetch the salt after the rice is eaten.** (Bengalese).

**'Tis too late to spare when the cask is bare.** (Dutch).

**To begin to dig a well when you feel thirsty.** (Marathi).

**To begin to put up a wedding awning after the wedding procession has reached the house.** (Marathi).

**To cut a stick when the fight is over.** (Japanese).

**To fetch water after the house is burned.** (Spanish).

**"Too late to be aware," quoth Beauty, when it's past.** (English).

**To search for water after the house is burnt.** (Marathi).

**To shut the stable door after the steed has been stolen.** (Osmanli).

**To stop the hole after the mischief is done.** (Spanish).

**What is the use of a doctor after the death of the patient.** (Bengalese).

**When all is consumed repentance comes too late.** (English).

When a thing is lost people take advice. (French).

When error is committed good advice comes too late. (Chinese).

When he had eaten and was reclining on the sofa, he said, " Thy bread has a smell of mastick." (Arabian).

When the calf is drowned they cover the well. (Dutch).

When the calf is stolen the peasant mends his stall. (German).

When the corn is stolen the silly body builds the dyke. (Gaelic).

When the cold weather was over he made himself a coat. (Marathi).

When the head is broken the helmet is put on. (Italian).

When the horse is starved you bring him oats. (English).

When the house caught fire they begin to dig a well. (Marathi, Hindustani).

When the oil is wanted for the lamp he yokes the bullock to the mill.—The mill is used for extracting the oil. (Marathi).

When the ship has sunk everyone knows how she might have been saved. (Italian).

When the thief has escaped men's wits expand. (Bengalese).

When the wine runs to waste in the cellar he mends the cask. (German).

When the wolf has run off with the child the door is made fast. (Hindustani).

When you are thirsty it's too late to think about digging a well. (Japanese).

When your horse is on a brink of a precipice it is too late to pull the reins. (Chinese).

Will you worship the sun after losing your eyes? (Telugu).

Ye rin for the spurtle when the pat's boiling ower. (Scotch).

You come a day after the fair. (English).

You plead after sentence is given. (English).

## KILL NOT THE GOOSE THAT LAYS THE GOLDEN EGG

A proverbial advice intended for speculators who in their desire to increase their income endanger the principal from which their income is derived.

The saying was derived from Æsop's fable of *The Goose that Laid the Golden Egg.* "A man and his wife had the good fortune to possess a goose which laid a golden egg every day. Lucky though they were they soon began to think they were not getting rich fast enough and, imagining the bird must be made of gold inside, they decided to kill it in order to secure the whole store of precious metal at once. But when they cut it open they found it was just like any other goose. Thus they neither got rich all at once, as they had hoped, nor enjoyed any longer the daily addition to their wealth."— *V. S. Vernon Jones' Translation.*

### ALLIED PROVERBS

**By filling it too much the sack burst.** (Basque).

**Covetousness as well as prodigality brings a man to a morsel of bread.** (English).

**Covetousness brings nothing home.** (English).

**Covetousness bursts the bag.** (English, Spanish).

**Every man has a goose that lays golden eggs if he only knew it.** (American).

**He has killed the goose that laid the golden egg.** (English).

**He that leaves certainty and sticks to chance, when fools pipe he may dance.** (English).

**In trying to save a drop of ghi (butter) he upset the ghi-pot.** (Bedaga).

**Like going to Benares and bringing back a dog's hair.** (Telugu).

**One may buy gold too dear.** (English, German).

**The cord of a violin is broken in stretching it too much.** (Basque).

**They quarrel about an egg and let the hen fly.** (German).

**To avoid the smoke do not throw yourself into the fire.** (Turkish).

**To fell a tree to catch a blackbird.** (Chinese).

**To gain a cat but lose a cow.** (Chinese).

**Too much good fortune is bad fortune.** (English).

**Too much tying loosens.** (English).

**Too much will soon break.** (German).

**Too much zeal spoils all.** (English, French).

**Who undertakes too much seldom succeeds.** (Dutch).

## LOOK BEFORE YOU LEAP

Consider first, act afterwards. Count the cost. Think before you speak.

Thomas Tusser is not, as has been supposed, the originator of this saying. He quoted it, so also did Heywood and Cervantes, who were his contemporaries, and Æsop told the story of *The Fox and the Goat* which is so strikingly suggestive of the thought conveyed in the adage that it could hardly have failed to have led to the formation of the proverb long before the Christian era.

SCRIPTURE REFERENCE: Luke, 14: 28–32.

Thus by these lessons, ye may learn good cheap
In wedding and all things to look or ye leap.
Ye have even now well overlooked me (quoth he),
And leapt very nigh me too. For I agree
That these sage sayings do weightily weigh
Against haste in all things, but I am at bay
By other parables, of like weighty weight,
Which haste me to wedding, as ye shall hear straight.

JOHN HEYWOOD, A.D. 1497–1580.

Look ere you leape, see ere you go,
It may be for thy profit so.

THOMAS TUSSER, A.D. 1524?–1580, *Five Hundred Points.*

"Before you can awaken my choler, will I lay yours asleep so fast that it shall never wake more, unless in the other world; where it is well known I am one who will let no man's fist dust my nose. Let every man look before he leaps."—MIGUEL DE CERVANTES SAAVEDRA, A.D. 1547–1616, *Don Quixote.*

In ancient times all things were cheape
'Tis good to looke before you leape
When come is ripe 'tis time to reape.

MARTYN PARKER, A.D. –1630, *The Roxburghe Ballads.*

Y' had best (quoth Ralpho). As the Ancients
Say wisely, have a care o' th' main chance,
And look before you ere you leap; For as you sow y' are like to reap.

SAMUEL BUTLER, A.D. 1600–1680, *Hudibras.*

"Indeed had not my nature in itself abhorred precipitancy, the accredited and much admired maxim of 'looking before we leap,' stood in the way of all such sudden apostacy. I adopted, therefore, the half measure of studying the subject denounced by my aunt, but of studying it by the light of the maxims which she herself prescribed."—JOHN W. CUNNINGHAM, A.D. 1780–1861, *Sancho Proverbialist.*

VARIANT PROVERBS

**Before you leap look at the ground.** (Malabar).
**Look before you leap for snakes among sweet flowers do creep.** (English).

**Look ere thou leap, see ere thou go.** (English).
**Take care before you leap.** (Italian).

### ALLIED PROVERBS

**A word that when spoken you would wish back, let it remain in your head.** (Ashanti).
**A wise man moves with one foot, stands fast with the other and does not quit the station he occupies without well considering that which he intends to go.** (Chinese).
**Before you marry consider what you do.** (Portuguese).
**Before you marry reflect—it is a knot you cannot untie.** (Spanish).
**Before you mount look to the girth.** (Dutch).
**Before you understand a thing do not catch fire and flash like Albanian powder.** (Osmanli).
**Every business ought first to be thought over.** (Gaelic).
**First consider, then begin.** (German).
**First think, then enter upon a work.** (Marathi).
**First weigh your words, then speak openly.** (Marathi).
**He that looks not or he loup, will fall ere he wit of himself.** (Scotch).
**His words accord not with his acts.** (Osmanli).
**I tread along with the greatest caution.** (Hindustani).
**Look at the river before you cross the ferry.** (Irish).
**Look at the wind before you lose the boat.** (Kashmiri).
**Look not at what is before you, look at your end.** (Osmanli).
**Measure your cloth ten times—you can cut but once.** (Russian).
**No one measures the river with both his feet.** (African).
**Prepare the companion before (taking) the road, and the food before the journey.** (Syrian).
**Say your say after reflection.** (Osmanli).
**The chameleon does not leave one tree until he has secured the other.** (Arabian).
**They first lay the foundation and then build the wall.** (Persian).

**Think of the going out before you enter.** (Arabian, Osmanli).

**You should look what you can swallow and what can swallow you.** (Telugu).

## LOOK NOT A GIVEN HORSE IN THE MOUTH

As the teeth of young horses come with their development and change with use their approximate age up to a certain time can be told by examination. Hence to look into the mouth of a horse that is presented as a gift indicates that the receiver suspects the good will of the donor and fears lest the animal being too old for work was bestowed not as a favor but as an easy means of disposal. The Arabians, who are good judges of horses, claim that it is not only a discourtesy to look a gift horse in the mouth, but that it is unnecessary as the eyes indicate sufficiently the animal's value. When the eyes are clear and flashing the horse is given as a favor and not for the owner's benefit; hence the Bedouin saying, "The eye of a good horse serves for a tooth." The Bengalese have another test by which to ascertain the value of a gift horse and declare that "One knows the horse by his ears, the generous by his gifts, a man by laughing and a jewel by its brilliancy."

While the proverb cannot be traced with any certainty further back than the fourth century it was probably in use at a much earlier date.

"Where gifts be given freely—east, west, north or south—
No man ought to look a given horse in the mouth,
And though her mouth be foul she hath a fair tail—
I consider this text, as is most my avail.
In want of white teeth and yellow hairs to behold,
She flourisheth in white silver and yellow gold.
What though she be toothless, and bald as a coot?
Her substance is shoot anker, whereat I shoot."

JOHN HEYWOOD, A.D. 1497–1580, *A Dialogue of the Effectual Proverbs.*

"A gift ought to rise in our esteem in proportion of the friendship and respect of the donor, not its intrinsic excellency or worth. To inquire into these is buying and selling, and making a bargain with a friend; 'tis setting a price upon your own merit, which most people value too high in themselves and too low in everybody else."—SAMUEL PALMER, A.D. 1710, *Moral Essays.*

"We may perhaps suppose that well known word which forbids the too accurate scanning of a present, 'One must not look a gift horse in the mouth,' to be of English extraction, the genuine growth of our own soil. I will not pretend to say how old it may be, but it is certainly as old as Jerome, a Latin father of the fourth century; who, when some found fault with certain writings of his, replied with a tartness which he could occasionally exhibit, that they were voluntary on his part, free-will offerings, and with this quoted the proverb, that it did not behoove to look a gift horse in the mouth; and before it comes to us we meet it once more in one of the rhymed Latin verses which were such great favorites in the middle ages:

Si quis dat mannos, ne quære in dentibus annos."

—ARCHBISHOP TRENCH, A.D. 1807–1886, *Proverbs and Their Lessons.*

"A mediæval writer tells us that 'A gyuen horse may not be loked in the tethe.' Rabelais says it must not, and the author of *Hudibras* says it must not; in fact there is an abundance of testimony to this effect, extending over centuries. The Frenchman says, 'A cheval donné il ne faut pas regarder aux dens'; the Portuguese says, 'Cavallo dado nao se repara a idade'; and the Spanish says, 'Caval donato non guardar in bocca,' and all over the world we find this delicacy of feeling advocated."—F. EDWARD HULME, A.D. 1841–1909, *Proverb Lore.*

VARIANT PROVERBS

**A gift cow—why has it no teeth?** (Marathi).
**A given horse look not at his teeth.** (Modern Greek).
**If anyone offers you a buffalo do not ask if she gives milk.** (Badaga).
**If you are given a horse you won't insist on examining its mouth.** (Belgian).
**The teeth of a gift horse are not inspected.** (Osmanli).
**The teeth of a horse presented are never observed.** (Turkish).
**They made him a present of a beast of burden and he examined its teeth.** (Modern Greek).
**When somebody gives you a donkey, you musn't examine the bridle.** (Mauritius Creole).

### CHARACTERISTICS OF HORSES IN PROVERBS

A blind horse goes straight forward. (German).

A dapple gray horse will sooner die than tire. (Scotch).

A galled horse will not endure the comb. (English).

A grunting horse and a groaning wife seldom fail their master. (English).

A lean horse does not kick. (Italian).

A nag wi' a waine and a mare wi' nane are no a gude pair. (Scotch).

A safe (useless) aiver was ne'er a gude horse. (Scotch).

Good luck for a gray mare. (English).

He is a horse with four white feet—that is, he is unlucky. (French).

He is a weak horse that maunna bear the saddle. (Scotch).

He's an auld horse that winna nicker when he sees corn. (Scotch).

He's a prude horse that winna carry his ain oats. (Scotch).

Horses are good of all hues. (Scotch).

If he (the horse) has one (white foot) buy him; if he has two, try him; if he has three, look about him; if he has four come without him. (Scotch).

It is a bad horse that does not earn his fodder. (Italian).

It is a good horse that never stumbles. (French).

It is a silly horse that can neither whinny nor wag his tail. (English).

It is certainly a good horse, but its circular marks are bad. (Tamil).

Little may an auld horse do if he maunna nicker. (Scotch).

Rub a scald horse on the gall and he'll wince. (English).

The best horse, the largest. (Welsh).

The biggest horses are not the best travelers. (English).

The blind horse is the hardiest. (English).

The gray mare is the better horse. (English).

The horse is judged by the saddle. (German, Chinese).

The horse that does not stumble is the best horse. (Tamil).

The wounded horse as soon as he sees the saddle trembles. (Modern Greek).

You can't judge of the horse by the harness. (English).

ALLIED PROVERBS

A cow given to a Brahmin as a religious gift cannot be expected to have retained its teeth—It must be accepted without asking any questions, though it be worthless by reason of age. (Guirati).

A gift cow eats thorns—i.e. It has no teeth. (Marathi).

A gift of pulse. "Clean it before you give it to me." A beggar's ungracious return for a meal. (Marathi).

A gift warm—i.e. A gift is bestowed and he asks to have it warm. (Marathi).

Better a blind horse than an empty saddle. (Dutch).

Better a poor horse than an empty stall. (Danish).

Do not trouble about the color of a gift horse. (Italian).

Like giving a horse in compensation to one who has been stripped. (Tamil).

One knows the horse by his ears, the generous by his gifts, a man by laughing and a jewel by its brilliancy. (Bengalese).

The eye of a good horse serves for a tooth. (Arabian).

The guest likes the bread which his host likes. (Bannu).

The old horse must die in somebody's keeping. (English).

They gave a cucumber to the beggar—"I do not like it," he said, "it is crooked." (Osmanli).

To dine upon charity and call out for sauce. (English).

To have a dinner given you for nothing and to ask for pepper. (Marathi).

What is roughness to the ear to the man who gets grain for nothing? (Telugu).

When a man is given a Putti of corn he complains of short measure. A Putti is 500 lbs. (Telugu).

Who will sell a blind horse praises the feet. (German).

Who wishes a horse without defects ought to go on foot. (Breton).

## MISERY LOVES COMPANY

There is an old Portuguese saying that "Another's misfortune does not cure my pain," yet people will ever seek help in their grief, for the sorrowing heart craves sympathy and encouragement.

The proverb is so in accord with human experience that it is vain to search for the time and place when it was first spoken. It belongs to all ages and all classes and conditions of men.

But the saying is not always used to indicate a natural craving for sympathy. It is sometimes quoted to express the selfish desire of one sufferer that another should suffer with him. "If I must be in trouble," he says to himself, "it would be a satisfaction to know that I am not alone in my misery." Many people dislike to hear of a neighbor's prosperity when they themselves are unfortunate or to learn of another's joy when they themselves are in grief. It was with this selfish side of the proverb in view that Æsop told the story of the Tunny fish that was chased by a Dolphin. The Dolphin continually gained on the Tunny fish when, just as it was about to seize its prey, they were both carried by the force of their flight upon a sand bank in an exhausted condition. Lying in helplessness on the beach the Tunny fish turned to its enemy and said, "I don't mind having to die now, for I see that he who is the cause of my death is about to share the same fate."

"Though ever so compassionate, we feel within I know not what tart, sweet, malicious pleasure in seeing others suffer; children themselves feel it:

> ''Tis sweet from land to see a storm at sea,
> And others sinking, whilst ourselves are free.'

Whoever should divest man of the seeds of these qualities would destroy the fundamental conditions of human life."—MICHAEL DE MONTAIGNE, A.D. 1533–1592, *Of Prophet and Honesty*.

"'I mean,' said Don Quixote, 'that when the head aches, all the members partake of the pain: so then, as I am thy master, I am also thy head; and as thou art my servant, thou art one of my members, it follows therefore that I cannot be sensible of pain, but thou too oughtest to be affected with it; and likewise, that nothing of ill can befall thee, but I must bear a share.''—MIGUEL DE CERVANTES SAAVEDRA, A.D. 1547–1616, *Don Quixote*.

> "Grief best is pleased with grief's society
> True sorrow is then feelingly suffered
> When with like semblance it is sympathized."

WILLIAM SHAKESPEARE A.D. 1564–1616, *The Rape of Lucrece*.

"Alas, the storm is come again! my best way is to creep under his gaberdine; there is no other shelter hereabout; misery acquaints a man with strange bed-fellows. I will here shroud till the dregs of the storm be past."—WILLIAM SHAKESPEARE, *The Tempest.*

"Who alone suffers most i' the mind,
Leaving free things and happy shows behind:
But then the mind much sufferance doth o'erskip,
When grief hath mates, and bearing fellowship."

WILLIAM SHAKESPEARE, *King Lear.*

"Tut, man, one fire burns out another's burning
One pain is lessen'd by another's anguish;
Turn giddy, and be holp by backward turning;
One desperate grief cures with another's languish:
Take thou some new infection to thy eye,
And the rank poison of the old will die."

WILLIAM SHAKESPEARE, *Romeo and Juliet.*

"I am convinced that we have a degree of delight, and that no small one, in the real misfortunes and pains of others."—EDMUND BURKE, A.D.1730–1797, *The Sublime and Beautiful.*

"I therefore purpose not, or dream,
Descanting on his fate,
To give the melancholy theme
A more enduring date;
But misery still delights to trace
Its semblance in another's case."

WILLIAM COWPER, A.D. 1731–1800, *The Castaway.*

"No bond,
In closer union knits two human hearts
Than fellowship in grief."
ROBERT SOUTHEY, A.D. 1774-1843, *Joan of Arc.*

"Most of our misfortunes are more supportable than the comments of our friends upon them."—CHARLES C. COLTON, A.D. 1780-1832, *Lacon.*

ALLIED PROVERBS

**A friend in need is a friend in deed.** (English).
**A friend is best found in adversity.** (English).
**A good companion makes heaven out of hell.** (German).
**Another's misfortune does not cure my pain.** (Portuguese).
**A true friend is known in the day of adversity.** (Turkish).
**" Bad company," said the thief, as he went to the gallows between the hangman and a monk.** (English).
**Between the blind soldier and his wall-eyed mare, providence has created friendship.** (Hindustani).
**Birds of a feather flock together.** (English).
**Company in distress makes trouble less.** (French).
**Company in misery makes it light.** (English).
**It is pleasant to die in company or to have companions in misfortune.** (Persian).
**Misfortunes make friends.** (Latin).
**Misfortunes make strange bed-fellows.** (English).
**My friend is he who helps me in time of need.** (German).
**One whose own barn is burned wishes the same misfortune to others.** (Persian).
**Pity him who turns his back on his own people.** (Gaelic).
**The afflicted cannot console the afflicted.** (Arabian).

## NAME NOT A ROPE IN HIS HOUSE THAT HANGED HIMSELF

In talking with others do not refer to personal nor family matters that would be likely to recall disagreeable events, or in any way cause annoyance to the person with whom you are conversing.

The proverb is intended to encourage prudence and courtesy in speech. "Whoso keepeth his mouth and his tongue keepeth his soul from troubles" (Prov., 21:23).

Tiruvallurar, the greatest of the Tamil poets, wrote:

> "The burns will heal: but festering stays,
> The wound a burning tongue conveys."

thus emphasizing the importance of self-control in speech.

The saying is probably derived from the ancient Hebrew proverb, "Should there be a case of hanging in one's family record, say not to him 'Hang up this fish.'"

"A fool is like a bottle broken in the bottom, for so is he broken in his heart, which is the bottom of a man; and as a bottle so broken keepeth nothing in it, so a fool uttereth all his mind. He hath no stopple for it, no care what to utter, what not, what now, what at another time, what to this man, what to that, but all is one to him, so all be out. Otherwise is the carriage of a wise man. He keepeth his mind in, he locks and bars it up."—MICHAEL JERMIN, A.D. 1659, *Comment on Prov.*, 29: 11.

"He that is wise will be extremely cautious in discourse in all mixed conversation, where he does not know either the good humor and virtues, or the weakness, infirmities and vices of his company; and there is very good reason for such a caution. No man of sense would desire to give an affront to strangers, or be thought to do it, and yet this is very difficult to prevent if we go suddenly into all the freedom of discourse without looking round the room and observing what may be acceptable and what not. . . . No man ought ever to make natural infirmities, or peculiar misfortunes, the matter of his discourse, or to be too free in making applications of a story among strangers—it may happen to touch too near. In general our conversation should always be employed on the virtues and good actions of men, or against vice, without reference to particular persons. . . . Thus I take it to be folly to rally and jest upon the deformities of a squint-eye, red hair, or a crooked back; to draw inferences, as some people are mighty fond of, that such a one's father hanged himself, another's broke and a third was so and so."—SAMUEL PALMER, A.D. 1710, *Moral Essays.*

VARIANT PROVERBS

**Dinna speak o' a raip to a chiel whose faither was hanged.** (Scotch).

**Do not show a man that is hanged a rope, nor a burnt man fire.** (Syrian).

**Don't mention a rope in the house of him who has been hanged.** (French, German, Italian, Spanish, Portuguese, Modern Greek).

**It is dangerous to mention ropes in the house of a man who was hanged.** (Spanish).

**Mention not a halter in the house of him that was hanged.** (English).

**Never speak of a rope in the house of a thief.** (Portuguese).

ALLIED PROVERBS

**A bad word is like the sound of a dome—The bad word is returned by reason of an echo.** (Persian).

**A bridle for the tongue is a necessary piece of furniture.** (English).

**A great spear wound is well to heal quickly; a severe tongue wound becomes a sore in the heart and healeth not.** (Afghan).

**A slip of the foot may be soon recovered, but that of the tongue never.** (English).

**A slip of the tongue is worse than that of the feet.** (Tamil).

**A tongue thrust is worse than a serpent's sting.** (Martinique Creole).

**A word once spoken, an army of chariots cannot overtake it.** (Chinese).

**Better a slip of the foot than of the tongue.** (French).

**Confine your tongue lest it confine you.** (English).

**Don't make beans come from the mouth**—Do not tell everything that is in your mind. (Osmanli).

**Don't mention the cross to the devil.** (Italian).

**He that knows not how to hold his tongue knows not how to talk.** (English).

**He that restrains not his tongue shall live in trouble.** (Ancient Brahmin).

**He who says what he likes hears what he does not like.** (English, Spanish).

**His ear does not listen to what comes out of his mouth**—He speaks without considering the import of his words. (Osmanli).

**If your foot slips you may recover your balance, but if your mouth slips you cannot recall your words.** (Telugu).

**It is a gude tongue that says nae ill.** (Scotch).

**It is more necessary to guard the mouth than the chest.** (German).

**Keep guard over the tongue that is in your mouth.** (Osmanli).

**May you never eat that leek which will rise up in your own throat**—May you never be forced to eat your own words. (Afghan).

**Open your mouth for something good.** (Osmanli).

**People should talk not to please themselves but those who hear them.** (English).

**Put a key on your tongue.** (Modern Greek).

**Should there be a case of hanging in one's family record, say not to him " Hang up this fish."** (Hebrew).

**Speaking without thinking is shooting without taking aim.** (English).

**Speak well of the dead.** (English).

**Speak well of thy friends, be silent as to thy enemies.** (German).

**Speak well of your friend, of your enemy neither well nor ill.** (Italian).

**Sugar flows from his mouth**—He speaks pleasantly of people. (Osmanli).

**Taste in the mouth, screaming in the throat—It was a pleasure for you to speak as you did but when you consider the results of your words you will regret having spoken as you did.** (Osmanli).

**The tongue breaketh bone, though itself have none.** (English, Modern Greek).

**The tongue has no bone yet it crushes.** (Turkish).

**The tongue slays more than the sword.** (Turkish).

**The tongue wounds more than a lance.** (French).

**To slip on the pavement is better than to slip with the tongue.** (Hebrew).

**Turn your tongue seven times before speaking.** (English).

**Two ears to one tongue, therefore hear twice as much as you speak.** (Turkish).

**Two words in speaking, two rounds in fastening.**

In splicing bamboos two rounds or more of rope or cane is required to fasten them together before the knot is tied. (Assamese).

**We heal the wounds of a knife but not those of the tongue.** (Turkish).

**You might hold the hand that strikes you but you cannot hold the tongue.** (Urdu).

**Your tongue runs before your wit.** (English).

NEVER RIDE A FREE HORSE TO DEATH

Never abuse privileges that have been granted as favors.

Though the date of this saying is unknown it was used before the sixteenth century. There never was a time when men have not been found who would not take advantage of the liberality of others and their acts have been freely expressed in proverbs. "Give them a pea," as the Guernsey folk say, "and they will take a bean," or "Invite them to your home for a while," as the natives of India declare, "and they will take possession of the whole house." A borrowed horse is to them a gift of service that may be used to the limit of the animal's endurance, hence the warning that the beneficiary should not abuse a benefactor's bounty.

"If I have told right, thou hast given thyself above a thousand stripes; that is enough for one beating; for, to use a homely phrase, the ass will carry his load, but not a double load; ride not a free horse to death."—MIGUEL DE CERVANTES SAAVEDRA, A.D. 1547–1616, *Don Quixote.*

"Henry Ware, with his benevolence and frigid manners, reminded men how often of a volcano covered with snow. But there was no deep enthusiasm. All his talent was available, and he was a good example of the proverb, no doubt a hundred times applied to him, of 'A free steed driven to death.'"—RALPH WALDO EMERSON, A.D. 1803–1882, *Journal, Aug. 10, 1843.*

ALLIED PROVERBS

**A borrowed horse and your own spurs make short miles.** (Danish, Italian).

**A dapple gray horse will sooner die than tire.** (Scotch).

**A little more breaks a horse's back.** (English).

**A gentle horse should na be o'er sair spurr'd.** (Scotch).

**A good horse has no need of the spur.** (Italian).

**A hired horse and your own spurs make the miles short.** (German, Dutch).

**A hired horse tired never.** (Scotch).

**A horse shall gang on Carrolside brae till the girth gaw his sides in twae.** (Scotch).

**All lay loads on a village horse.** (English).

**Another man's horse and your own spurs outrun the wind.** (German).

**Another man's horse and your own whip can do a great deal.** (Danish).

**Beggars mounted run their horses to death.** (English).

**Do not spur a willing horse.** (English, Italian, French, German, Latin).

**Gee on! hired horse.** (Welsh).

**Give them a pea and they will take a bean.** (Guernsey).

**Invite them to your home for a while and they will take possession of the whole house.** (India).

**Milk the cow but don't pull off the udder.** (Dutch).

**Mount not a horse that does not belong to you—Boast not of things of which you are ignorant.** (Syriac).

**The horse that draws always gets the whip.** (German, French, Italian).

## NEVER BUY A PIG IN A POKE

The word "poke," meaning a bag, is of Celtic origin and has given us the words "pouch" and "pocket." The miller's cart of mediæval days was called a "poke cart" because it was often filled with bags of meal.

The phrase, it is said, was often used in olden times by purchasers of small pigs when the peasants brought them in strong bags to the trading places, for it was a common trick of dishonest sellers to substitute a cat or some other small animal for a sucking pig and an examination of a package was a wise precaution. When on opening the bag a fraud was discovered and a cat escaped the tradesman was said to have "let the cat out of the bag." John Wycliffe said that peace should be in the church without strife of doggies in a poke.

Among poor peasants the selling of a fully grown pig was fraught with much anxiety for the money received was often necessary for the purchase of household supplies and payment of rents so that any failure to secure full payment might lead to want and much suffering. This fact gives significance to the saying, "A hog upon trust grunts until it is paid for" which was current at the time.

The origin of the proverbial admonition to refrain from buying a pig in a poke is obscure. It may have come from a common trade custom as indicated above or it may have arisen, as Professor Alexander Negris maintains, from "the practice in Greece," during the Mahometan dominion of selling pork in the night time, which was done with the greatest secrecy, to avoid giving offence to the tyrant."

While similar admonitions are found in many lands, the English form is more frequently used, both because of its quaintness and alliteration.

"Blind bargains" have always been regarded as unfair; an honest seller is willing to show his goods and a prudent purchaser should know for what he spends his money.

"Down ran the blody streem upon his brest;
And in the floor with nose and mouth to-broke
They walweden as pigges in a poke;
And up they goon, and down they goon anon,
Till that the miller stumbled at a ston."

GEOFFREY CHAUCER, A.D. 1328–1400, *Canterbury Tales.*

"And a thousand fold would it grieve me more
That she, in my fault, should die one hour before
Than one minute after; then haste must provoke,
When the pig is proffered to hold up the poke."

JOHN HEYWOOD, A.D. 1497–1580, *A Dialogue.*

"But your teeth must water—a good cockney coke!
Though ye love not to buy the pig in the poke,
Yet snatch ye at the poke, that the pig is in,
Not for the poke, but the pig good cheap to win."

JOHN HEYWOOD.

"I will never buy the pig in the poke;
There's many a foul pig in a fair cloak."

JOHN HEYWOOD.

"In doing of either let wit beare a stroke
For buying or selling of pig in a poke."

THOMAS TUSSER, A.D. 1524–1580,
*Five Hundred Points of Good Husbandry.*

"However honest people, in their right wits, do not use to go to market to buy a pig in a poke. They do not lay their money out at a venture, upon what they do not see, handle and know very well, before the bargain is struck."—OSWALD DYKES, A.D. 1707, *Moral Reflections.*

"Examine the article before you part with your money. If you do not do so, and are taken in, you will have yourself to blame. If the pig in the poke should turn out to be very lean, it will be no wonder. If it had been fat the seller would have allowed you to see it."—CHARLES H. SPURGEON, A.D. 1834–1892, *The Salt Cellars.*

VARIANT PROVERBS

**A pig in a poke.** (Modern Greek).
**Buy no cats in bags.** (Belgian).
**I'll ne'er buy a blind bargain or a pig in a poke.** (Scotch).

It is folly to buy a cat in a sack—i.e. a game bag. (French).
To buy the cat in the bag. (German, Welsh).

ALLIED PROVERBS

A cat is not sold in a bag, but openly produced. (African, Accra).

Do not look upon the vessel, but upon that which it contains. (English).

Don't bite till you know whether it is bread or a stone. (Italian).

Nocturnal venison is not fat—i.e. Game caught in the night is poor. (Oji).

The horse is in the stable and you declare his price in the market. (Hindustani).

To buy a cat for a hare. (French).

To settle the price of a buffalo while she is lying in the water. (Marathi).

When the pig is proffered hold up the poke. (English).

When they give you a heifer make haste with the halter. (Spanish).

## 3

### ONE SWALLOW DOES NOT MAKE A SUMMER

One drop of water does not make a shower, one virtue does not make a saint, one battle does not decide the fate of war, one misdoing does not make a vagabond, one profitable venture does not make a successful business career.

In days of old the people of England expected swallows to make their appearance about the middle of April and the fifteenth day of the fourth month was therefore set apart as "Swallow Day," yet they were wise enough to realize that birds could not create seasons and that one swallow would not make a summer any more than one woodcock would make a winter.

There are several reasons why the swallow should have been selected by the makers of this proverb, rather than any other bird. It attracts attention by its graceful movement and is loved because of its solicitous provision for the comfort of its mate. No male bird is more tender of its mate, particularly at nesting time. He provides not only for her wants but takes her place in the nest that she may fly abroad for needed exercise. When the birdlings appear he is ready to assist her in caring for them until they leave the nest.

Even after they have entered independent lives, both he and his mate seem to retain an interest in them, for it is said, when they meet in the air the parent birds pause in flight to lovingly touch the beaks of their children.

Another reason why it was said that "One swallow does not make a summer" may have been that one is seldom seen. Swallows are gregarious; they go in flocks and live in colonies. So pronounced is this trait that when the fledglings leave their nest they keep together feeding about the same place.

Perhaps the main reason is found in the fact that the swallow has always been closely associated with superstition. In centuries past men were wont to regard the bird as a bringer of good and ill luck. Among the Romans it was sacred to the household gods and was under special protection. To kill one meant that the slayer would meet with dire misfortune. Its early appearance in the spring assured the old Slavonians of an abundant harvest and also protected them from fire and lightning. Bohemian maidens looked for the coming of the bird with both hope and fear, for they believed that the girl who was first to see one would be married before the close of the year, but the girl who saw two would be compelled to wait. In Ireland the swallow is called the "Devil's Bird" because it is said to pluck the hair of destiny from men's heads which dooms them to perdition. The peasants of Germany once thought that the flight of the bird beneath a cow would sometimes lead to its death, or in case it should live would cause it thenceforth to give bloody milk which was known as "Swallow Milk." Our own ancestors were glad to have swallows build their nests under the eaves of their houses because their presence brought good luck. There is an old belief that they fly to the seashore and bring their fledglings a stone which gives them sight.

"Oft in the barns they climbed to the populous nests on the rafters,
Seeking with eager eyes that wondrous stone, which the swallow
Brings from the shore of the sea to restore the sight of its fledglings;
Lucky was he who found that stone in the nest of the swallow."

HENRY W. LONGFELLOW, A.D. 1807–1882, *Evangeline.*

There is an old Norwegian tradition that the swallow obtained its name at the cross—that when Jesus died it flew above the head crying "Svala! svala!" and was thenceforth known as *Svalow* which means the bird of consolation. Still another tradition is preserved in France that declares the swallow removed the crown of thorns from the brow of Christ and in doing so pierced its own breast, which accounts for its ruddy hue.

The origin of the proverb is unknown. It was quoted by Horace the Latin poet before the

Christian era. It was also used by Aristotle three centuries and more before the coming of our Lord. It may have been suggested from Æsop's fable of *The Spendthrift and the Swallow.*

The oldest form of the proverb substitutes spring for summer.

> "I did lately hear
> How flek and his make use their secret haunting,
> By one bird, that in mine ear was late chaunting.
> One swallow maketh not summer, (said I), men say."
>
> JOHN HEYWOOD, A.D. 1497–1580, *A Dialogue.*

"*Pimon:* With all my heart, gentlemen both· and how fare you?

*First Lord:* Ever at the best, hearing well of your lordship.

*Second Lord:* The swallow follows not summer more willing than we your lordship.

*Timon* (*Aside*): Nor more willingly leaves winter; such summer birds are men."—WILLIAM SHAKESPEARE, A.D. 1564–1616, *Timon of Athens.*

"I could never yet be a friend to the Roman Auguries, nor have any faith for their fond, foolish and credulous observations taken from the flying, feeding, chirping, chattering or singing of crows, pies, owls, eagles, vultures, buzzards and such like birds: I do not know whether there were any swallows among 'em; but this I am confident of, that the Grecians were much in the right on't, to say, that one swallow makes no summer. . . . A swallow's flying abroad early in the spring is not a sufficient direction to make me leave off my clothes, in hope of fine weather, or dress myself up in a volatile air, upon the expectation of a warm summer, for fear of catching a mistake and meeting with a cold reception upon such an over-hasty credulity . . . But this I may positively assert, according to the general opinion of all writers, as well as Sophocles, the Prince of the Tragic Poets; that, as one inhabitant does not make a city, nor one man a multitude, so neither can one silly swallow rationally convince a wise, a cautious or a considerate person of the approach of summer."—OSWALD DYKES, A.D. 1707, *Moral Reflections.*

"All the false as well as foolish conclusions from a particular to a universal truth, fall under the censure of this proverb. It teaches that as he that guesses at the course of the year by the flight of one single bird, is very liable to be mistaken in his conjecture; so also a man cannot be denominated rich from one single piece of money in his pocket, nor accounted universally good from the practice of one single virtue, nor temperate because he is stout, nor liberal because he is exactly just: that one day cannot render a man completely happy in point of time, nor one action consummate his glory in point of valor. In short the moral of it is, that the right way of judging of things, beyond imposition and fallacy, is not from particulars but universals."—NATHAN BAILEY, A.D. 1721, *Diverse Proverbs*

"We are but too ready to accept the first isolated sign of success as a proof of its aggregate presence, or forthcoming; whereas any one actual and entire success requires a combination of favorable circumstances—with a sharp sprinkling of unfavorable too, by way of spurs and spices—more numerous and intricate than could ever be present, or even seen after they had occurred."—*Household Words*, February 28, 1852, *Commenting on the Proverb*.

"The Greek original of 'One swallow does not make a spring,' which is as old as Aristotle and seems to be the basis of an allusion in Aristophanes, ought to have weight in the question which has found its way into *Notes and Queries*, whether for 'spring' we ought to read 'summer.' Mrs. Ward in her *National Proverbs in Five Languages* does not decide the question, though she proves the wide acceptance of the proverb. The difference seems to resolve itself into one of climate. Of the Greek form, another evidence is preserved in a painted vase representing some ladies looking up at a bird, while from the mouth of one of them proceeds a scroll bearing the words, 'See the swallow! It is already spring.'"—*London Quarterly Review*, July, 1868.

"Yes—one foul wind no more makes a winter than one swallow makes a summer. I'll try it again. Tom Pinch has succeeded. With his advice to guide me I may do the same."—CHARLES DICKENS, A.D. 1812–1870, *Martin Chuzzlewit*.

"When, wild with delight, I saw a swallow glancing through the sunny springtime air, I ran to tell my father. Can I forget how he too, who had been a 'snapper-up of unconsidered trifles,' seeming not to share in my gladness, looked up and said warningly, 'One swallow does not make a summer.'"—LOUISE V. BOYD in *Arthur's Magazine, 1873.*

"It's surely summer, for there's a swallow:
Come one swallow, his mate will follow,
The bird-race quicken and wheel and thicken."

CHRISTINA G. ROSETTI, A.D. 1830–1894, *Bird Song.*

VARIANT PROVERBS

**A single flower or a single swallow does not always announce the Spring.** (Armenian).
**One actor cannot make a play.** (Chinese).
**One basket of grapes does not make a vintage.** (Italian).
**One brier does not make a hedge.** (Italian).
**One cloud does not make a winter.** (Osmanli).
**One crow does not make a winter.** (German, Dutch).
**One day of great heat never yet made a summer.** (Breton).
**One devil does not make hell.** (Italian).
**One finger does not make a hand nor one swallow a summer.** (Portuguese).
**One flower does not make spring.** (Latin, Osmanli).
**One flower makes no garland.** (English).
**One horseman does not raise a dust cloud.** (Bannu).
**One rain won't make a crop.** (Negro—Tide-water section of Georgia).
**One stone does not make a stone wall.** (Osmanli.)
**One swallow does not make a spring nor one woodcock a winter.** (English).

**One tree does not make a forest.** (Negro—Tide-water section of Georgia).

ALLIED PROVERBS

**One dose will not cure nor one feed make fat.** (Gaelic).
**One grain fills not a sack but helps his fellows.** (English).
**One makes not a people—nor a town.** (African—Accra).
**What dust will rise from one horseman.** (Bannu).
**When one man has his stomach full it cannot satisfy every man.** (Vai-West Africa).

60

## OUT OF THE FRYING PAN INTO THE FIRE

The proverb is applied to people who in their endeavor to extricate themselves from one difficulty complicate themselves in another and greater difficulty; or who, laboring under hard conditions, seek relief in an employment where the work is much more severe.

The origin of the saying is not known. It is used in various forms in different parts of the world. In its old Latin form: "Out of the smoke into the flame" it predates the fourth century for we find it quoted by Amianus Marcellinus, the Roman historian. In its Greek form which is the same as the Latin it was used by Lucian the satirical writer in the second century.

The English equivalent—"Out of the frying pan into the fire" seems to have a direct reference to fish that fall into the flame when being cooked.

John Heywood (A.D. 1497–1580) wrote:

"I mislike not only your watch in vain,
But also, if ye took him, what could ye gain?
From suspicion to knowledge of ill, forsooth!
Could make ye do but as the flounder doeth—
Leap out of the frying pan into the fire,
And change from ill pain to worse is worth small hire."

A writer in *Blackwoods Magazine* (1864) gives expression to the same idea in the stanza:

> "The fish that left the frying pan,
> On feeling that desire, sir,
> Took little by their change of plan,
> When floundering in the fire, sir."

Several of Æsop's fables illustrate the thought of the proverb. Among them may be noted *The old Woman and her Maids, The Ass and his Master* and *The Stag and the Lion.*

In modern times we find it illustrated by a West African practice. On cold nights, it is said, the Negroes of the gold coast huddle close to a fire for warmth. Sometimes the smoke from the burning logs annoys them and in half wakeful condition they call to their companions who are near the blaze, to remove the smoking log. Should the log be removed and the smoke continue, the request is repeated and another log is thrown aside. This being done a number of times the fire goes out and there is no warmth. In relieving themselves of the annoyance of smoke they have the greater annoyance of cold. This occurs so often that the practice gave rise to the Oji proverb—"Throw it away! Throw it away! Then we shall soon sleep without fire."

On the Afghan frontier a story is told of a certain Hindoo, who, being ordered by a Mohammedan king to repeat when attending him the words "Ram, Ram," the requirement so annoyed the Hindoo that he determined to escape from the tyranny of such a useless procedure, so he fled and, being captured, was sold into slavery, hence the Pashto saying—"I was escaping from the Ram and fell on hard work."

A pictorial illustration of the proverb is found in Barber's *Hand Book* (1859) where a man is represented as seeking to escape from a wolf. In his endeavor to keep beyond the animal's reach he came to a precipice and is shown as hanging on a rock above the yawning chasm and near to the wolf's savage teeth. The stanza beneath the picture tells the story of the man's dilemma thus:

> "See here a man doth true courage lack,
> He flies apace—a wolf is on his track;
> Nearer he comes—the man doth swifter flee;
> The verge he gains; he leaps into the sea:
> Out of one danger into one more great,
> The foolish creature finds his certain fate."

"The short and the long is, I take it to be the wisest course to jog home and look after our harvest and not to run rambling from Ceca to Mecca, lest we 'leap out of the frying pan into the fire,' or 'out of God's blessing into the warm sun.'"—MIGUEL DE CERVANTES SAAVEDRA, A.D. 1547–1616, *Don Quixote.*

> "Thus must I from the smoke into the smother;
> From tyrant Duke into tyrant brother:
> But heavenly Rosalind!"

WILLIAM SHAKESPEARE, A.D. 1564–1616, *As You Like It.*

"This proverb is usually applied to persons who, impatient under some smaller inconvenience, and rashly endeavoring to extricate themselves, for want of prudence and caution, entangle themselves in difficulty greater than they were in before."—NATHAN BAILEY, A.D. 1742.

"Although the world is so changeful and uncertain, that quiet, amongst all its rarities, seems the thing most rare; there are many persons who appear to have more than they like of it, and are so impatient for novelty, that they are continually leaping out of the frying pan of their own tormenting restlessness, into the fire of positive calamity. By changing for the sake of change they expect trouble to give them ease, and find out to their cost, that the cure is worse than the complaint."—JEFFERYS TAYLOR, A.D. 1827, *Old English Sayings.*

"One may make more haste than good speea, in escaping from the plague, by breaking one's neck in jumping out of a window. Some persons fairly kill themselves to save their lives. They leap out of the frying pan into the fire, not because there was nothing better that they could do, but because they would not give themselves time to do it. Many things are repented of at lesiure, merely because they were done in haste."—JEFFERYS TAYLOR, *Old English Sayings.*

"No one was ever yet compelled to commit sin, small or great, since there is always the alternative of suffering. He who prefers moral to physical harm, of two evils chooses the greatest; he beyond a question leaps out of the frying pan into the fire."—JEFFERYS TAYLOR, *Old English Sayings.*

"In the common affairs of life, we ought to be careful about getting out of the frying pan into the fire. He that will get into debt, in order to save himself some little trouble, privation or economy, will find that he has taken a greater evil for a lesser one. Better to live on bread and water than to be harassed about debts which cannot be paid."—JOHN W. BARBER, A.D. 1798–1885, *Hand Book.*

VARIANT PROVERBS

**Avoiding the rain we meet a tempest.** (Turkish).
**Fleeing from smoke he falls into fire.** (Osmanli).
**Flying from the bull he fell into the river.** (Spanish).
**From leaking to under the water spout.** (Syrian).
**From the fear of the rain he flies under the spout.** (Persian).
**He fled from the rain and sat down under the water spout.** (Arabian).
**He fled from the sword and hid in the scabbard.** (African—Youba).
**He ran from the wolf and fell in with the bear.** (Russian).
**I escaped the thunder and fell into the lightning.** (English).
**In avoiding Charybdis he fell into Scylla.** (Latin).
**I was escaping from the Ram and fell on hard work.** (Pashto).
**Out a-do watah, inside a-putto-putto—i.e. Out of the water, inside the mud.** (British Guiana).

**Out of the briers into the thorns.** (Gaelic).
**Out of the cauldron into the fire.** (Irish—Ulster).
**Out of the fire into the embers.** (Gaelic).
**Out of God's blessing into the warm sun.** (English).
**Out of the kettle into the fire.** (Gaelic).
**Out of the mire into the brook.** (Italian).
**Out of the mucksy into the pucksy—i.e. Out of the muck-heap into the quagmire.** (English).
**Out of the smoke into the flames.** (Latin, Greek).
**Out of the peat-pot into the gutter.** (Scotch).
**To come out of the fireplace and fall into the oven.** (Marathi).
**To escape from the fire and fall into the hot ashes.** (Marathi).
**To fall from the frying pan into the burning coals.** (Italian).
**To fall from the frying pan into the coals.** (Portuguese).
**To leap from the frying pan and throw oneself into the coals.** (French).

ALLIED PROVERBS

**Being burnt out of my home I fled to the jungle where I found a fire twice as fierce.** (Kumaun, Garhwal).
**From fame to infamy is a beaten road.** (English).
**From fear of the ghost to clasp the corpse.** (Malayan).
**From the Bel (fruit) to the Acacia (fruit), from earth to dust.** (Hindustani).
**Having escaped falling into the well he jumped into the fire.** (Tamil).
**He fell from one bath-furnace to another—i.e. He fell from one trouble to another.** (Osmanli).
**He fled from death and fell into it.** (Arabian).
**He that is wounded with the prickles of Bel goes under the Acacia.—One has prickles, the other thorns.** (Hindustani).

**He who was hurt by the Bel went for refuge under the Bubool and he that was hurt by the Bubool fled to the Bel.**

The Bel fruit is so large that it would hurt a man should it fall on his head; its rind is so hard that crows cannot pierce it with their bills; while the Bubool has prickles that would wound the feet. (Hindustani).

**In avoiding one evil we fall into another, if we use not discretion.** (Latin).

**In avoiding one vice fools rush into the opposite extreme.** (Latin).

**In escaping from the bull he fell into the brook.** (Spanish).

**In shunning the bear he fell into the pit.** (Arabian).

**It is said that the snake afraid of the charmer sought the friendship of the rat.** (Hebrew).

**I trod in the mud and hung myself in the thorn bush—i.e. I consented to take trouble for a prospective benefit and got into more or worse trouble.** (Osmanli).

**No sooner had I got free from the net when I fell into the cage.** (Persian).

**One river is colder than the other.** (Kashmiri).

**The cure may be worse than the disease.** (English).

**The goat was fleeing from the wolf and spent the night in the butcher's house.** (Pashto).

**Throw it away! throw it away! Then we shall soon sleep without fire.** (Oji).

**To avoid the smoke do not throw yourself into the fire.** (Turkish).

**To call the tiger to chase away the dog.**

The Chinese generally apply this proverb to the Tartars who more than two centuries ago were called in to put down a rebellion and made themselves masters. (Chinese).

**To fall into the jaws of the tiger after escaping from the mouth of the alligator.** (Malayan).

To go from Ceca to Mecca, and from bad to worse—i.e. To go from one pilgrimage to another. (Spanish).

(When they say) " Throw it away! Throw it away! Then we shall soon sleep without fire. (Oji).

While keeping a tiger from the front door, the wolf enters in at the back. (Chinese).

## PEACOCK, LOOK AT YOUR LEGS

The peacock though possessed of a beautiful tail has insignificant legs and feet.

The saying is applied to proud people who seem to be unconscious of their faults and failings.

No one knows the age or origin of this saying. According to an East Indian tradition the peacock originally had beautiful legs and feet, but having been cheated out of them, he continually mourned his loss and grew so ashamed of those that he possessed that he felt humiliated whenever anyone looked at them. If by chance he happened to see them himself, particularly when dancing, he was sure to weep. From this tradition there arose the Kumaun and Garhwal proverb, "The peacock looking at his feet wept." The story is that the peacock, being proud of his beautiful legs and feet, as well as of his tail, arranged to dance before the partridge, provided the partridge would afterwards show its ability in the same way, which it agreed to do. The peacock therefore danced with the greatest skill but the partridge seeing the graceful movements of its companion knew that it could not do so well and refused to keep its promise and take turn unless the peacock would consent to trading legs. Being of a kindly disposition and feeling flattered by the suggestion the peacock readily assented to the proposition. Having thus obtained the peacock's legs and feet the partridge flew away to the jungles.

There is a Hindustani proverb that seems to have been derived from the same story. The Hindu, when he sees a man of ability displaying marked talents among people who do not appreciate them, says "Who has seen the peacock dance in the forest."

"The peacock hath an unsteadfast and evil shaped head, as it were the head of a serpent, and with a crest. And he hath a simple pace, and small neck and areared, and a blue breast, and a tail full of eyes distinguished and high with wonder fairness, and he hath foulest feet and rivelled. And he wondereth of the fairness of his feathers, and deareth them up as it were a circle about his head, and then he looketh to his feet, and seeth the foulness of his feet, and like as he were ashamed he letteth his feathers fall suddenly, and all the tail downward, as though he took no heed of the fairness of his feathers. And as one saith, he hath the voice of a fiend, head of a serpent, pace of a thief. For he hath an horrible voice."—BARTHOLOMEW ANGLICUS, A.D. 1263? *Encyclopedia.*

"The proud sun-braving peacock with his feathers,
Walks all along, thinking himself a king,
And with his voice prognosticates all weathers,
Although God knows but badly he doth sing;
But when he lookes downe to his base blacke feete
He droppes, and is asham'd of things unmeete."

R. CHESTER, *Love's Martyr.*

PROVERBS ABOUT THE PEACOCK

**A dancer is never a good scholar because he guides his feet (like the peacock) better than a pen.** (English).

**As proud as a peacock.** (English).

**Bachelor, a peacock; betrothed, a lion; married, an ass.** (Spanish).

**Fly pride, says the peacock.** (English).

**He is as proud as a peacock and calls for ram's milk.** (Modern Greek).

**If peacocks cry in the night there is rain to fall.** (English).

**If the peacock cries when he goes to roost and indeed much at any time it is a sign of rain.** (English).

**If you exclaim, " O peacock! O peacock! " will it give you its feathers.** (Spanish).

**I like writing with a peacock's quill because its feathers are all eyes.** (English).

**March comes wi' adders' heads and gangs wi' peacocks' tails.** (Scotch).

**Peafowl utter loud cries before a storm and select a low perch.** (English).

**Proud as a peacock, all strut and show.** (English).

**The peacock cries before the rain.** (English).

**The peacock has too little on his head and has too much on his tail.** (German).

**The peacock looking at his own feet wept.** (Kumaun, Garhwal).

**The sluggard like the peacock is afraid of rain.** (Karanese).

**The squalling of a peacock by night often foretells a rainy day.** (English).

When all men praised the peacock for his beautiful tail, the birds cried out with one consent—"Look at his legs! and what a voice!" (Japanese).

When the peacock and guinea fowls scream and turkeys gobble expect rain. (English).

When the peacock's distant voice you hear, are you in want of rain? Rejoice, 'tis almost here. (English).

When the peacock loudly bawls, soon we'll have both rain and squalls. (English).

Who has seen the peacock dance in the forest? (Hindustani).

9, 121, 140, 167.

## PHYSICIAN, HEAL THYSELF

The demand that a diseased man should heal himself before offering to cure others is found in proverbial forms everywhere. The Italians, French, Spaniards, Germans and Arabs all use the phrase—"Physician, heal thyself." It is so natural to ask a healer to first cure his own malady that students have been unable to discover from whence the proverb came and where it was first spoken. It seems to have always been in common use. Five and a half centuries before Christ Æsop told the story of a frog who had laid claim to being a physician, whose skill was so much greater than others that he could cure all diseases; but his claim was soon challenged by a fox, who tauntingly called after him—"Say, Doctor, why do you proclaim that you can heal others when you cannot straighten your own crooked legs, nor cure the blotches and wrinkled skin?"

When Jesus preached in His own home town his auditors wondered at His "words of grace." They could not deny His power as a public speaker nor question the purity of His message, but they were not ready to accept Him as the promised Messiah for He was of humble birth. How could the son of Joseph the carpenter speak with authority? Jesus knew their thoughts and said, "Doubtless ye will say unto me this parable, 'Physician, heal thyself,' whatsoever we, have heard done at Capernaum, do also here in thine own country." Then, as though one proverb had suggested another, He explained that prejudice was the real cause of their unbelief, and quoted the well-known saying: "No prophet is acceptable in his own country."

Notwithstanding the continued advancement in knowledge regarding the treatment of disease and the increasing skill of physicians, few proverbs speak approvingly of doctors; the reason being that they, like other men, are frail and subject to maladies that cannot be cured. So that the taunt will ever be flung—"Physician, heal thyself."

But the proverb is not always applied to physicians. It is often used in referring to men who offer to help others when they are unable to help themselves, or who claim consideration which is not their right, because of known defects in character or lack of ability. "The Panre (teacher) would teach others," say the Behar peasants, "but he himself stumbles."

"Why do you note the splinter in your brother's eye, and fail to see the plank in your own eye? How can you say to your brother—'Let me take out the splinter from your eye' when there lies the plank in your own eye? You hypocrite! Take the plank out of your own eye first, and then you will see properly how to take the splinter out of your brother's eye."—MATTHEW 7: 3-5, *Moffats' Translation.*

"Do not forget that you are Cicero; one who has been used always to prescribe for and give advice to others; do not imitate those paltry physicians who pretend to cure other peoples' diseases, yet are not able to cure their own; but suggest rather to yourself the same lesson which you would give in the same case—SERVIUS SULPICIUS, B.C. 105-43.

"Physicians pretending to cure the diseases of others, and are themselves loaded with complaints, are the immediate objects of the censure contained in this adage; but it may also be applied to persons railing against vices to which they are themselves addicted."—ROBERT BLAND, A.D. 1814, *Proverbs.*

"He (Jesus) had described the various ills from which His hearers were suffering and directed their attention to Himself as the physician sent to heal them. This is what the proverb cited refers to. Thus 'You are going even to turn to ridicule what you have just heard, and say to me—Thou who pretendest to save humanity from its misery begin by delivering thyself from thine own."—FREDERICK GODET, A.D. 1812-1900, *Commentary on Luke 4: 23.*

### VARIANT PROVERBS

**A healer of others, himself diseased.** (Latin).
**Before healing others heal thyself.** (Wolof—West Africa).
**If you can pull out, pull out your own gray hairs.** (Oji—West Africa).
**Physician, heal thy lameness.** (English).
**The doctor has a ringworm on his nose.** (Assamese).
**The Panre would teach others, but he himself stumbles.** (Behar).

### ALLIED PROVERBS

(See proverbs under "The pot calls the kettle black.")

**A good example is the best sermon.** (English).
**An ounce of practice is worth a pound of preaching.** (English).
**Example does more than much teaching.** (German).
**Example is better than precept.** (English).
**Example teaches more than precepts.** (English).
**Good example is half a sermon.** (German).
**Good preachers give fruits not flowers.** (Italian).
**He is a good preacher who follows his own preaching.** (German).
**He is past preaching who does not care to do well.** (French).
**Point not at other's spots with a foul finger.** (English).
**Practice is better than precept.** (English).
**Practice what you preach.** (English).
**Precept begins, example accomplishes.** (French).
**The Panre would teach others but he himself stumbles.** (Behar).
**There are many preachers who don't hear themselves.** (German).
**Why beholdest thou the mote in thy brother's eye, but considerest not the beam in thine own eye.** (Hebrew).

## PROVERBS ABOUT PHYSICIANS

**A broken apothecary, a new doctor.** (English).

**A half doctor near is better than a whole doctor afar.** (German).

**A lucky physician is better than a learned one.** (German).

**A new doctor, a new apothecary.** (English).

**Better wait on the cook than the doctor.** (English).

**Doctors make the very worst patients.** (English).

**Each physician thinks his pills the best.** (German).

**Every man at forty is either a fool or a physician.** (English).

**He who has suffered is the physician.** (Modern Greek).

**Feastings are the physician's harvest, Christmas.**

It may have been that the word "Christmas" at the end of the proverb was originally placed at the beginning. (English).

**Honor a physician before thou hast need of him.** (English).

**If doctors fail what shall avail.** (English).

**No good doctor ever takes physics.** (Italian).

**No man is a good physician who has never been sick.** (Arabian).

**That city is in a bad case whose physician has the gout.** (Hebrew).

**The barber must be young and the physician old.** (German).

**The best surgeon is he who has been hacked himself.** (English).

**The disobedience of the patient make the physician seem cruel.** (English).

**The doctor seldom takes physic.** (English, Italian).

**The physician can cure the sick but he cannot cure the dead.** (Chinese).

**The physician cannot drink medicine for the patient.** (German).

**You need not doubt, you are a doctor.** (English).

PROVERBS THAT DISPARAGE PHYSICIANS

**A new doctor, a new grave digger.** (German).

**An ignorant doctor is no better than a murderer.** (Chinese).

**A loquacious doctor is successful.** (Tamil).

**A physician is an angel when employed, but a devil when one must pay him.** (German).

**A young physician should have three graveyards.** (German).

**Do not dwell in a city whose Governor is a physician.** (Hebrew).

**Fond of lawyer, little wealth; fond of doctor, little health.** (Spanish).

**God healeth and the physician has the thanks.** (English).

**God keep me from judge and doctor.** (Turkish).

**God is the restorer of health and the physician puts the fee in his pocket.** (Italian).

**He who kills a thousand people is half a doctor.** (Tamil).

**Hussars pray for war and the doctor for fever.** (German).

**If the doctor cures the sun sees it; if he kills the earth hides it.** (Scotch).

**If you have a friend who is a doctor take off your hat to him, and send him to your enemy.** (Spanish).

**If you have a friend who is a physician send him to the house of your enemy.** (Portuguese).

**It is God that cures and the doctor gets the money.** (Spanish).

**Leaches kill with license.** (English).

**No physician is better than three.** (German).

**One doctor makes work for another.** (English).

**Physicians' faults are covered with earth and rich men's with money.** (English).

**Physicians are costly visitors.** (English).

**The blunders of physicians are covered by the earth.** (English, Portuguese).

**The doctor is often more to be feared than the disease.** (French).

The doctor says that there is no hope and, as he does the killing, he ought to know. (Spanish).

The doctor's child dies not from disease but from medicine. (Tamil).

The earth covers the mistakes of physicians. (Italian, Spanish).

The earth hides as it takes the mistakes of physicians. (Spanish).

The patient is not likely to recover who makes the doctor his heir. (English).

The physician owes all to the disease and the disease nothing to the physician. (English).

The physician owes all to the patient and the patient owes nothing to him but a little money. (English).

The physician takes the fee but God sends the cure. (German, Spanish).

Time cures more than the doctor. (English).

'Tis not the doctor who should drink physic. (Italian).

When the physician can advise the best patient is dead. (German).

When you call a physician call the judge to make your will. (German).

While the doctors consult the patient dies. (English).

With respect to gout the physician is but a lout. (English).

Who has a physician has an executioner. (German).

## SET A BEGGAR ON HORSEBACK AND HE WILL GALLOP

Exalt a boor and he will become proud and arrogant.

A man who acquires wealth suddenly is apt to spend his money freely and indulge in wild extravagances.

While the origin of this proverb is not positively known it probably came from the pretensions of liberated slaves. In olden times the slave class was made up of war captives, victims of seizure, some who chose slavery for support and those who were forced into servitude through debt or crime. Many captives of war, particularly those who were taken by the Romans, were educated in the schools and skilled in the arts but the great mass of bondmen were ignorant and coarse in their feelings, mere "Hewers of wood and drawers of water." No more vivid picture of pride without cause could have presented itself to the ancients than the assumption of a liberated slave who sought to impress others with his importance by assuming the ways of the free born. Claudius declared that "nothing is more obnoxious than a low person raised to a high position" and Publius Syrus said that "Fortune by being too lavish of her favors on a man only makes a fool of him." It is a common saying among the negroes of Ashanti, Africa, that "When a slave is freed he will call himself a Sonneni," that is, of exalted rank—the Sonna being the highest class.

A curious prayer proverb comes from the district of Bannu in the Punjab, India, where the Almighty is addressed as follows: "Mayest thou not give a poor wretch a goat to catch hold of by the legs." As the legs of a goat are held when it is milked it is thought that a poor wretch would abuse the animal should he own one, as the degraded everywhere abuse authority when they have it in possession.

BIBLE REFERENCES: Deut. 31: 20; 32: 15; Neh. 9: 25, 26; Prov. 26: 1, 8.

"Hath that poor monarch taught thee to insult?
It needs not, nor it boots thee not, proud queen,
Unless the adage must be verified,
That beggars mounted run their horse to death."

SHAKESPEARE, A.D. 1564–1616, *King Henry VI.*

"A proud beggar when he is once mounted so high, as to keep his coach—which was only invented for cripples—to carry him in triumph above the earth, thinks it below him to look down upon his inferiors, and inconsistent with his grandeur, to take notice of little people that stand in the way of his impetuous career or imperious contempt."—OSWALD DYKES, A.D. 1707. *Moral Reflections*;

"In short every page or shipkennel who formerly waited upon my Lord or my Lady Somebody, that has got preferment and money, sets up for a gentleman now-a-days, and is as proud as any beggar in the proverb upon horseback that gallops headlong without either fear or wit upon the precipice of ambition and the brink of ruin."—OSWALD DYKES, A.D. 1707. *Moral Reflections.*

> "Such is the sad effect of wealth—rank pride—
> Mount but a beggar, how the rogue will ride."
>
> JOHN WOLCOTT, A.D. 1738–1819.

"There is an old and vulgar saying about a 'beggar on horseback' which I would not for the world have applied to these reverend philosophers; but I must confess that some of them, when they are mounted on those fiery steeds are as wild in their covetings as was Phaeton of yore when he aspired to manage the chariot of Phœbus."—WASHINGTON IRVING, A.D. 1783–1859, *Knickerbocker History of New York.*

"Set a beggar on horseback and he'll ride to the devil." The direction in which he will ride depends entirely on the character of the beggar—a poor man suddenly risen to power. Some sink over the other side of the horse and drop into utter sloth and pampered sensualism but others do their best to ride well and sometimes succeed. Masaniello and Rienzi did not ride long in the best way; but several patriots who have rapidly risen from obscurity to power have set noble examples."—*Household Words*, February 7, 1852.

"Of the danger of unearned elevation we have two—the coarse English: "Set a beggar on horseback and he will ride to the ——," and the Italian: "Everything may be borne but good fortune." Most of them, however, are of a more healthy and satisfactory character, showing that however capricious the fickle goddess may be she is looked to with hope, and sometimes for justice. The English think that "Every dog has his day" and that "There are as good fish in the sea as ever came out of it." The grave Roman averred in more classical language that "The sun of all days has not yet gone down"; the Italian that "The world is for him that has patience" but the Persian saying is the most beautiful and the most faithful—"A stone that is fit for the wall is not left in the way"—that tells men to deserve the favors of fortune by being fit to receive them, and cherishes both effort and hope."—*Eliza Cook's Journal*, Feb. 19, 1853.

ALLIED PROVERBS

**A beggar ennobled does not know his own kinsman.** (Italian).

**A beggar's son struts like a peer.** (Hindustani).

A clown enriched knows neither relation nor friend. (French).

A lion growls not in a den full of straw but in a den of meat. (Hebrew).

A little lizard does not know its mother. (Nigeria).

A man begs and then gets up on an elephant. (Kashmiri).

A man well mounted is always proud. (French).

A novice was dressed in breeches and looked at them every step. (Modern Greek).

A poor man's child with a fine name—i.e. A boorish man apes the gentleman. (Bengalese).

As soon as mulatto is able to own an old horse he will tell you that his mother wasn't a nigger. (Martinique Creole).

A two legged mounting a four legged. (Kashmiri).

A wild boar in place of a pig would ravish the town, and a slave made king would spare nobody. (Youba—Africa).

Begging and riding upon a horse! A proud beggar. (Kashmiri).

Beggars mounted ride a horse to death. (English).

But yesterday out of the shell, today he despises the shell. (Turkish).

Entering by the eye of a needle and coming out by the elephant's stable door. (Kashmiri).

Everything may be borne but good fortune. (Italian).

First your walking stick and then your pet daughter. Having asked to be your equal he wants to marry your daughter. (Kashmiri).

Give a cup to the low and he swells himself with water—i.e. He is puffed up with pride. (Panjabi).

He descends (like) the foot of a crow, and ascends (like) the foot of a camel.

According to Arabian custom, guests when eating with their fingers from a common dish consider it good manners to take only a small portion at a time and hold their fingers close together for that purpose. An ill-bred person will show his condition by trying to follow the example of others, putting his fingers in the dish like the foot of a crow, but withdrawing them with a fist full, making his hand look like the foot of a camel. (Arabian).

**He has no trousers and yet orders a tent.** (Persian).

**He has put on a sword and says that he is a servant of the king.** (Persian).

**He'll gang mad on a horse whose proud in a ponnie.** (Scotch).

**He sprang from a chestnut shell and he does not admire his husk.** (Osmanli).

**He swells himself like a turkey cock.** (Osmanli).

**He who is on horseback no longer knows his own father.** (Russian).

**His family had no cow for seven generations, but he takes a " Kariya " and goes milking.**

A "kariya" is a bamboo chunga or milk pail. He makes a great show of milking. (Assamese).

**If the plowman becomes a " lord " yet he is not then even fit to sit upon the matting.** (Kashmiri).

**Just put a mulatto on horseback and he'll tell you his mother wasn't a negress.** (Louisiana Creole).

**Mayest thou not give a poor wretch a goat to catch hold of by the legs.** (Pashto).

**No pride like that of an enriched beggar.** (English, French).

**Put a beggar on horseback and he does not trot, but he gallops.** (Dutch).

**Set a beggar on horseback and he will ride to the devil.** (English).

**She who from being a slave is become the mistress pierces the bath basin with stones; he who from being a servant is now a muezzin, shakes down the minaret with his voice.**

A muezzin is a mosque chanter. (Osmanli).

So is it worn, twixt the pack-saddle and the straw cloth. (Gaelic).

The ass is the same but the pannel different. (Persian).

The bejeweled leg of a leper. (Malayan).

The blown out parrot fish that has only wind inside it. (Malayan).

The bug that mimics the tortoise. (Malayan).

The cup fell into the hands of one who never saw one and she drank till she died. (Hindustani).

The clown saw himself in plush breeches and was insolent as could be. (Spanish).

The dog of the master of the house mounts upon the chief sofa. (Osmanli).

The dog saw himself in fine breeches.—He would not recognize other dogs. (Spanish).

The gourd grew and lengthened its neck. (Moroccan).

The horn in ivory mountings. (Malayan).

The man in boots does not know the man in shoes. (English).

The mean man being exalted regards the earth as a potsherd. (Bengalese).

The more riches a fool has the greater fool he is. (English).

The onion grew and became round and forgot its former state. (Arabian).

The peasant saw himself in fine breeches and he was as insolent as could be. (Spanish).

The plated ware that shows its nature when scratched. (Malayan).

There is no pride like a beggar grown rich. (French).

The snake that apes the dragon. (Malayan).

The tortoise that affects arboreal habits. (Malayan).

The Turk, if he be mounted on a horse, thinks " I am a bay." (Osmanli).

The worm that plays the serpent. (Malayan).

They ask the mule, " Who is your father? " He says "The horse is my uncle." (Osmanli).

Time made (him) come forth from the mud. (Osmanli).

**What is past is past.** (Persian).

**What! You follow the trade of a barber and pretend to be independent?—A fling at one who being in some lowly business puts on the air of importance.** (Persian).

**When a beggar gets on horseback the devil cannot outride him.** (German).

**When a clown is on a mule he remembers neither God nor the world.** (Spanish).

**When a Donko becomes rich he runs mad.**

A Donko is one of a negro tribe in the interior of Western Africa. The Donkos furnish the Oji people with most of their slaves. (Oji).

**When a man becomes rich the town goes to ruin.—He loses all his public spirit in his effort to please himself.** (Oji).

**When a slave becomes a freeman he will drink rain water —i.e. He will become so lazy that he will drink water that is nearest at hand.** (Oji).

**When a slave girl becomes mistress she does not mind sending her slave girls out in bad weather.** (Hindustani).

**When a slave is emancipated he will call himself a nobleman.** (Oji).

**When a slave is freed he will call himself Sonneni.** (Ashanti).

**When claninclo get ye-ye-tickle he t'ink hese'f gubnah.** (British Guiana).

**When fortune smiled on a mean person he ordered an umbrella to be bought at midnight.** (Telugu).

**When he had filled his belly he began to vex the poor.** (Hindi).

**When the goat goes to church he does not stop till he gets to the altar.** (Old Irish).

**When the poor man grows rich he beholds the stars at noonday.—i.e. He is purse proud and insolent.** (Bengalese).

When the slave is freed he thinks himself a nobleman. (Oji).

When wert thou changed into a queen, O pawn?—The reference is to a game of chess. (Arabian).

Wondrous God's power! Wondrous God's caprice! The muskrat oils his head with jasmine essence. (Hindustani).

Yesterday he came out of his egg, today he does not admire its shell. (Osmanli).

## STILL WATERS RUN DEEP

It has been thought that this saying is an adaptation from the French novel *Le Gendre* but the Roman historian Quintus Curtius in the first century declared that the Bachrians used the proverb so that it must have been quoted more than two thousand years ago.

"Silent and quiet conspirators," says Brewer, "are the most dangerous" as "Still waters run deep." This opinion seems to be shared by people of all climes. The Portuguese bid us "Beware of the man who never speaks and the dog that never barks" and the Russians tell us that "In a still pool swarm devils."

The patriarch of Uz, knowing his own pain and grief, chided his friends for trying to minister to his comfort in their ignorance and called on them to be silent, saying, "Oh, that ye would altogether hold your peace! and it would be your wisdom" (Job 13:5).

Yet it must not be forgotten that, like nearly all folk sayings, it is not always true. Talkers are not always fools, wise men are not always quiet. "Waves will rise on silent waters" and the restless sea continually beats against the shore.

"Even a fool when he holdeth his peace is counted wise; when he shutteth his lips, he is esteemed as prudent."—PROVERBS 17:28.

> "Smooth runs the water where the brook is deep;
> And in his simple show he harbours treason.
> The fox barks not when he would steal the lamb.
> No, no, my sovereign; Gloucester is a man
> Unsounded yet and full of deep deceit."

WILLIAM SHAKESPEARE, A.D. 1564–1616, *King Henry VI, Part 2.*

> "Deep waters noiseless are; and this we know,
> That chiding streams betray small depth below.
> So when love speechless is, she doth express
> A depth in love and that depth bottomless."

—ROBERT HERRICK, A.D. 1591–1674.

"As when the door is shut it cannot be seen what is within the house: so the mouth being shut up by silence, the folly that is within lieth undiscovered; and as in glasses and vessels so in men, the sound which they make showeth whether they be cracked or sound. An ass is known by his ears (saith the Dutch proverb) and so is a fool by his talk. As a bird is known by his note and a bell by his clapper, so is a man by his discourse. Plutarch tells us that Megabysus, a nobleman of Persia, coming into Apelles', the painter's, work house, took upon him to speak something there concerning the art of painting and limning but he did it so absurdly that the apprentices jeered him and the master could not bear with him."—JOHN TRAPP, A.D. 1601–1669, *Comment on Job* 13:5.

"A wise man will be of few words, as being afraid of speaking amiss. He that has knowledge and aims to do good with it is careful when he does speak to speak to the purpose, and therefore says little, that he may take time to deliberate upon it. He spares his words because they are better spared than ill spent.

"This is generally taken for such a sure indication of wisdom that a fool may gain the reputation of being a wise man if he have but wit enough to hold his tongue, to hear and see and say little. If a fool hold his peace men of candor will think him wise, because nothing appears to the contrary and because it will be thought that he is making observations on what others say, and gaining experience, and is consulting with himself what he shall say that he may speak pertinently. See how easy it is to gain men's good opinion and to impose upon them. But when a fool holds his peace God knows his heart and the folly that is bound there; thoughts are words to Him and therefore He cannot be deceived in His judgment of men.—MATTHEW HENRY, A.D. 1662–1714, *Comment on Proverbs* 17:28.

"It has been safely enough alleged that of two men equally successful in the business of life, the man who is silent will be generally deemed to have more in him than the man who talks. The latter 'shows his hand'; everybody can tell the exact length of his tether; he has trotted himself out so often that all his points and paces are matters of notoriety. But of the taciturn man little or nothing is known. *Omne ignotum pro magnifico*: 'The shallow murmur, but the deep are dumb.' Friends and acquaintances shake their heads knowingly and exclaim with an air of authority that 'so and so' has a great deal more in him than people imagine. 'They are as often wrong as right; but what need that signify to the silent man? He can sustain his reputation as long as he likes by the simple process of holding his tongue.'"—FRANCIS JACOX, A.D. 1874, *Scripture Proverbs*.

"It is written among the Proverbs of Solomon that 'Even a fool when he holdeth his peace is counted wise.' Even the fool that shutteth his lips is esteemed a man of understanding. The wise king declares in another place that a fool's mouth is his destruction and that his lips are the snare of his soul. Let him keep his mouth closed and his folly is an unknown quantity; out of sight out of mind. Let him keep his lips shut and wisdom shall be imputed unto him. Of him lookers-on will say, a discreet man that—For they are only lookers-on, not listeners. To listen would break the spell. As it is they are apt to count him as deep as he is still. Do not still waters run deep?"—FRANCIS JACOX, *Secular Annotations*.

VARIANT PROVERBS

**Deepest waters stillest go.** (English).

**It is the shallowest water that makes the most noise.** (Irish—Ulster).

**It is the smooth waters that run the deepest.** (Irish—Ulster).

**Quiet waters, deep bottoms.** (Belgian).

**Shaal waters mak the maist din.** (Scotch).

**Silent men, like still waters, are deep and dangerous.** (English).

**Steady and deep.** (Hindustani).

**Smooth waters run deep.** (English).

**The deepest rivers flow with the smallest noise.** (Latin).

**There is no worse water than that which sleeps.** (French).

**Waters that are deep do not bubble.** (English).

**Where water is stillest it is deepest.** (Gaelic).

ALLIED PROVERBS

**A silent dog will bite the heels.** (Tamil).

**A smooth river washes away its banks.** (Servian).

**As the river sleeps.** (Telugu).

**Barking dogs seldom bite.** (English).

**Believe not that the stream is shallow because its surface is smooth.** (Latin).

**Beware of a man who never speaks and of a dog who never barks.** (Portuguese).

**Beware of a silent dog and still water.** (English).

**Beware of the smooth currents of a river and of a man's glances on the ground—still waters run deep and a man who looks down is not to be trusted.** (Osmanli).

**Dumb dogs and still waters are dangerous.** (German).

**Empty vessels give the greatest sound.** (English).

**Every devil can hunt his own swamp**—See "**In a still pool swarm devils.**" (Russian).

**From a silent man and from a dog that does not bark deliver us.** (Spanish).

**From smooth (or still) water God preserve me; from rough (or running) I will preserve myself.** (Italian, Spanish).

**In a still pool swarm devils.**

The reference is to the Vodyanoy or water sprite. (Russian).

**In the coldest flint there is hot fire.** (English).

**It is the empty car that makes the greatest noise—when in motion.** (Irish—Ulster).

**It is the empty cart that makes the noise.** (Irish—Armagh).

**It is the water which stands there calm and silent that takes (drowns) a man.** (Ashanti).

**Mistrust the water that does not warble and the stream that does not chirp.** (Armenian).

**Nothing rattles in the kettle except the bones—Shallow people do the most talking.** (Syrian).

**Still waters breed worms.** (Italian).

**Take heed of still waters, the quick pass away.** (English).

**The empty kettle sings, not the full one.** (Old Sanskrit).

**The empty pot rattles, the full one is silent.** (Panjabi).

**The greatest resonance is in the empty barrel** (Irish—Armagh).

**The most covered fire is the strongest.** (French).

**The stillest humors are always worst.** (English).

**Under white ashes there is glowing coal.** (Italian).

**Water beneath straw.** (Syriac).

**Where the stream is shallowest greatest is its noise.** (Gaelic).

## STRETCH YOUR LEGS ACCORDING TO YOUR COVERLET

Know your limitations and go not beyond them.

The saying is said to have had its origin in the following old Palistinean folk story: A certain old man, realizing that he could not live long desired to commit the management of his property, which was large, to one of his three sons who were associated with him in business. Not knowing which was the most capable to assume the responsibility he decided to test them by a ruse. Providing himself with a quilted cotton coverlet that was too short for his bed he feigned illness and sent for each of his sons in turn to come and nurse him, beginning with the oldest. The first had scarcely taken his place in the sick room before the old man complained that his feet were cold and that the coverlet, or ilhalf, as it was called, was not spread over them; whereupon the son drew it down over his feet, but in so doing uncovered his neck and shoulders. This seemed to displease the old man for he at once became enraged and declared that it was quite as important to have his chest and arms covered as his feet; so the young man drew the ilhalf up again, at the same time asked his father if he might go and get a larger one as there were plenty in the house. "No!" retorted the old man in apparent anger, "I am too weak to bear any greater weight on my body." The son patiently remained by his father's bedside all day and the next night drawing the ilhalf up and down according to his wishes and returning kindness and service for fretful murmurings and open complaints. Then the second son was called and passed through a like experience, dutifully obeying his father's orders and patiently enduring his father's faultfindings. He, like his brother, suggested a larger covering but was not permitted to go for it. At last the youngest son was sent for, and ministered to his father with the same patient durance as did his brothers, but observed that the old man, who constantly complained of weakness, was not so weak but that he could eat large meals with a relish. This led him to suspect that his father was deceiving him by feigning illness. Excusing himself for a few moments he went into the garden and secured a flexible rod from a pomegranate tree. Concealing it from sight he waited for the old man to speak. It was not long before he began as before to grumble over his cold extremities; but instead of seeking to appease his father the young man seized the rod and brought it down on the bed with great violence, close to the old man's feet, saying as he did so, "Very well, father! stretch your legs according to your coverlet." The old man was so surprised and frightened that he jumped out of bed, and, when his temper had subsided, commended the young man for his shrewdness and refusal to allow anyone to impose upon him. Then he committed to him all his affairs.

"For the bed is shorter than that a man can stretch himself on it; and the covering narrower than that he can wrap himself in it."—ISAIAH 28:20.

### VARIANT PROVERBS

**A man should stretch out his feet after looking at the bedclothes.** (Kashmiri).
**Everyone stretches his legs according to the length of his coverlet.** (English, Spanish, German, Portuguese).
**Extend not your feet beyond your blanket.** (Modern Greek).
**Extend your feet according to the length of your sheet.** (Hindustani).
**In proportion to the length of thy garment stretch out thy leg.** (Arabian).
**Make your soup according to your bread.** (French).
**Stretch thy leg as long as thy bed.** (Arabian).
**Stretch thy leg as long as thy carpet.** (Arabian).
**Stretch thy leg as long as thy cloak.** (Arabian).
**Stretch thy leg as long as thy cover.** (Arabian).
**Stretch thy leg as long as thy rug.** (Arabian).
**Stretch your arm no further than your sleeve will reach.** (English, Dutch).
**Stretch your feet only as far as your covering goes.** (Pashto).
**To the measure of your bed stretch your feet.** (Syrian).

ALLIED PROVERBS

According to his pinions the bird flies. (Danish).
According to the bread must be the knife. (French).
Everyone counts as much as he has. (German).
Everyone must row with the oars he has. (German).
Everyone signs as he has the gift and marries as he has the luck. (Portuguese).
Everyone to his own calling and the ox to the plow. (Italian).
He is a fool who spends more money than he receives. (French).
He who spends more than he should shall not have to spend when he would. (English).
Make a plaster as large as the sore. (English).
Make not the tail broader than the wings. (English).
Make not your sail too big for your ballast. (English).
One must cut his coat according to his cloth. (German, English, Dutch).
One must plow with the horses one has. (German).
We must spend according to our income. (Italian).

## THE POT CALLS THE KETTLE BLACK

There seems to be a strange proclivity in many people to see in their fellow men the faults that mar their own characters and criticize them for indulging in habits against which they themselves are obliged to fight their hardest battles. This proclivity is so general that all nations have found it necessary to adopt some proverbial phrase to use when a man is heard severely criticizing others for sins of which he himself is guilty, or when the faultfinder's life is known to be such as to open him to the charge of inconsistency. Over two thousand years ago Æsop declared that every man carried two bags about with him, one hanging in front and the other behind; that the one in front was filled with his neighbors' faults and the one behind was filled with his own faults, and that accounted for the fact that no one was ever able to see his own defects but was always conscious of the defects of others. Jesus charged the people who were gathered about Him on the mountainside not to judge others lest they should in like manner be judged. "Why beholdest thou," said He, "the mote that is in thy brother's eye, but considerest not the beam that is in thine own eye?" (Matt. 7:3).

The most careful research fails to throw any light on the origin of this saying. The thought found expression over two thousand years ago in many curious aphorisms that have changed their form by constant repetition but that have never lost their original meaning.

"And so he that sees a mote in another man's eye, should do well to take the beam out of his own; that people may not say—The pot calls the kettle black-arse, and the dead woman is afraid of her that is fleaed."—MIGUEL DE CERVANTES SAAVEDRA, A.D., 1547–1616, *Don Quixote*.

"In other men we faults can spy,
And blame the mote that dims their eye;
Each little speck and error find;
To our own stronger errors blind."

JOHN GAY, A.D. 1685–1732, *Fables*.

"Judge not! The workings of his brain
And of his heart thou canst not see;
What looks to thy dim eyes a stain,
In God's pure light may only be
A scar, brought from some well-won field,
Where thou wouldst only faint and yield."

A. A. PROCTOR, A.D. 1825–1864.

VARIANT PROVERBS

**A pig came up to a horse and said, " Your feet are crooked and your hair is worth nothing."** (Russian).

**" Crooked Carlen " quoth the cripple to his wife.** (Scotch).

**Death said to the man with his throat cut, " How ugly you look."** (Catalan).

**" Get away ! " The crow mocked the pig for his blackness.** (Chinese).

**One ass nicknamed another " Long Ears."** (German).

**Said the jackdaw to the crow, " Get away, nigger."** (Spanish).

**Said the pot to the kettle, " Get away black face."** (Spanish).

**Said the raven to the crow, " Get out of that, Blackamoor."** (Spanish).

**The ass said to the cock " Big-headed."** (Modern Greek).

**The clay pot wishes to laugh at the iron pot.** (Trinidad Creole).

**The colander said to the needle, " Get away, you have a hole in you."** (Hindoo).

**The cow rails at the pig for being black.** (Chinese).

**The crow mocked the pig for his blackness.** (Chinese).

**The earthen pot wishes to laugh at the iron pot.** (Haytian).

**The frying pan says to the kettle, "Avaunt, Black brows."** (English).

**The griddle calling the pot black bottom.** (Irish—Ulster).

**The kiln calls the oven " Burnt house."** (English).

**The kettle reproaches the kitchen spoon. " Thou Blackee," he said, " Thou idle babbler."**

The kitchen spoon here referred to is made of wood. (Arabian).

**The kettle calls the pot black-arse.** (English).

**The kettle calls the saucepan " smutty."** (Turkish).

**The lame man laughs at the legless.** (Bulgarian).

**The mortar complaining to the drug.** (Telugu, Malay).

**The mud laughs at the puddle.** (Mauritius Creole).

**The pan says to the pot " Keep off or you'll smutch me."** (Italian).

**The pot calls the pan burnt-arse.** (English).

**The pot punishes the kettle; you are both black.** (Bohemian).

**The pot reproaches the kettle because it is black.** (Dutch).

**The pot upbraids the kettle that it is black.** (Dutch).

**The pot said to the pot, " Your face is black."** (Osmanli).

**The raven bawls hoarsely to the crow " Get out of that, Blackamoor."** (Spanish).

**The raven said to the rook, " Stand away, black coat."** (English).

**The sal is laughing at the singi, " You are as worthless as I am, therefore there comes no suitor for either of us."**
The sal and the singi are Assamese fishes. The proverb is applied to young women who do not know how to weave and spin. (Assamese).

**The saucepan laughs at the pipkin.** (French, Italian).

**The shovel insults the poker.** (Russian).

**The shovel scoffs at the poker.** (French).

**The sieve says to the needle, " You have a hole in your tail."** (Bengalese).

**The sieve with a thousand holes finds fault with the sup.**
The "sup" is a basket used in sifting grain. (Behar).

**" Thou art a little bird," said the raven to the starling.** (English).

ALLIED PROVERBS

**At the foot of the lighthouse it is dark.** (Japanese).

**Chase flies away from your own head.**
A retort to a critic. (Japanese).

**Dirty nosed folk always want to wipe other folks' noses.** (French).

**Do not ridicule the short and thin bearded as long as thou thyself are without a beard.**
This proverb is now obsolete. (Arabian).

**" Fly pride," says the peacock.** (English).

**" God helps the fool," said the idiot.** (English).

**He sees the speck in another's eye but does not the film in his own.** (Hindustani).

**He sees not the beam in his own eye, he sees the fragments that are in the eyes of other people.**

The fragments referred to in the proverb are small pieces of straw. (Osmanli).

**He who has done eating will say, " He who eats at night is a sorcerer."** (Oji—West African).

**It is said that a young palm leaf is laughing at the dry leaf because it is falling off.** (Tamil).

**Let everyone sweep the snow from his own door and not busy himself with the frost on his neighbor's tiles.** (Chinese).

**Man is blind to his own faults but keen sighted to perceive those of others.** (Latin).

**Take the pestle from your own eye, then take the mote from another's.**

By pestle and mote the people of Western India intended to refer to a certain heavy wooden instrument commonly used by them in pounding and a very small blade of spear grass that is apt to adhere to the clothing. (Marathi).

**The blind of one eye perceives not the film on her own eye but sees the speck on another's.** (Hindustani).

**The defects in the eyelash are not apparent to the eye. (Tamil).**

**The kettle blackens the frying pan.** (French).

**The kettle blackens the stove.** (French).

**The man without clothes busying himself in making jackets for dogs.** (Singalese).

**The mortar's complaint to a drug.** (Malayan).

**The raven chides blackness.** (English).

**" The roach has come out of the flour barrel," said the women of color who whitened their faces with rice powder.** (Mauritius Creole).

**The vulture says that the civet cat stinks—the vulture is said to have a bad odor.** (Ashanti).

**They know not their own defects who search for defects in others.** (Sanskrit).

They that live in glass houses should not throw stones. (English).

Though he sees a splinter in people's eyes he does not see the beam that is in his own eye. (Osmanli).

Throwing water at the buttocks of others when one's own are wet. (Assamese).

We ourselves have dirty noses and yet are laughing at other people. (Marathi).

When one inquired what the ugly man was doing—he was counting all the good looking people. (Telugu).

When your house is of glass do not throw stones at your neighbor's house. (Kurdish).

82

## THERE'S MANY A SLIP TWIXT THE CUP AND THE LIP

This proverb is very old though it is not true that it "is probably the oldest of all familiar English sayings," as a writer has recently declared. It is believed to have originated in Greece and spread from that country to one district after another until it is now used in almost every land. The following story is said to have given rise to the saying, also to the French phrases: "Between the hand and the mouth the soup is often spilt" and "Wine poured out is not swallowed."

Ancæos, the son of Poseidon, Supreme Lord of the sea, according to Greek mythology was a harsh man and acted toward his slaves with the greatest severity. At times he was so cruel that it seemed to them almost impossible to endure his treatment. Under the burden of his inhumanity one of them prophesied that he would never be permitted by the gods to taste again the wine from his vineyard. When the prophecy was repeated to him he laughed at the seer and continued his harsh treatment. Finally the season for wine-making returned and, when the grapes were gathered and pressed Ancæos called for a cup of the newly made beverage, repeating the prediction of the slave that he would never be permitted by the gods to drink. When the wine was brought he sent for the seer that he might in his presence drink thereof and jeer at him and taunt him for his foolish augury. The man came as he was ordered and Ancæos lifted the cup and repeated to him his prophecy. "There's many a slip twixt the cup and the lip," returned the slave. At that moment a messenger rushed into the room with the tidings that a large wild boar had entered the vineyard and was laying it waste. Ancæos quickly returned the glass to the table and ran out to stay the ravages of the boar and preserve his vines but the task was more difficult than he had thought. He was killed in his encounter with the animal and the slave-prophet's words became a proverb.

"The ground of a certain rich man brought forth: and he reasoned within himself, saying, what shall I do because I have not where to bestow my fruits. And he said, this will I do: I will pull down my barns and build greater; and there will I bestow all my grain and my goods. And I will say to my soul, Soul, thou hast much goods laid up for many years; take thine ease, eat, drink and be merry. But God said unto him, Thou foolish one, this night is thy soul required of thee, and the things which thou hast prepared, whose shall they be? So is he that layeth up treasure for himself, and is not rich toward God."—LUKE 12:16–21, Revised Version.

> "Oft expectation fails, and most oft there
> Where most it promises; and oft it hits
> Where hope is coldest; and despair most fits."

WILLIAM SHAKESPEARE, A.D. 1564–1616, *All's Well that Ends Well.*

> "But Mousie, thou art no thy lane,
> In proving foresight may be vain:
> The best-laid schemes o' mice and men,
> Gang aft a-gley,
> And lea'e us naught but grief and pain,
> For promised joy."

ROBERT BURNS, A.D. 1759–1796, *To a Mouse.*

### VARIANT PROVERBS

**Between the hand and the chin.** (Latin).
**Between the hand and the mouth the soup is spilt.** (French).
**Many things happen between the cup and the lip.** (Greek).
**There's many a slip from the hand to the mouth.** (Irish).
**The soup is often lost between the hand and the mouth.** (French, Italian, Spanish, Portuguese).
**Twixt the spoon and the lip the morsel may slip.** (Dutch).
**Wine poured out is not swallowed.** (French).

### ALLIED PROVERBS

**All things come not to pass which the mind has conceived.** (Latin).
**Between the mouth and the spoon great trouble often arises.** (Latin, French).

**Between two stools the breech comes to the ground.** (French, Dutch).

**Between wording and working is a long road.** (German).

**He is to be married, they say; but sometimes the marriage ring slips from one's finger.** (Mauritius Creole).

**Hope is a good breakfast but a bad supper.** (English).

**No one so sure but he may miss.** (Dutch).

**The monkey says that what has gone into the belly is his, but what is in his mouth is not his.** (Oji).

**The unlooked-for often comes.** (German).

**What one swallows is his own but not what he is chewing.** (Gaelic).

## THE WEAKEST GO TO THE WALL

The meaning of this proverb is obscure. As commonly understood it indicates that in the struggle of life those who are least able to protect themselves are driven back from places of opportunity to be finally crushed. Walter K. Kelly, commenting on the saying, had this thought in mind when he reminded his readers that in a crowd the wall was the worst place for anyone to be. Quoting the Dutch proverb, "Where the dam is lowest the water first runs over," he says that "people overrun and oppress those who are least able to resist," thus confirming what he believed was the true teaching of the saying.

According to J. O. Halliwell, "To go to the wall" meant in olden times to be set aside or slighted, which is less severe than to be crowded and crushed by competition.

But there are several other explanations that are more pleasing—for example: The aged go to the wall for support, the blind reach out their hands to the wall for guidance and feeble folk generally have a sense of security and protection close to its sheltering stones. "In a fray the weak are strong," says an Italian proverb. They flee to the wall and are safe.

A correspondent of the Westminister *Gazette*—June 8, 1918—gives still another explanation. "I had it from a Scotchman of no mean literary ability," he says that "in the Middle Ages, when roads and pavements as we know them were not in existence, the roads received most of the waste and refuse from the adjoining houses, and generally collected all the filth of the town or city. The causeys or causeways were at some considerable height above the road, and it was the custom of a kindly minded person or a gentleman to see that children, women, and old people were placed against the wall to be saved from the splashing filth from the road, or the possible danger of falling into it." This explanation conforms to that of Nathan Bailey (A.D. 1721) who declared that the saying was "a compliment paid to the female sex or those to whom one would show respect by letting them go nearest the wall or houses upon a supposition of its being the cleanest."

Perhaps the best explanation is found in the church practice of our forefathers who required the strongest people among the worshippers to stand and later permitted them to be seated on benches and at the same time provided stone seats along the wall for the weak. In advocacy of this view a writer in *Notes and Queries* quoted this passage from Miller's *Rambles Round the*

*Edge Hills:* "On the north and west side of the north aisle the old stone seats against the wall of the church remain. In those days there were no seats in the midst of the church and the congregation stood or knelt. When the clergyman commenced his sermon he used to say: 'Let the weakest go to the wall,' hence the proverb so strangely perverted from its original meaning."

Mr. J. A. Sparvel Bayly, writing about old English parochial churches, says, "A stone bench, in some instances, ran round the north, south and west walls, to which the weary might retire for a while. In Chaldon church, Surrey, a long low stone seat ran along the wall of the south isle, until 1871, when it was 'restored' away; and in Acton church, near Nanturich, there is still a stone bench along the wall of the south aisle."

"We grope for the wall like the blind; yea, we grope as they that have no eyes; we stumble at noonday as in the twilight; among them that are lusty we are as dead men."—ISAIAH 59: 10.

> "The weaker goeth to the pot: Yea, and God wot,
> Some the weaker for oft going to the pot."
>
> JOHN HEYWOOD, A.D. 1497-1580, *Epigrams.*

In the above epigram Heywood used the word pot in the first line to indicate either total destruction, or to the melting pot of the refiner.

"*Gregory:* That shows thee a weak slave, for the weakest goes to the wall.

"*Samson,* 'Tis true; and therefore women, being the weaker vessels, are ever thrust to the wall; therefore I will push Montague's men from the wall and thrust his maids to the wall."—WILLIAM SHAKESPEARE, A.D. 1564–1616, *Romeo and Juliet.*

"In the days of our forefathers the streets were narrow and there were no pavements; while discharging pipes and running gutters by the sides of the walls made the center of the road a more agreeable place for the traveler. Wheeled conveyances of diverse sorts passing and repassing forced the foot passenger to the side of the road, and any tumult or street fight would drive the conquered pell-mell to take refuge in the houses or to the shelter of the wall out of the rush. Hence the proverb: The weakest goes to the wall. In *Romeo and Juliet* Sampson and Gregory are found in the market place of Verona and the former declares: 'I will take the wall of any man or maid of Montague's'; to whom the latter unsympathetically replies, 'That shows thee a weak slave, for the weakest go to the wall.'"—F. EDWARD HULME, A.D. 1841–1909, *Proverb Lore.*

VARIANT PROVERBS

**The weaker goes to the pot.** (English).
**The weakest gaes to the wa'.** (Scotch).

### ALLIED PROVERBS

**A white wall is the fool's writing paper—he writes his name there.** (English, French, Italian).

**Every weak person who contends with a stranger falls so as not to rise again.** (Persian).

**In the fray the weak are strong.** (Italian).

**The cudgel of the powerful must be obeyed.** (Hindustani).

**The fallen are cudgelled repeatedly.** (Behar).

**The ill clad are put against the wind.** (French).

**The water overflows a low wall—i.e. Misfortune overcomes the weak.** (Persian).

**The weakest always is wrong.** (Italian).

**The weakest has the worse.** (English).

**The weakest must hold the candle.** (French).

**To be weak is to be miserable.** (English).

**Where the dam is lowest the water first runs over.** (Dutch).

**Where the dyke is lowest men go over.** (English).

**Where the hedge is lowest men may soonest over.** (English).

**Whether the melon falls upon the knife or the knife on the melon the melon is the sufferer.** (Hindustani).

84

## THEY THAT LIVE IN GLASS HOUSES SHOULD NOT THROW STONES

It is said that Charles Dickens remarked when in conversation with a pompous young man who denounced the sins and follies of the human race, "What a lucky thing it is that you and I do not belong to it."

People often condemn others for the sins in which they themselves indulge. The faults that seem small in one's own life appear large in the lives of a neighbor, The critic, who is also a reformer, is of great use in the world but mere fault-finders benefit no one. To be just one must not only know the truth but the whole truth. There are times when it is necessary to condemn the course of others but condemnation should be devoid of bitterness and tempered with compassion.

The proverb probably came originally from Spain, where there are many folk sayings of similar import. "He that has a roof of glass should not throw stones at his neighbors" is a familiar phrase among the people of the peninsula.

It is believed by many people that the proverb

was first used by James I (VI of Scotland) but as Chaucer, who died a century and a half before the union of the two crowns was effected, quoted the saying, James I, could not have been its author. Chaucer quoted it thus: "Frothy (therefore) who that hath an heed (head) of verre (glass). Fro cast of stones war him in the werre (let him beware)."

The following story is frequently given in proof that James I was its author: When the governments of England and Scotland were united a large number of Scotchmen came to London. Their presence was offensive to many Englishmen and a movement was started to annoy them. The leader of the movement was the Duke of Buckingham who lived in a house that had many windows and that was known as the "glass house." One of the ways by which the malcontents sought to harass the newcomers was by going about after dark and breaking the windows of their houses. This so enraged the Scotchmen that they retaliated by visiting Buckingham's mansion in St. Martin's Fields and, under cover of the night, shattered all the glass that could be reached. The Duke went at once to the King and complained of the treatment he had received; whereupon the sovereign said to the court favorite, "Steenie, Steenie, those who live in glass houses should be carefu' how they fling stanes."

If there is any truth in the story James I only quoted a well-known saying.

"Whoso casteth a stone on high casteth it on his own head; and a deceitful stroke shall make wounds. Whoso diggeth a pit shall fall therein; and he that setteth a trap shall be taken therein. He that worketh mischief, it shall fall upon him, and he shall not know whence it cometh."—ECCLESIASTICUS 27:25–27.

"How is it that no man tries to search into himself, but each fixes his eyes on the wallet of the one who goes before him?"—PLAUTUS B.C. 254?–184. Referring to Æsop's fable of two bags that Jupiter is said to have hung on men, the one in front being filled with the faults of the wearer's neighbor and the one on the back with the wearer's vices.

"He who accuses another of wrong should look well into his own conduct."—PLAUTUS.

"Frothy, who that hath an heed of verre
Fro cast of stones war him in the werre."

GEOFFREY CHAUCER, A.D. 1340–1400, *Troilus & Cressida.*

"Then Eld took heart and was hastily shriven
And waved away Wanhope and fought with Life,
And Life fled away to Physic for help,
Besought him succour and used his salves,
Gave gold, good measure that gladdened his heart.
The doctors gave him a glass house to live in.
Life believed that leechcraft should stay the steps of Eld
And with drink and drugs drive away Death."

WILLIAM LANGLAND, A.D. 1330–1400, *Piers Plowman.*

"Think but how vile a spectacle it were,
To view thy present trespass in another.
Men's faults do seldom to themselves appear;
Their own transgressons partially they smother;
This guilt would seem death-worthy in thy brother
O, how are they wrapp'd in with infamies,
That from their own misdeeds askance their eyes."

SHAKESPEARE, A.D. 1564–1616, *The Rape of Lucrece.*

"There's some wi' big scars on their face,
Point out a prin scart on a frien';
And some, black as sweeps wi' disgrace,
Cry out, the whole world's unclean."

JAMES HOGG, A.D. 1770–1835.

VARIANT PROVERBS

**He that has a roof of glass should not throw stones at his neighbor.** (Spanish, Danish, Italian, German, Dutch).

**He that hath a body made of glass must not throw stones at another.** (English).

**He who lives in a house of glass should not throw stones at people.** (Hebrew, Arabic).

**If you have a head of glass do not throw stones at me.** (Spanish).

**Let him that hath a glass skull not take to throwing stones.** (Italian).

**Let him that hath glass panes not throw stones at his neighbor's house.** (Spanish).

**Let him that hath glass tiles not throw stones at his neighbor's house.** (Spanish).

**When your house is of glass do not throw stones at your neighbor's house.** (Kurdish).

**Who hath glass windows of his own must take heed how he throws stones at his house.** (English).

## ALLIED PROVERBS

**Barefoot men should not walk on thorns.** (English).

**Don't laugh at me, you will catch the contagion.**
This is an admonition to those that laugh at the misfortunes of others. (Assamese).

**Don't use ridicule, some of it is sure to fall on your own head and feet.** (Bannu).

**Evil that cometh out of thy mouth fleeth into thy bosom.** (English).

**He has need o' a clean pow that ca's his neighbor nitty now.** (Scotch).

**He that courts injury will obtain it.** (Danish).

**He that flings dirt at another dirtieth himself most.** (English).

**He that goes barefoot must not plant thorns.** (English).

**He that hath a head of wax must not walk in the sun.** (English).

**He that hath horns in his bosom, let him not put them on his head.** (English).

**He that hurts another hurts himself.** (English).

**He that mischief hatcheth, mischief catcheth.** (English).

**He that strikes with his tongue must ward with his head.** (English).

**He who threateneth hunteth after revenge.** (English).

**He who throws a stone above himself may have it fall on his own head.** (German).

**If dogs (busybodies) go about they must expect the stick.** (Japanese).

**Look out as you move for there are many uneven places within your own body and you might slip into one of them.** (Assamese).

**Oil your own wheel first.** (Bengalese).

**O Mother-in-law should you accuse me and bring a reproach on yourself in return.** (Telugu).

**One stone is enough to destroy a house which is made of glass.** (Persian).

**Spit a-de sky, he say fall a-you face.** (British Guiana).

**Spit at the sun and the spittle will fall on your own face.** (Hindustani).

**Sweep away the snow from thine own door and heed not the frost upon the neighbor's tiles.** (Chinese).

**The threatener sometimes gets a drubbing.** (French).

**They that do what they should not, should hear what they would not.** (English).

**They wha will break rude jists maun put up wi' rude answers.** (Scotch).

**They who play with edged tools must expect to be cut.** (English).

**Threats are arms for the threatened.** (Italian).

**What you put into the pot you will take out in the ladle.** (Arabian).

**Who has a head of wax must not come near the fire.** (French).

## TO CARRY COALS TO NEWCASTLE

To take material of any kind to a place where it abounds, or to give to another that of which he has plenty.

The origin of the saying is unknown. The form is evidently English and has been in use by the English people since the sixteenth century but the thought has been expressed in some adage everywhere for untold ages. The old Rabbis declared that when Moses first demanded that the children of Israel should be delivered from Egyptian bondage he wrought miracles in attestation of his right to prompt obedience as a messenger of Jehovah, but Pharoah ridiculed him and said that miracles proved nothing in Egypt as the magicians there were masters of the art. Then he asked, "Art thou bringing straw to Eprayne?" and calling some children from school bade them perform some wonders in magic before Moses, which they did. Pharoah's wife, the Rabbis tell us, also wrought miracles. Having thus disproved Moses' claim as he supposed, Pharoah asked Moses whether any man could be considered wise who "carried muria to Spain, or fish to Acco"; whereupon Moses answered by repeating proverb for proverb saying, "Where there is a market for greenstuff, there I take my greenstuff."

Aristophanes, the comic poet of Greece, who lived over three hundred years before Christ, spoke of "Carrying owls to Athens" where the image of the bird of night was stamped on the coins and where it was held sacred.

It was common during the middle ages to speak of any superfluous act or bestowment as "carrying indulgences to Rome."

One of the strangest forms that the proverb has ever taken is that used by the natives of Africa speaking the Oji language. Knowing that mushroom gatherers are in the habit of looking for a supply of the fungus on anthills where it is frequently found growing, they laugh at any one who gathered mushrooms elsewhere and foolishly put them on such hills for safe-keeping. They therefore speak of men who seek a market for their goods in a place where similar goods abound, or who give to others that of which the recipient has an abundance: "Nobody gathering mushrooms deposits them on an anthill."

Perhaps the most humorous form that the proverb takes is that which has been adopted by the French who use the expression—"To jump into the water for fear of rain," thus presenting to the mind a picture of a man who fearing that he will be overtaken by an approaching storm flees to a river or lake and leaps therein so as to be under cover when the rain begins to fall.

Disraeli tells us in his *Curiosities of Literature* that the saying was borrowed by the English and applied to themselves. "It may be found," he declares, "among the Persians: In the 'Bustan' of Sadi we have *Infers piper in Hindostan*—'To carry pepper to Hindostan.' Among the Hebrews, 'To carry oil to the city of olives'; a similar proverb occurs in Greek."

SCRIPTURE REFERENCES: Gen. 33:8, 9; Exod. 36:5–7; Matt. 13:12; 25:29; Mark 4:25; Luke 6:38; 8:18; 19:26.

"He betook himself to the town of Ephraim, twenty miles north of Jerusalem and five north-east of Bethel, on the margin of the wilderness of Judea. Ephraim is unknown to fame. It was situated in a wheat growing district, and the Jews had a proverb, 'Carry straw to Ephraim," much like our 'Carry coals to Newcastle."—DAVID SMITH, A.D. 1866, *In the Days of His Flesh.*

"Proverb literature testifies to a universal abundance of that class of gifts which provoke a 'thank you for nothing.' 'Coals to Newcastle' is our national expression but for such superfluous presents the Greeks had many a mocking adage."—*London Quarterly Review*, July, 1868.

VARIANT PROVERBS

**A farthing to the millions of Crœsus.** (Greek).

**Carrying saut to Dysart and puddings to Tranent.**

Sometimes this saying is used only in part and treated as two proverbs. (Scotch).

**Carry vegetables to the town of vegetables.** (Hebrew).

**Like selling needles in the blacksmith's street.** (Telugu).

**Like selling pots in Potter's Street.** (Telugu).

**Putting salt into the sea.** (Gaelic).

**Selling needles at the iron mungers.** (Bengali).

**Sending salt to the salt pit.** (Welsh).

**That were sending butter to a dairyman's house.** (Gaelic).

**That were sending wood to Lochaber.** (Gaelic).

**To add a farthing to the riches of Crœsus.** (Latin).

**To act cupbearer to the frogs.** (Greek).

**To carry apples to Alcinous.** (Greek).

**To carry blades to Damascus.** (Asiatic).

**To carry box to Cytorus.** (Greek).

**To carry brine to Apamæa and fish to Acco.** (Hebrew).

**To carry cockles to St. Michael.** (French).

**To carry cumin seed to Kirmin.** (Persian).

**To carry fish to the Hellespont.** (Greek).

**To carry indulgences to Rome.** (English).

**To carry leaves to the woods.** (French).

**To carry muria to Spain or fish to Acco.** (Ancient Hebrew).

**To carry oil to the city of olives—sometimes quoted "To carry oil to Olivet."** (Hebrew, Greek).

**To carry owls to Athens.** (Greek).

**To carry peppers to Hindustan.** (Persian).

**To carry straw to Ephraim.**

Ephraim being the wheat growing district of Palestine. (Ancient Hebrew).

**To carry the clod to the plowed field.** (Greek).

**To carry water to the river.** (French).

**To carry wood to the forests.** (Latin).
**To carry wood to the mountain.** (Spanish).
**To cart water to the Thames.** (English).
**To offer honey to one who owns beehives.** (Spanish, Portuguese, Italian).
**To pour water into the Severn.** (Welsh).
**To send enchantments to Egypt.** (Hebrew).
**To send fir to Norway.** (Dutch, Danish).
**To send water to the sea.** (French, Portuguese, German, Dutch, Spanish, Osmanli).
**To sell shells to those who come from St. Michel.** (French).
**To show the path to one who knows it.** (Welsh).
**To throw brine into the sea.** (Welsh).
**To throw water into the river.** (Persian).

ALLIED PROVERBS

**Cress is not sold to the cress seller, nor tarragon to him who vends tarragon.** (Osmanli).
**Do not sell sun in July.** (Italian).
**It is foolish to show glow worms by candle light.** (Italian).
**Nobody gathering mushrooms deposits them on an ant-hill.** (Oji—Africa).
**Of what use is a torch at midday?** (Hebrew).
**Sending ducks to fetch the geese from the water.** (Welsh).
**The beggar stands at the beggar's door.** (Panjabi).
**The healthy seeking a doctor.** (Welsh).
**The lamb teaching the sheep to graze.** (Welsh).
**The light of a lamp amid the glare of a torch.** (Assamese).
**To carry a lantern in midday.** (Hebrew).
**To grease a lump of lard.** (Welsh).
**To jump into the water for fear of rain.** (French).
**To light a lamp amid the glare of a torch.** (Assamese).
**To sell honey to buy sweet things.** (Welsh).
**To sell the sow and buy bacon.** (Welsh).
**To show the sun with a torch.** (French).

**To sink a well by the riverside.** (German).

**When it rains everybody brings drink to the hens.** (Armenian).

**Where there is a market for greenstuff, there I take my greenstuff.** (Ancient Hebrew).

## TO ROB PETER TO PAY PAUL

To take from one and give to another.

The proverb is very old. Its origin is unknown. Many believe that it was not used earlier than 1560. On Dec. 17, 1550, the abbey church of St. Peter's, Westminster, was made a cathedral. Ten years later the Westminster lands were so wasted that they became insufficient to support the cathedral and were therefore in part sold and the money used to repair St. Paul's Cathedral, London. It has been thought that the proverb came into use at that time. But Walter W. Skeat says truly that such a derivation of the proverb is a mere guess and quoted the phrase as found in Lanfranc's *Science of Cirurgie* written about the year 1400 where the following expression is found: "For sum medicyne is for Peter that is not good for Poule, for diuersite of complexioun." The two names Peter and Paul being used not with reference to the apostles but in a general sense and because of the alliteration. He further reminds us that Heywood in 1562 quoted the proverb—"Rob Peter to pay Paul," which is the true form with no application to the Westminster incident. It is not at all improbable that when the repairs were made in St. Paul's Cathedral the proverb, being well known, was quoted in referring to the work.

It may have been that the English form—"To rob St. Peter to pay St. Paul"—was an adaptation of the French saying—"To strip St. Peter to clothe St. Paul"—which probably was first used as a robing proverb and referred to the indiscriminate use of vestments on St. Peter's and St. Paul's days.

"He always looked a given horse in the mouth, leaped from the cock to the ass and put one ripe between two green. By robbing Peter he paid Paul; he kept the moon from the wolves and hoped to catch larks if ever the heavens should fall."—FRANÇOIS RABELAIS, A.D. 1490?–1553.

"Like a pickpurse pilgrim ye pry and ye prowl
At rovers, to rob Peter and pay Poule
Iwys, I know, or any more be told,
That draf is your errand, but drink ye wolde."

JOHN HEYWOOD, A.D. 1497–1580.

"Rob Peter to pay Paul: Thou sayest I do,
But thou robbest and poulst Peter and Paul too."

JOHN HEYWOOD.

"I dwell from the city in suburbs at rowles;
I pray to St. Peter to bring me near Powles.
Alas, thou pray'st all in vain, poor silly fool—
Peter will set no hand to bring thee to Poule."

JOHN HEYWOOD.

VARIANT PROVERBS

Give not Peter so much to leave St. Paul nothing. (English).
He robs Peter to pay Paul. (Hindustani).
He takes from St. Peter and gives to St. Paul. (English).
Plunder Peter and pay Paul. (Irish-Ulster).
To strip St. Peter to clothe St. Paul. (French).
To take from St. Peter and give to St. Paul. (French).

ALLIED PROVERBS

From whom did you gain? From my brother—that is no gain. (Pashto).
He cut from the skirt and added to the shoulder. (Persian).
He has cut from the beard and joined (it) to his moustache. (Osmanli).
He plucked from his beard and added to his moustache. (Persian).
He plucked from the beard and added to the whiskers. (Persian).
He put Uhmud's cap upon Muhmood's head. (Persian).
He rieves the kirk to theek the choir. (Scotch).
It is no use starving the horse to fatten the mule. (Chinese).
Peter in, Paul out. (Scotch).
Praise Peter but don't find fault with Paul. (English).
Starving Mike Malcolm to fatten big Murdock. (Gaelic).
The thatch of the kiln on the mill. (Gaelic).
They took it off from his beard and put it into the moustache. (Arabian).
Tie the kiln to thatch the mill. (Scotch).
To dig toward the East in order to fill up a hole towards the West is giving oneself useless trouble. (Chinese).
To kill crows and throw them to kites. (Telugu).
To make one hole to fill up another. (Spanish).
To steal oil from one temple in order to light a lamp in another. (Marathi).
To strip one altar to cover another. (Italian).
Who praiseth St. Peter doth not blame St. Paul. (English).

36

## WHAT CAN'T BE CURED MUST BE ENDURED

This truism was in common use before the Christian era. Plautus said that "if you cultivate a cheerful disposition in misfortune you will reap the advantages of it" and Publius Syrus declared that one "must endure that which cannot be altered." But the saying is not generally used merely to state a fact, but rather to encourage those who despond because of trouble or rebel against adverse conditions. It is therefore a proverb of inspiration for the faint-hearted. The Scriptures carry the thought further and bid us profit by our adversities. "We triumph even in our troubles," wrote the Apostle Paul "knowing that trouble produces endurance, endurance produces character and character produces hope—and hope which never disappoints us, since God's love floods our hearts through the Holy Spirit which has been given to us."—ROMANS 5: 3–5, *Moffat's Translation.*

An old and wise saw advises:

"If there is a remedy find it
If there is none ne'er mind it."

"Judging by the stupendous grandeur of the

revelation—therefore lest I should be over elated there has been sent to me like the agony of impalement Satan's angel dealing blow after blow lest I should be over elated. As for this, three times have I besought the Lord to rid me of him; but his reply has been 'My grace suffices for you, for power matures in weakness.' Most gladly therefore will I boast of my infirmities in the bearing of insults, in distress, in persecutions, in grievous difficulties—for Christ's sake; for when I am weak then I am strong."—II CORINTHIANS 12:7–10, *Weymouth's Translation.*

"To bear troubles is a light thing; to endure them to the end is a heavy thing."—SENECA, B.C. 4?–A.D. 65.

"Whatever you suffer deservedly should be borne patiently; the punishment which comes to one undeserving of it comes as a matter of bewailing."—OVID, B.C. 43–A.D. 17.

"Why courage then! what cannot be avoided
'Twere childish weakness to lament or fear."

WILLIAM SHAKESPEARE, A.D. 1564–1616, *Henry VI., Pt. III.*

"Alas! I show'd too much
The rashness of a woman; he is touch'd
To the noble heart. What's gone and what's past help
Should be past grief; I beseech you, rather
Let me be punish'd, that have minded you
Of what you should forget."

WILLIAM SHAKESPEARE, *A Winter's Tale.*

"Follow after that which He calls you unto;

and you will find light arising unto you in the midst of darkness. Has he a cup of affliction in one hand?—Lift up your eyes and you will see a cup of consolation in the other. And if all stars withdraw their light whilst you are in the way of God, assure yourself that the sun is ready to rise."—JOHN OWEN, A.D. 1616–1683.

"God, perhaps, is pleased to visit us with some heavy affliction, and shall we now, out of a due reverence of his all governing wisdom patiently endure it? Or out of a blind presumption of our own endeavor by some sinister way or other to rid ourselves from it?"—ROBERT SOUTH, A.D. 1633–1716.

"This is a consolatory proverb applicable to persons under the pressure of some inevitable calamity; and advises to make a virtue of necessity, and not aggravate but alleviate the burden by patient bearing."—NATHAN BAILEY, A.D. 1721, *Diverse Proverbs.*

"Nothing but mirth can conquer fortune's spite;
No sky is heavy if the heart be light:
Patience is sorrow's salve; what can't be cured,
So Donald right areads, must be endured."

CHARLES CHURCHILL, A.D. 1731–1764, *The Prophecy of Famine.*

ALLIED PROVERBS

**Gnaw the bone which is fallen to thy lot.** (English).
**If I live I can exist on Balusukura.** (Telugu).
**If it can be nae better it's weel it's nae waur.** (Scotch).

Nothing is grievous which necessity enjoins. (Latin).

Of what use is it to call on one who is drowned. (Persian).

There is no misfortune out of which some good fortune may not be got. (Welsh).

There is nothing for it now but resignation—generally used by the Persians after the death of kindred or friends. (Persian).

Whatever comes is endured. (Osmanli).

What is done can't be undone. (Danish).

What was hard to bear is sweet to remember. (Portuguese).

Where remedies are needed sighing avails nothing. (Italian).

### CONTRADICTING PROVERB

What you can't have, abuse. (Italian).

## WHEN IN ROME DO AS THE ROMANS DO

Suit your behavior or appearance to the country in which you dwell.

Adapt yourself to circumstances.

Monica and her son, Aurelius Augustus, better known as Saint Augustine, having learned that Saturday was observed as a fast day in Rome, when it was not so observed in Milan, went to St. Ambrose for advice as to the proper course to pursue when visiting the Imperial City. St. Ambrose thinking it wise to conform to the practices of others in matters non-essential answered, "When I am here (in Milan) I do not fast on Saturday, when in Rome I do fast on Saturday." This reply of St. Ambrose is said to have given rise to the saying—"When in Rome do as the Romans do."

Pandit Ganga Datt Upreti, who resided for many years in the secluded district of Kumaun and Garhwal in India, gives the following amusing stories current among the people, that illustrate this proverb:

"A man once arrived in a foreign country to visit a friend. He inquired for the road leading to his friend's house from a boy standing by, telling him that on arrival at his host's house he would give him plenty of sweetmeats. The boy led him there. The man before entering his friend's house gave him one rupee to buy sweetmeats. The boy did not accept it, saying that it was not enough. The man, for fear of disgrace, offered him five rupees but still the boy refused and, becoming very obstinate, began to quarrel with him. He was at a loss what to do. At last the noise of the quarrel reached his friend who came out and inquired into the whole matter and then told him the proverb—'One ought to adopt the guise of the country in which he lives'—and gave him advice adapted to the occasion. The man according to his friend's advice bought some sweetmeats for one pice, and then divided them into two portions—i.e. one greater and the other smaller. Putting a portion in each hand he told the boy to take whichever he pleased. The boy took the greater portion with satisfaction and then went away."

"Once a man happened to arrive in a village which was peopled only with noseless men (who had had their noses cut off for some crime). No sooner had he arrived than he was ironically addressed by the nickname 'Nacku,' or the man having a nose. As the stranger was obliged to stay there for his livelihood he was contemptuously treated and tormented by the villagers until he also had his nose cut off."

The Hindoos are very loth to give up the ways

of their ancestors particularly in religious matters and their proverbs reflect that trait of character. The Pashto proverbs—"Do not go on the road which neither your father nor your mother goes," "Forsake your village, but not its ancient usages," and "Though the head should go a habit goes not"—all indicate this unwillingness to change. There is a proverbial complaint that is addressed to men about to remove their residence to another district or country that further shows this characteristic. One Hindoo will say to his departing friend in a tone of regret—"Wherever you live you will observe their customs," as though the influence of the new home might cause him to depart from the ways of his ancestors, and a father addressing a wayward son will conclude his remarks with the saying—"You have now followed a novelty which neither your father nor your grandfather knew." While the people of India are unwilling to give up the ways of their ancestors they are often prone to change when thrown among foreigners. Mr. S. S. Thorburn of the Indian Civil Service, says that a Mohammedan in the Bennu district seldom misses praying five times a day and always in as public manner as he can, but once let him separate himself from his own people, where no tale-bearing eyes are upon him, he'll forget his beads and his genuflexions.

The European Turks have a quaint way of advising men regarding a departure from accustomed practices. They say one to another—"Go to your father and make salutation to him"—that is, do as you please about the matter.

"Their host bewailed himself exceedingly that he could offer him no wine: 'Had he but known four and twenty hours before he would have had some, had it been within the circle of forty miles round him. But no gentleman could do more to show his sense of the honor of a visit from another, than to offer him the best cheer his house offered.' When there are no bushes there can be no nuts and the way of those you live with is that you must follow."—WALTER SCOTT, A. D. 1771–1832, *Waverley*.

"To 'do at Rome as they do at Rome' is a sage maxim of antiquity which teaches us that in whatever spot of the globe we may chance to be, it is our duty kindly to accommodate ourselves to the prevailing custom."—JOHN W. CUNNINGHAM, A.D. 1780–1861, *Sancho*.

"They are in a double fault, 'that fashion themselves to this world,' which Paul forbids, and like Mercury, the planet, are good with good, bad with bad. When they are at Rome they do there as they see done, Puritans with Puritans, Papists with Papists; *omnium horarum homines*, formalists, ambidexters, lukewarm Laodiceans. All their study is to please, and their god is their commodity; their labor to satisfy their lusts, and their endeavors to their own ends. Whatever they pretend or in public seem to do 'withe the fool in their hearts, they say there is no God.'"—ROBERT BURTON, A.D. 1759–1796, *Anatomy of Melancholy.*

### VARIANT PROVERBS

**At Rome do as Rome does.** (French).
**He that has Rome must keep Rome up.** (Gaelic).
**When you are in Rome do as you see.** (Spanish).
**You may not sit in Rome and strive with the Pope.** (Scotch).

### ALLIED PROVERBS

**At Benares he was a Benares-man, at Mathura he was a Mathura-man.**
This proverb is applied to time servers. (Marathi).
**Do as most men do and men will speak well of thee.** (English).
**Do as others do and few will mock you.** (Danish).
**Go out and see how the people act.** (Ancient Hebrew).
**Go with many, eat with many.** (Pashto).
**Hast gone into the city conform to its laws.** (Ancient Hebrew).
**I came down stairs in the dark and washed my face in a water pot filled with water. This must be done in the house—i.e. I adapted myself to the place in which I lived.** (Kashmiri).
**If there is darkness in the place to which you have gone, do you also close your eyes.** (Osmanli).
**If you go among other people, be like them.** (Marathi).
**In the place of roses do you be a rose, and where there are thorns do you be a thorn.** (Persian).
**Never wear a brown hat in Friesland.** (Dutch).
**One ought to adopt the guise of the country in which he lives.** (Kumaun, Garhwal).

**One ought to look at the country of one eyed men with only one eye.** (Kumaun, Garhwal).
**Recite according to the book.** (Chinese).
**Suit your appearance to the country.** (Behar).
**The law of the state is law.—i.e. The law of a state is binding on a foreigner therein as well as a native, even though he be a Jew.** (Ancient Hebrew).
**The manner of the folk one lives among will be followed.** (Gaelic).
**The reply of a Turkish question should be in Turkish.** (Persian).
**The way of those you live with is that you must follow.** (Scotch).
**Thy neighbor is thy teacher.** (Arabian).
**When you are in town if you observe that people wear the hat on one side, wear yours likewise.** (Armenian).
**Wherever you are do as you see done.** (Spanish).
**Wood in the town cooks the pot in the town.** (Ibo-Nigeria-Africa).

## WHEN THE CAT IS AWAY THE MICE WILL (OR MAY) PLAY

This proverb is found in all lands.

When the restraints of law are withheld or relaxed the people yield to evil propensities and commit crime.

When children are not under supervision and control they say and do that which they ought not.

When mechanics are without oversight they grow careless and negligent in work—"The master's eye will do more work than both his hands."

When there is no steersman at the helm the boat will drift.

Liberty without restraint leads to license.

The inhabitants of Western India declare that when the gods become false those who study the Vedas grow wicked. A similar belief is held by the Marathi people who say—"God is not in the shrine and the censer dances about."

> "For once the eagle England being in prey,
> To her unguarded nest the weasel Scot
> Comes sneaking and so sucks her princely eggs,
> Playing the mouse in absence of the cat,
> To tear and havoc more than she can eat."

WILLIAM SHAKESPEARE, A.D. 1564–1616, *King Henry V.*

300

### VARIANT PROVERBS

**The cat is absent and the mice dance.** (Modern Greek).
**When the cat is gone the mice dance.** (Belgian).
**When the cat is away the mice have room to play.** (Welsh).
**When the cat is not in the house the rats (or mice) dance.** (Italian).
**When the cat is not the mice are awake.** (French).
**When the cat's away it is jubilee with the mice.** (Dutch).
**When the cat's away the mice give a ball.** (Martinique Creole).
**When the cat shall leave home the mice shall have leave to dance.** (Irish-Farney).
**When the cats leave town (or home) the mice dance.** (Irish-Ulster).
**When the cat sleeps the mice play.** (Dutch).
**When there is no cat mice dance.** (Indian-Kumaun, Garhwal).

### ALLIED PROVERBS

**A blate cat makes a proud mouse.** (Scotch).
**A blind cat catches only a dead rat.** (Chinese).
**God is not in the shrine and the censer dances about.** (Marathi).
**If you have money to throw away set on workmen and don't stand by.** (Italian).
**Lamps out, the turban vanishes—when the ruler dies or is deposed the people commit crime.** (Hindustani).
**The eye of the master fattens the steed.** (English).
**The master's eye is worth both his hands.** (English).
**The master's eye maketh the horse fat.** (English).
**The master's eye puts mate on the horse's banes.** (Irish-Ulster).
**The mewing of the cat has silenced the mice.** (Modern Greek).
**There is a thick mist so sing as you please.** (Hindustani).
**Under misrule they play the fool.** (Hindustani).

**Well knows the mouse that the cat's out of the house.** (Scotch).

**Were the cat at home it were worse for you.** (Welsh, Irish).

**What wots the mouse, the cat's out of the house.** (Scotch).

**When the cat dies the mice rejoice.** (Ashanti, Oji-West African).

**When the cat is blind the rat becomes bold.** (Marathi).

**When the cat is safe in the forest the rat says—"She's my wife."** (Hindustani).

**When the king is away the queen is free to act as she likes. (Behar).**

91, 117, 274, 287

## WHO KEEPS COMPANY WITH A WOLF LEARNS TO HOWL

(See "A man is known by the company he keeps" and "Birds of a feather flock together.")

The origin of this proverb is unknown. It may have come from the ancient superstition that people were sometimes temporarily converted into wolves. In olden times the dread of wolves was so great, particularly among the pastoral people, that the strange and terrible hallucination known as lycanthropy, or wolf madness, prevailed in many lands and among all classes. It spread among the people like an epidemic. The ignorant and educated alike declared that human beings could, by the aid of supernatural agencies, be changed into wolves and go about as wild beasts, roaming the forests, walking on their hands and feet, howling, tearing open graves, molesting unarmed travelers, stealing and eating children, etc. The dread of such a transformation was so great that whole communities lived in constant fear lest they should suffer injury from the assaults of wolfmen. Some people, out of vengeance for fancied injuries, accused their neighbors of werwolfery and caused them to be brought before the courts, and tried; not infrequently the hapless victims of such an accusation were adjudged guilty and condemned to severe punishment. Strange as it seems, the delusion took such a strong hold on the people that many declared themselves to be guilty and gave circumstantial evidence of their transformation.

Many wild and impossible stories of wolf madness were repeated in mediæval times but all of them find an explanation in the heated imagination of the people or in the acts of men who were mentally unbalanced.

"In the fifteenth century a council of theologians, convoked by the Emperor Sigismund, gravely decided that the *loup-garow* was a reality."—E. COBHAM BREWER, A.D. 1810–1897.

"If thou wishes to get rid of any evil propensities, thou must keep far from evil companions." —SENECA, B.C. 4–A.D. 65.

"Bad company is like a nail driven into a post, which after the first or second blow, may be drawn out with little difficulty; but being once driven up to the head, the pinchers cannot take hold to draw it out, but which can only be done by the destruction of the wood."—ST. AUGUSTINE, A.D. 354–430.

"A parent or guardian should always reflect upon the consequences of placing a child or a ward here or there. Some company is as infectious and more mischievous than the plague; and no account can be given for the odd choice that some people make in the disposition of a son who are extremely solicitous about the good breeding of a dog. We should therefore recommend good company to youth by our own example, and putting them into it, that they may early taste the satisfaction of virtuous society and resist the insinuating arts of the vicious."—SAMUEL PALMER, A.D. 1710.

"Frequent intercourse and intimate connection between two persons make them so alike that not only their dispositions are moulded like each other, but their very faces and tones of voice contract a similarity."—JOHANN C. LAVATER, A.D. 1741–1801.

"No company is far preferable to bad because we are more apt to catch the vices of others than virtues as disease is far more contagious than health."—CHARLES C. COLTON, A.D. 1780–1852.

Mr. John Foster in his *Life of Dickens* has a curious story of "a distinguished writer," their common friend, and "a man of many sterling fine qualities; but with a habit of occasional free indulgence in coarseness of speech," who once met at dinner at Lausanne "a stately English baronet" and his "two milksop sons" who were being educated into manhood with exceptional purity and innocence; at which crisis of their career "our ogre friend" encountered these lambs and, "as if possessed by a devil, launched out into such frightful and appalling impropriety—ranging over every kind of forbidden topic and every species of forbidden word, and every sort of scandalous anecdote—that years of education in Newgate," affirms the author of *Oliver Twist*, "would have been as nothing compared with their experience of that one afternoon. After turning paler and paler, and more and more stony, the baronet, with a half suppressed cry, rose and fled." The best meaning, really the worst, of the story is, that the sons, intent on the ogre, remained behind instead of following their father, and are supposed to have been ruined from that hour.—FRANCIS JACOX, A.D. 1874.

"It is important to prevent children in particular from associating with those who have personal defects lest they should adopt them. It is still more necessary to guard them against the infection of depraved morals which are more readily imbibed, take deeper root and are with greater difficulty removed than those affecting only the person."—JOHN BRAND, A.D. 1744–1806.

VARIANT PROVERBS

**A calf that goes with a pig will eat excrement.** (Tamil).
**A fowl brought up with a pig will eat dirt.** (Tamil).
**Amongst the honorable a man becomes honorable; amongst the base, base.** (Bannu).
**Grapes derive their color from grapes.** (Persian).
**He who walks with the virtuous is one of them.** (English).
**If you sit down with a lame man you will learn to halt.** (Modern Greek).

If you sit with one who squints before evening you will become cat-eyed. (Modern Greek).

Keep company with good men and good men you'll imitate. (Chinese).

Keep company with good men and good men you'll learn to be. (Chinese).

Live with him who prays and thou prayest; live with the singer and thou singest. (Arabian).

Live with one who plays and thou playest. (Arabian).

Live with the singer and thou singest. (Arabian).

The manners of the flock one lives among will be followed. (Gaelic).

The servant of a king is like a king. (Hebrew).

Who follows a thief learns to steal. (Ibo-Nigerian).

Who lives with a cripple learns to limp. (English, Dutch, Portuguese).

With the good we become good. (Dutch).

OTHER PROVERBS RELATING TO INFLUENCE

A bad friend is like a smith, who if he does not burn you with fire will injure you with smoke. (Arabian).

A collector of mummies will be one. (Japanese).

A crow learned to walk like a cuckoo and forgot his own walk. (Kashmiri).

A crow tried to acquire the strut of the partridge and forgot even its own—On the Afghan frontier a red-legged partridge is regarded as very graceful while the crow is thought to be a type of awkwardness. (Pashto).

A little buttermilk, the size of a pearl, to a whole pail full of milk. (Telugu).

A monkey sees its fellow jump and jumps too. (Nigerian).

A single scrap of spoiled meat taints the whole meat. (Chinese).

A thief knows a thief and a wolf knows a wolf. (English).

A thief knows a thief's ways. (Hindustani).

Approach the perfumer and thou wilt be perfumed. (Hebrew).

**A wise man associating with the vicious becomes an idiot; a dog traveling with good men becomes a rational being.** (Arabian).

**Bad companions quickly corrupt the good.** (German).

**Bad company is friendship with a snake fencing with a sword.** (Telugu).

**Blackness leaves the coal when the fire enters—that is, the evil becomes good by good association.** (Bengalese).

**Carry wood behind the owner of property—i.e. Follow the prosperous and you will prosper.** (Hebrew).

**Do not approach the black, there will be black contagion. (Osmanli).**

**Evil companionships corrupt good morals.** (Greek).

This proverb was probably in common use in the first century. St. Paul quoted it in I Cor. 15: 33. (Greek).

**Follow the owl and he will lead you into a ruined place.** (Arabian).

**He who goes to Ceylon becomes a demon.** (Bengalese).

**He who intimately frequents people for forty days becomes one of their number.** (Obsolete Arabian).

**He who introduces himself between the onion and its peel goes forth with the onion smell.** (Arabian).

**He who lies down with dogs will get up with fleas.** (English, French, Italian, Spanish, Danish).

**He who mixes himself with draff will be eaten by the swine.** (Dutch).

**He who sits among the rubbish must not be surprised if pigs devour him.** (Serbian).

**He who speaks good hears good, he who speaks bad hears bad.** (Osmanli).

**If there be a Balija man as small as a clove of garlic, he will ruin the whole village.** (Telugu).

**If you wrestle with a collier you will get a blotch.** (English).

**Near putrid fish you will stink.** (Chinese).

Near putrid fish you will stink, near the epidendrum you will be fragrant. (Chinese).

Near to the perfumer is fragrance. (Hebrew).

Near vermillion one gets stained pink; near ink one gets stained black. (Chinese).

On account of the teacher the pupil has eaten—i.e. Out of respect to his teacher the pupil reflects his honors. (Hebrew).

One bad goat will spoil the herd. (Vai-West African).

One ill weed mars the whole pot of pottage. (English).

One rotten apple in the basket infects the rest. (Dutch).

One scabby goat infects the flock. (Persian).

One scabby sheep's enough to spoil the flock. (English, Italian, French).

Play with dogs and you will get fleas. (Martinique Creole).

Should there be two dry logs and a fresh one together, the dry logs set the fresh one on fire. (Hebrew).

The character of a man depends on whether he has good or bad friends. (Japanese).

The goat and its companions eat palm leaves. (Nigerian).

The governor took us and the scent came into the hand.—i.e. He shook hands with us. (Hebrew).

The pickpocket is the thief's brother. (Hindustani).

The qualities of a tree depend on those of the seed from which it sprung and those of a man on the company he keeps. (Persian).

The rotten apple spoils its companions. (Spanish).

Thy neighbor is thy teacher. (Arabian).

Unless you had touched garlic your fingers would not have smelt. (Telugu).

Vice and virtue arise from our associations. (Bengalese).

Whatever goes into a salt mine becomes salt. (Persian).

What is near vermillion becomes stained red; what is near ink becomes stained black. (Chinese).

When one plum beholds another it sets forth color. (Persian).

**When the crow is your guide he will lead you to the corpses of dogs.** (Arabian).

**When we strike mud we get smeared over.** (Malabar).

**Who lives with a blacksmith will at last go away with burnt clothes.** (Afghan, Bannu).

**Who play wid de puppy get bit wid de fleas.** (British Guiana).

**Who talks with a smith receives sparks.** (Kurdish).

**With whom you are, such one you are.** (Dutch, Serbian).

**You only stink your hand by killing a muskrat.** (Bengalese).

349

## YOU A LADY AND I A LADY, WHO WILL PUT THE SOW OUT

If there is no one but you or me to perform the task and I cannot do it by reason of my social position, how is the work to be done?

This old proverb is generally used when urging someone to perform a hard or disagreeable task. The service must be rendered by one or the other and as neither one thinks that he has the ability or time what is to be done? It is sometimes quoted ironically by one member of a family to another in seeking to induce him to perform some disagreeable task. Its origin is unknown.

Among the Behar peasants it is customary to speak disparagingly of people who leave any special line of work in which they are engaged and to which they are adapted that they may enter some other calling that has taken their fancy. In referring to such people they instinctively think of one of their religious customs and ask: "Who will search the pots and pans for food if all the dogs go on a pilgrimage to Benares?" or in other words, who is going to do the work of the world if everyone becomes a religious pilgrim?

"There is and always must be some rough

work to be done in the world; work which, though rough, is not therefore in the least ignoble; and the schemes, so daintily conceived, of a luxurious society, which repose on a tacit assumption that nobody shall have to do this work, are touched with a fine irony in this Arabic proverb: *If I am master, and thou art a master, who shall drive the asses?*"—RICHARD CHENEVIX TRENCH, A.D. 1807–1886.—*Proverbs and their Lessons.*

VARIANT PROVERBS

**I am an esquire, you are an esquire, who will harness the horses?** (Osmanli).

**I am a queen, and you are a queen, so who is to fetch the water?** (Hindustani).

**If I am master, and you are a master, who shall drive the asses?** (Arabian).

**I stubborn and you stubborn, who is to carry the load?** (Spanish).

**I the mistress, and you the young lady, who will sweep the house?** (Spanish).

**The mother-in-law is great, the daughter-in-law is also great, the pot is burnt, who will take it off the fire?** (Kashmiri).

**You a gentleman, and I a gentleman, who will milk the cow?** (Turkish).

**You a lady, I a lady, who shall drive the hogs afield?** (Gallican).

**You are a queen, I am queen, but who will husk the millet?** (Kumaun, Garhwal).

**You stout, and I stout, who will carry the dirt out?** (English).

ALLIED PROVERBS

**Every ass thinks himself worthy to stand with the king's horses.** (English).

**Gentry sent to market will not buy one bushel of corn.** (English).

**If all get into the palanquin who will be the bearers?** (Hindoo, Telugu, Gallican).

**If everyone becomes Lord, who shall turn our mill.** (Armenian).

**It is hard to be high and humble.** (English).

## YOU CANNOT MAKE A SILK PURSE OUT OF A SOW'S EAR

You cannot change nature. You cannot perform an impossible task.

The age and origin of the proverb is unknown.

It is sometimes said: "You cannot make a horn of a pig's tail nor a silk purse of a hog's ear." The sow's ear is often referred to in old maxims. A few will be sufficient to indicate their character: "He has the right sow by the ear" (German). "To come sailing in the sow's ear" (English). "It is not every man who takes the right sow by the ear" (Danish). "To take the wrong sow by the ear" (English).

*Peter Prim's Pride*, a child's book published in 1810, contains an illustration of the proverb, "You cannot make a whistle out of a pig's tail." The illustration represents a maid and hairdresser trying in vain to adorn a large and gross-looking woman, dressing her hair in a way that will give her the appearance of refinement.

In the secluded districts of Kumaun and Garhwal, India, the people are accustomed to say in referring to dullards who have failed to profit by educational advantages: "In order to make the tail of a dog straight it was put in a hollow bamboo and kept there for twelve years, but when it was taken out of the bamboo it again became crooked." The same thought is expressed in the Bible: Eccles., 1:15; 7:13; Jer., 13:23.

There is an old East Indian story of the Mohammedan King Akbar, who in the spirit of fun, said to Birbal, the Brahman minister, "Birbal make me into a Brahman." On hearing the demand the minister asked for time that he might consider the matter and see what he could do to accomplish the king's conversion.

A few days thereafter Birbal, hearing that Akbar was intending to take a drive, ascertained the direction in which he was to go, procured a donkey and led it to the roadside where the king would pass. There he waited till he saw him coming, when he began to vigorously curry the donkey as though he were engaged in a very important business.

When the king saw the Brahman thus engaged he stopped and laughingly inquired why he was occupied in such a foolish business; whereupon Birbal explained that his labor was not foolish for he was turning a donkey into a horse. "Turning a donkey into a horse," repeated the king, "How can you do that?"

"If that cannot be done, replied Birbal, "How do you expect to turn a Mohammedan into a Brahman?"

"A crow was filled with envy on seeing the

beautiful white plumage of a swan, and thought it was due to the water in which the swan constantly bathed and swam, so he left the neighborhood of the altars, where he got his living by picking up bits of the meat offered in sacrifice, and went and lived among the pools and streams, but though he bathed and washed his feathers many times a day, he didn't make them any whiter, and at last died of hunger into the bargain."—ÆSOP, B.C. 561?, *The Crow and the Swan, V. S. Vernon Jones' Translation.* See also Æsop's fable of *The Eagle, the Jackdaw and the Shepherd.*

"A bad man, though you treat him friendly, will perpetually be taking on again his old disposition. He is like the tail of a dog, which though you bend it down with utmost care by emollients and unguents, will always return again to its old shape."—FROM THE PANCHATANTRA, *predating the Christian era.*

> "Each is bounded by his nature,
> And remains the same in stature,
> In the valley, on the mountain:
> Scoop from ocean or from fountain
> With a poor hand or a richer
> You can only fill your pitcher."
>
> SAADI, A.D. 1184–1291.

> "Nultow (Thou wilt not) never, late me (nor) skete (soon),
> A goshauk maken of a kete (kite),
> No faucon (falcon) make (en) of busard (buzzard),
> No hardy knight make of coward."
>
> *From King Alisaunder*, A.D. 1300.

"You cannot make my lord, I fear,
A velvet purse of a sow's ear."

JOHN WOLCOT, A.D. 1738–1819, *Lord B. and His Motions.*

"A sow's ear may somewhat resemble a purse, and a curled pig's tail may somewhat resemble a twisted horn; but a sow's ear cannot be made into a silk purse, nor a pig's tail into a cow's horn."—E. COBHAM BREWER, A.D. 1810–1897, *Phrase and Fable.*

"All the education in the world will not change a strong original nature, or law of nature; it may modify and improve; but the inherent—the raw material—will always remain the same. 'What is bred in the bone will come out in the flesh.'"—*Household Words*, Feb. 28, 1852.

ALLIED PROVERBS

**A black rug cannot be made white by means of soap.** (Persian).

**A carrion kite will never make a good hawk.** (English).

**A chicken will not be produced from an earthen egg.** (Persian).

**A hog in armor is still a hog.** (English).

**A hog in a silk waistcoat is still a hog.** (English).

**A pestle cannot be made into a bow.** (Marathi).

**A pig's tail will never make a good arrow.** (Spanish, Portuguese).

**Can you make a pipe of a pig's tail.** (English).

**Chamois leather is not made of camel's hide.** (Persian).

**Don't expect good faith from a low born man; reeds will never become sugar cane.**

This proverb is taken from the old Pashto poet—Abdul Hamid. (Pashto).

**Every block will not make a bedstead.** (English).
**Every man's nose will not make a shoeing horn.** (English).
**Every reed will not make a pipe.** (English).
**How can a good sword be made from bad iron?** (Persian).
**It is hard making a horn of an ape's tail.** (English).
**It is hard making a good web of a bottle of hay.** (English).
**It is ill making a blown horn of a tod's tail.** (Scotch).
**Jack will never make a gentleman.** (English).
**Of a pig's tail you can never make a good shaft.** (English, Portuguese).
**String cannot be made from stone.** (Marathi).
**Spears are not made of bulrushes.** (English).
**The bust of Mercury cannot be cut from every wood.** (Latin).
**The world would not make a race horse out of a donkey.** (Irish).
**Though iron may be heated ever so much it will not become gold.** (Tamil).
**You cannot make a good archbishop of a rogue.** (Danish).
**You cannot make a good coat of bad wool.** (Spanish).
**You cannot make a good hunting horn of a pig's tail.** (English, Danish).
**You cannot make a hawk of a buzzard.** (French).
**You cannot make a horn of a pig's tail.** (English).
**You cannot make a sieve of an ass's tail.** (Greek, German).
**You cannot make a whistle out of a pig's tail.** (English).
**You cannot make hawks of kites.** (Gaelic).
**You cannot make velvet out of a sow's ear.** (English).

### OTHER PROVERBS OF IMPOSSIBILITY

**A dog's tail never became straight.** (Persian).
**A donkey's tail is not a horse's tail.**

This proverb is used to indicate the same as "You cannot make a silk purse out of a sow's ear." (Mauritius Creole).

**Asking wool of a goat and the making of a piece of cloth of a pucan.** (Irish).

**A thing cannot be at the same time both true and false.** (Chinese).

**A thousand men cannot undress a naked man.** (Modern Greek).

**A toad propping a bedpost firmly.** (Chinese).

**Can you change the shape of a dog's tail?** (Tamil).

**Can you obtain musk from a polecat?** (Tamil).

**Heather bells do not bear cockle shells.** (Scotch).

**I cannot run and sit at the same time.** (English).

**I cannot sell the cow and have the milk.** (Scotch).

**I cannot spin and weave at the same time.** (English).

**Is it possible to cover a kittle drum with the skin of a mouse?** (Behar).

**It is ill making a deadly enemy out of a gude friend.** (Scotch).

**Ivory does not come from a rat's mouth.** (Chinese).

**Nae man can baith sup an' blaw thegither.** (Scotch).

**Nae man can make his ain hap—i. e. Can arrange his own destiny.** (Scotch).

**No man can call again yesterday.** (English).

**No man can flay a stone.** (English).

**No one can be caught in places he does not visit.** (Danish).

**No one can blow and swallow at the same time.** (German).

**No one is bound to do impossibilities.** (French, Italian).

**One actor cannot perform a play.** (Chinese).

**One cannot be and have been.** (French).

**One cannot be both old and young at the same time.** (German).

**One cannot be in two places at once.** (English).

**One cannot drink and whistle at the same time.** (Italian).

**One cannot ring the bells and walk in the procession.** (French).

**One cannot wash a blackamoor white.** (German).

**One can't shoe a running horse.** (Dutch).

**One foot cannot stand on two boats.** (Chinese).

**Pounding an ass to make him a horse.** (Bengalese).

**Should even the water of life fall from the clouds you would never get fruit from the willow.** (Persian).

**That which has been eaten out of the pot cannot be put in the dish.** (Danish).

**The eyebrow of the new moon will not become green with the dye of the sky.** (Persian).

**The water of the river does not mount up to the ridge pole.** (Persian).

**The water that comes from the same spring cannot be both pure and salt.** (English).

**The wonderful and the impossible have collided.** (Kaffir).

**To believe a business is impossible is the way to make it so.** (English).

**You cannot clap with one hand.** (Chinese).

**You cannot coax de mornin' glory to climb de wrong way roun' the cornstalk.** (Negro—Plantation Proverb).

**You cannot damage a wrecked ship.** (Italian).

**You cannot draw blood from a turnip.** (Italian).

**You cannot draw wine out of an empty cask.** (German).

**You cannot drive a windmill with a pair of bellows.** (English).

**You cannot get blood from a stone.** (English).

**You cannot get oil out of a wall.** (French).

**You cannot pull hard with a broken rope.** (Danish).

**You cannot shade off the sun with one hand.** (Chinese).

**You cannot shear the sheep closer than the skin.** (Danish).

**You cannot strip two skins off one cow.** (Chinese).

**You cannot take a cow from a man that has none.** (Danish).

**You cannot eat your cake and have it too.** (English).

**Wash a dog, comb a dog, still a dog is but a dog.** (French).

### CONTRADICTING PROVERBS

**By labor fire is got out of a stone.** (German, Dutch).

**It is always the impossible that happens.** (French).

**Labor conquers all things.** (Latin).

**Labor makes bread out of stone.** (German).

**Madam, if it is possible, it is done; if it is not possible it shall be done.** (French).

**Nothing is so difficult but we may overcome it by perseverance.** (Scotch).

**Nothing is difficult to a willing mind.** (Italian, English, French).

**Nothing is impossible to pains and patience.** (English).

**Persevere and never fail.** (English).

**The gods sell everything for labor.** (English).

**The will does it.** (German).

**To a brave heart nothing is impossible.** (French).

**To him that wills ways are not wanting.** (English).

**Where there is a will there is a way.** (English, Spanish, Italian).

# AUTHORS QUOTED

## BIBLE REFERENCE

*Old Testament*



*New Testament*

# Curiosities in Proverbs

By

Dwight Edwards Marvin

More than 2000 folk sayings translated from more than seventy languages and dialects. The volume is not a mere compilation, but also a study of proverb lore which shows the real significance of the sayings of the people, and the reason for their repetition from one generation to another. There is an alphabetical and topical index whereby the location of any particular proverb may be readily ascertained.

CPSIA information can be obtained
at www.ICGtesting.com
Printed in the USA
LVHW091935131020
668706LV00013B/43

9 789354 17277